Admired
and Understood

Admired and Understood

The Poetry of Aphra Behn

M. L. Stapleton

DELAWARE

Newark: University of Delaware Press

Associated University Presses
2010 Eastpark Boulevard
Cranbury, NJ 08512

Associated University Presses
P.O. Box 338, Port Credit
Mississauga, Ontario
Canada L5G 4L8

The paper used in this publication meets the requirements of the American National Standard for Permanence of Paper for Printed Library Materials Z39.48-1984.

Library of Congress Cataloging-in-Publication Data

Stapleton, M. L. (Michael L.), 1958–
    Admired and understood : the poetry of Aphra Behn / M.L. Stapleton.
        p.   cm.
    Includes bibliographical references and index.
    ISBN 0-87413-849-3 (alk. paper)
    1. Behn, Aphra, 1640–1689—Poetic works.   2. Women and literature—England—History—17th century.   I. Title.
    PR3317.Z5 S73   2004
    821'.4—dc21   2003010950

PRINTED IN THE UNITED STATES OF AMERICA

Thou canst not touch the freedom of my mind.
—Milton, *A Mask Presented at Ludlow Castle* [*Comus*], 663

Contents

Acknowledgments   9
Abbreviations   11
A Note on Texts   13

Introduction: The Middle-Aged Poetess Presents
Herself   17
1. "A Fancy strong may do the Feat": The Structure
    of *Poems upon Several Occasions*   43
2. Notions of the Lyric and Pindaric: The Debt to
    Cowley   65
3. The Debt to Daphnis: Theocritus, Horace,
    Lucretius   86
4. Behn's Godlike Rochester and Libertinism   119
5. The Juniper-Tree in Behn's Pastoral World   143
6. "Swoln to Luxurious Heights": *A Voyage to the Isle
    of Love*   164

Afterword: Welcome Mischiefs   198
Notes   203
Bibliography   228
Index   239

Acknowledgments

Parts of chapter 4 appeared in article form as "Aphra Behn, Libertine" in *Restoration: Studies in English Literary Culture, 1660–1700* 24 (2000): 75–97. I thank the current editor, Professor J. Douglas Canfield of the University of Arizona, for permission to use certain portions of the essay, as well as his academic institution, under whose aegis the journal is now published. I must also thank the previous editor, Professor J. M. Armistead of the Tennessee Technological University, whose encouragement and kindness at an early stage of the project made its completion possible.

My primary debt, joyfully acknowledged, is to my dear brother and friend of three decades, Mr. Douglas F. Peacock, whose bibliographical expertise, especially with the Wing catalog, was invaluable.

Abbreviations

To REDUCE THE NUMBER OF NOTES, THE PRESENT STUDY USED the following abbreviations for these four frequently cited multivolume works:

CE: J. E. Spingarn, ed., *Critical Essays of the Seventeenth Century*, 3 vols. (Oxford, 1907; reprint, Bloomington: Indiana University Press, 1963).

K: Walter P. Ker, ed., *The Essays of John Dryden*, 2 vols. (Oxford: Clarendon Press, 1900).

S: Montague Summers, ed., *The Works of Aphra Behn*, 6 vols. (London, 1915; reprint, New York: Benjamin Blom, 1967).

W: Janet Todd, ed., *The Works of Aphra Behn*, 7 vols. (Columbus: Ohio State University Press, 1993).

A Note on Texts

THE EDITION OF BEHN'S POETRY PRIMARILY USED IN THIS STUDY is *Poems upon Several Occasions: With A Voyage to the Island of Love, By Mrs. A. Behn* (London: Printed for R. Tonson and J. Tonson, 1684), Wing #1757, the copy photographed at Harvard University. I have also made use of Summers and Todd. Both twentieth-century editions of the poetry (Summers, vol. 6; Todd, vol. 1) present difficulties for the scholar. Summers has no line numbers but preserves the unity of Behn's 1684 collection as well as the commendatory verses and presents the reader with what is, in effect, a diplomatic transcript of that edition, limiting his explanatory notes to names and dates. Todd uses line numbers and is more fulsome in her explanatory notes, but reorganizes Behn's entire corpus of poetry chronologically and therefore does not preserve the unity of 1684 or include the commendatory poems. Therefore it seemed best to me to rely on the 1684 *Poems*, using Todd's line numbers and supplying these for the commendatory verses she does not include but that Summers does. References to Behn's prose are taken from Todd's edition, with volume and page number following in parentheses. Citations from the plays are also from Todd's edition, but include act, scene, and line numbers only, without volume or page numbers.

Admired
and Understood

Introduction: The Middle-Aged Poetess Presents Herself

For *Punk* and *Poetess* agree so Pat,
You cannot well be *This*, and not be *That*.
　　　　　—Robert Gould, "The Poetess: A Satyr,
　　　　　Being a Reply to *Silvia's Revenge*," c. 1689

she—poor lady!—considered herself a poet first of all.
　　　　　—Edward Wagenknecht, "In Praise of Mrs. Behn," 1934

GOULD'S NOTORIOUS SATIRE, DIRECTED SPECIFICALLY AT "EPHE-lia" and Aphra Behn, encapsulates the general late-seventeenth-century attitude toward women writers and specifically, women poets, one that we can see persisted well into the twentieth. A recent commentator has argued that Gould's frequently cited opinions "do not represent the unanimous verdict of a monolithic culture" and have been misread as typical of Restoration readers.[1] Granted, the ingenuity of the invective is remarkable, which may account for modern fascination with it. Yet the commentator does not acknowledge the apparent cause of Gould's scorn. Behn refuses to invest her work with an avowedly moral function, perhaps unforgivable in light of the work of Katherine Philips, of whom Gould unconditionally approves. Small wonder, then, that recent scholarship argues ceaselessly that Carolean literary culture, mostly male, naturally regarded authorship as a masculine prerogative as well as activity, a concept Behn herself appears to validate when she refers to her own writing as "my Masculine Part the Poet in me."[2] For a woman to transgress on this manly prerogative invited the type of scorn generally directed at those such as Behn who invaded such well-marked territory. To defend it then as now, men used women's gender and sexuality

17

against them. Some twentieth-century critics perpetuate
Gould's scorn as well as Wagenknecht's condescension. A
standard history of the period slightingly refers to the author as "Mrs. Behn," calls her "indecent," and even suggests
that "masculine gallantry" accounts for the bad habit of
viewing her work "too kindly."[3] Therefore, despite the examples of Philips and Anne Killigrew, a "woman who lived
a public life in the seventeenth century, whether as a publishing writer, a playwright, or an actress, was sexually suspect, as available for hire as any prostitute because she was
not the exclusive *private* property of a man," as Laurie
Finke puts it so well.[4] Behn knew she could not escape la-
boring as a poet in the wake of this ridiculous syllogism and
ignored it, surely hardened by her years in the theater and
its hostility to women who sought to do more than display
the contours of their hips and thighs in breeches. Worse
still, argues Gerald MacLean, the Stuart regime forced
women to resubmit to the strictures of gender that they had
partially escaped during the Interregnum, thanks to the Puritan insistence on the inclusion of women's voices in the
public sphere, when "speaking and writing both as women
and socially responsible agents" was the norm.[5]

That Behn so ardently supported a monarchy that sought
to repress these voices is surely bizarre. Janet Todd calls
her "a snobbish high Tory."[6] Although Angeline Goreau
seeks to justify this cultural schizophrenia by reconciling
Behn's monarchical absolutism with her feminism, Ros Ballaster argues instead that her "success lay in her dual articulation of Tory myth and feminocentric individualism."[7]
However one chooses to read this social paradox, one must
admit that Behn's position as woman poet was extremely
tenuous and certainly caused her anxiety, as she articulates
in her critical writings. If one considers the discouraging
reemergence of the handicap that MacLean delineates, as
formidable in some ways as a corset must have been, it is
remarkable that any woman wrote or attempted to gain access to Restoration literary culture, sexually suspect as
women were. Then again, perhaps the obstacles created the
determination, even the rage, to overcome them. Behn's
roles as spy and wanderer as well as playwright and poet
reflect this determination, one of "moral and intellectual

venturing," an "imaginative, political and intellectual au-
dacity."[8] At any rate, she did not appreciate the equation of
her profession with the world's oldest. If one reads the entire sentence from which the aforementioned "Masculine
Part" reference is taken,[9] one will see that sarcasm out-
weighs servility, as it does in an antiphonal description of
herself in relation to a hero of her fictions. Of Oroonoko, she
says, "his Mis-fortune was, to fall in an obscure World, that
afforded only a Female Pen to celebrate his Fame" (W 3:88).
Her poetry itself also expresses this tendency, sarcasm
perhaps infusing "What in strong manly Verse I would
express, / Turns all to Womannish Tenderness within" ("To
Mr. Creech," 13–14). Her resentment arises not because the
public scorns her attempts at uniqueness, but because she
is trying so hard to fit in, hoping to be "By all admir'd and
understood" ("A Farewel to Celladon," 2) as a poet, disdain-
ing to be "Stinted to Singularity" ("To Mr. Creech," 105).[10]

I

'Tis an unprofitable Art, to those who profess it; but you,
who write only for your Diversion, may pass your Hours
with Pleasure in it, and without Prejudice, always avoiding (as I know you will) the Licenses which Mrs. Behn allowed herself, of writing loosely, and giving (if I may
have leave to say so) some Scandal to the Modesty of her
Sex. I confess, I am last Man who ought, in Justice to ar-
raign her, who have been myself too much a Libertine in
most of my Poems, which I should be well contented I
had Time either to purge or to see them fairly burned.
But this I need not say to you, who are too well born, and
too well principled, to fall into that Mire.
—John Dryden to Elizabeth Thomas, c. 1699[11]

For it was as a poet that Behn hoped to be accepted, respected, remembered, and not as one who, having fallen
into the mire, allowed herself the license to write "loosely"
(incautiously as well as unchastely).[12] The careful construction of Poems upon Several Occasions: With a Voyage to the Island of Love (1684) suggests no less.[13] To paraphrase Richard
Helgerson's concept of the young Edmund Spenser in The
Shepheardes Calender, the middle-aged poetess in effect

presents herself to her literary culture and shows it what she can do.[14] The main purpose of this study is to analyze and to explain exactly how she does this—how she attempts to demonstrate to her peers that she is master of an impressive number of literary forms, stanzaic types, and poetic topoi and that she partakes of the literary theory they practice. I also seek to account for her view of her gender and relate it to her conception of herself as a poet, which various commentators have also attempted to do: Finke's "double-dressing," the "strategy of exploiting and confounding traditional gender roles within a single persona," Paul Salzman's "staging," and Elizabeth Spearing's "femini[ni]ty as a masquerade."[15] Behn seems all too aware that she is doomed to be stinted to singularity because of her unusual profession. Nonetheless, she refuses to allow this corset, so to speak, to constrict her unduly in her quest to be admired and understood. She even uses it to her advantage—a woman who wanted to be known as Astraea (and hoping to find her *aurea mediocritas*) may not have thought of singularity as altogether stinting.

Even the commendatory verses to *Poems upon Several Occasions* reflect this duality about her conception of her gender and her extreme care in presenting herself. Since she seems to have overseen every other detail of her book, it is unlikely that this important feature was left to chance.[16] This editorial activity on her part was almost certainly a reaction to Philips's posthumous *Poems* (1678), whose six commenders (one female) all comment on her stature and singularity as Poetess.[17] Nine poems preface Behn's collection, two by John Cooper, one by John Adams, one by Thomas Creech, two anonymous (one of these perhaps by her publisher, Jacob Tonson), one by a J. W., one by a F. N. W., and the last by Henry Watson. All address these same themes and prepare the reader for what is to follow. They, essentially, provide Behn with a masculine escort if not an apology, one that she solicited, very much in the spirit of the escort provided for Philips. The first poem, Cooper's "To Mrs. *Behn*, on the publishing of her Poems," dated the previous year (25 November 1683), invites us to overhear a direct address, a respectful series of compliments:

> With all the *thought* and *vigour* of our Sex
> The moving *softness* of your own you mix.
> The *Queen* of Beauty and the *God* of Wars
> Imbracing lie in thy due temper'd Verse,
> *Venus* her sweetness and the force of *Mars*.
>
> (22–26)[18]

This first escort stresses singularity as he attempts not to condescend. Like Adams, who explains, "Yet neither sex do you surpass alone, / Both in your Verse are in their glory shown," ("To the excellent Madam *Behn*, on her Poems," 16–17), Cooper, anticipating his audience's misperception that Behn's femininity is constraining or debilitating, addresses the issue directly and forcefully corrects it. He explains how she fuses her female nature with the qualities of the dominant sex in an image that foretells the heterosexual eroticism in the collection. One does not dominate the other; one is not subordinate to the other. Thomas Sprat makes much the same aesthetic point in praising Cowley fourteen years earlier: "there is a kind of variety of Sexes in Poetry as well as in Mankind: that as the peculiar excellence of the Feminine Kind is smoothnesse and beauty, so strength is the chief praise of the Masculine" (*An Account of the Life and Writings of Mr. Abraham Cowley*, 1668 [CE 2: 129]). Cooper claims that thought, vigor, and softness are all "due temper'd" by Behn's own virtues as a poet, her sweetness and force thrashing away in Vulcan's net, on display for all:

> Thus thy luxuriant Muse her pleasure takes,
> As *God* of old in *Eden's* blissful walks;
> The Beauties of her new Creation view'd,
> Full of content She sees that it is *good*.
>
> (27–30)

The first adjective (cf. *luxuria*, lust) and the verb phrase suggests that Behn enjoys arousing the prurient interest, a point that other escorts such as Creech and Adams make in their commendatory verses: "I see the Banks with Love-sick Virgins strow'd, / Their Bosoms heav'd with the young fluttering Gods" ("To the Authour, on her Voyage to the Island of Love," 37–38); "who e'er so sweetly could repeat / Soft lays of Love, and youths delightfull heat?" ("To *Astraea*, on her Poems," 25–26). But then Cooper, in a surprising and ingenious twist worthy of his subject, compares her to the ever-creating Almighty, even capitalizing the pronoun to underscore the point. She must have been delighted.

One of the anonymous commenders, who identifies himself as male, provides what is probably the best introduction to Behn's volume. His "Upon these and other Excellent Works of the Incomparable *Astraea*" explains her stance as a poet the most clearly. The nine-part, 235-line irregular Pindaric ode, very much like those Behn herself writes, explains how she wishes to be perceived. No bearded drudge of the schools, replete with "senseless Jargon and perplexing Rules" (15), Behn exemplifies "What Divine Nature can in Woman doe" (18). In this she is singular, better than Philips, and without undue sexual display or other forms of bad taste. She will not "rob the Learned Monuments of the dead" or use "foreign aid" (24–25), a somewhat disingenuous comment when one considers that no poet, especially Behn, can be innocent of such robbery or aid. Nevertheless, the commender expands his praise to stress that Behn is not beholden to the insulting sex: "doubly Curst be he that thinks her Pen / Can be instructed by the best of men" (35–36). Again, her debt to Cowley, Rochester, and Creech renders this untrue, but the commender presses on. She in theory made Creech a better poet: "her sweeter Muse did for him more, / Than he himself or all *Apollo's* sons before" (117–18). Her diversity, the product of her feminine sensibility, surpasses masculine poetic uniformity:

> While most of our dull Sex have trod
> In beaten paths of one continued Road,
> Her skilfull and well manag'd Muse
> Does all the art and strength of different paces use
>
>   (103–6)

The passage argues for the superiority of the feminine in poetry, in comparison with the more guarded assessments of Cooper and Adams, who both describe her verse as possessing "A Female Sweetness and a Manly Grace" ("To *As-*

failed to be sufficiently enlightened by our notions of feminism or political loyalty. Perhaps the failure lies elsewhere.
As N. H. Keeble has proposed, what we might mistakenly
view as self-effacement can actually be read as "a strategy
to secure the liberty to create and to publish" one's own
"autonomous subject," evidence in itself of such a "text's
self-assertiveness."[20] The lack of a comprehensive treatment of her poetry, especially an account of her self-presentation in *Poems upon Several Occasions,* is a lacuna that this
study attempts to fill.[21]

Since most accounts of Behn's poetry concentrate on the
issues of gender and sexuality that are perceived to lie
within, poems such as "The Disappointment" and "To the
fair *Clarinda*" receive most of the critical attention, perhaps
to the detriment of her other work. More general commentary tends to read Behn into her poetry, or to use it to
psychoanalyze her, circumscribing her within the aforementioned issues. Ballaster argues that Behn "repeatedly
inscribes herself into her tales of love, compulsively turning her reader's gaze from the amorous couple to the amatory narrator, who then uncannily retreats or withholds
herself from view, in order to set the pursuit in train again";
she is a kind of narcissist, the subject and object of her own
poetry.[22] Dorothy Mermin suggests that such a phenomenon
was inevitable in Restoration literary culture because
Behn's career itself proved that publication was "a kind of
sexual self-display," a lesson not lost on her successors,
who were much more modest, even "safely unambitious."[23]
However, these later poets keenly observed and learned
from what Salzman describes as Behn's "masquerade of
gender," which aided her in her search for "the possible
representation of a female sense of self."[24] This Behn, feminist, self-absorbed to the point of narcissism, and anticipatory of certain poststructuralist discourses, saw herself as
a guerilla cultural critic, one who, as Carol Barash puts it,
"challenges literary conventions by exaggerating the femaleness of her characters and narrators," calling "the
reader's attention to the conventions within which her cultural narratives operate."[25] Robert Markley makes an almost identical claim about Behn, that she "simultaneously
deconstructs and idealizes the discourses of sexual and

romantic love, reconstructing them in opposition to the mercenary economies of financial self-interest and the exploitation of women."[26] Similarly, Spearing views Behn as the cultivator of a "distinctive, and distinctively feminine, participation in power-relationships involving text and reader."[27] Ultimately, Judith Kegan Gardiner's generalization summarizes how virtually all of these critics view their subject's poetical work, a site in which "traditional tropes of heterosexual love present a longing for community, for a society in which the radical values of liberty, equality, and fraternity would be possible for women and defined in women's terms."[28]

I agree with much of the foregoing in principle; it informs much of what follows here. Indeed, Behn's poetical work demonstrates a strong interest in female community, as her subsequent "Our Cabal" and her legendary devotion to her circle of writing friends both demonstrate. Therefore, it is equally obvious that her poetry helped define an emerging feminine subjectivity, as Virginia Woolf's famous injunction concerning flowers, graves, and debts suggests.[29] And, since she inscribes herself in her poetry as a woman aware of being observed and judged, some element of sexual self-display will be evident. Her forty-five poems (as well as *A Voyage*) in her collection could be viewed as advertisements for herself no less than the nine commendatory poems that precede them.

However, to concentrate exclusively on such issues limits Behn, removes her from her milieu, and stints her to singularity just as definitely as Gould does. Again, Behn sought to be admired and understood by all, like her male contemporaries. Sir Robert Howard assures his readership that he "was resolv'd . . . not to appear singular" (Preface to *Four New Plays*, 1665 [CE 2:103]) in presenting himself. Edward Phillips adopts equivalent language: "if I have differ'd ought from the received opinion, I can safely aver that I have not done it out of affectation of singularity" (Preface to *Theatrum Poetarum*, 1675 [CE 2:272]). Behn's deliberate attempt to cultivate a *lack* of singularity in much of her verse implicitly expresses her rather fervent wish to be regarded as a Poet such as Howard and Philips rather than as punk-poetess, as if she were consciously attempting to fulfill Dryden's ideals about the proper cultivation of easy and natural wit, "a propriety of thoughts and words; or, in other terms, thoughts and words elegantly adapted to the subject" (*The Author's Apology for Heroic Poetry and Poetic License*, 1677 [K 1:190]). Creech's couplet in his commendatory poem, "what you fire burns with a constant flame, / Like what you write, and always is the same" ("To the Authour, on her Voyage to the Island of Love," 53–54) may have been the highest validation for her. At times, she calls the reader's attention to conventions "within which her cultural narratives operate," not so much to show him or her how subtly she overturns such conventions but how eagerly she attempts to fulfill them. What may, for example, seem to be "exaggerating the femaleness of her characters and narrators" may also be, simply put, her conception of the feminine—to her, this is what women are like. The sexual self-display that became so distasteful in the succeeding age (and remains very much so in many quarters) may not have been something she adopted with clenched teeth as we would, such as the title and second couplet of the other anonymous commendatory poem (which Tonson later owned to writing),[30] framed in the language that a contemporary talk-show host would introduce a movie star: "Such pains took Nature with your Heav'nly Face, / Form'd it for Love, and moulded every Grace" ("To the Lovely Witty *Astraea*, on her Excellent Poems," 3–4). It may be unnerving for us to consider the possibility that she *liked* it.[31]

Examining such issues in her poetry is essential to understanding how she wished to present herself in *Poems upon Several Occasions*. Yet, again, other considerations, such as her debts to her predecessors and her attempts to be conventional, are equally essential to achieving such an understanding of one who strove to achieve poetical constancy by keeping her flame the same. Chapter 1 analyzes the remarkable unity of the forty-five poems in Behn's collection. At times, the structure is solid enough to suggest that *Poems upon Several Occasions* forms a giant corona, or circle of poems. Not only are virtually all of the pieces related to one another, but they seem to have been placed in a very definite order, as though the reader would not just sample but read through them. Chapters 2, 3, and 4 examine the roots of her poetics in those of Cowley and Rochester, as well as in Creech's excellent translations from Horace, Lucretius, and Theocritus. Behn sought to be a part of her own writerly community with contemporaries such as Edward Ravenscroft and Thomas Flatman, and also sought to situate herself within the traditions of her illustrious predecessors and redefine them for herself: Cowley's notions of the Pindaric as it applies to occasional verse and poetical freedom; Rochester and libertinism; Horace, Theocritus, and Lucretius (filtered through Creech), and pastoral. And, of course, Cowley, Rochester, and Lucretius inform Behn's conception of love and how a poet evokes it, so important to understanding how she chooses to present herself. Chapter 5 is devoted to "On a *Juniper-Tree*" and accounts for its centrality in her canon and, to some extent, how these masters and their traditions inform it. The last chapter analyzes *A Voyage to the Isle of Love*, itself obviously a series of linked poems, as designed to be where it is in *Poems upon Several Occasions;* it also can be related quite easily to the corona that precedes it.

Writing about Behn's dramatic corpus is quite an enterprise in itself, so I have taken care to avoid becoming sidetracked into writing extensively on the plays. One could certainly write a book-length study on the interpenetrations of *Poems upon Several Occasions* and the comedies. Inevitably, however, to engage in such a comparison here would duplicate the critical phenomenon of relegating the poetry to the type of minor status that has rendered it superfluous over the last three centuries. Therefore, I limit my discussion of the plays to parts of Chapter 4, the section devoted to Rochester and libertinism, since, in my judgment, her comedies constitute the chief site of her engagement with this issue along with her poetry. Throughout this book, I am mindful of Behn's struggle to negotiate between universal approbation and singularity because it informs her other difficulties as a poet: writing freely but not loosely; thinking of her writing itself as her masculine part, even though she is always conscious of her female pen; and, of course, her attempts to learn from the theorists of her own day by reading or by a type of osmosis concerning translation, imitation, and literature itself. For this reason, my text is somewhat liberally endowed with quotations from Restoration literary criticism, drama, and poets not in the mainstream of the book. This was, after all, Behn's milieu. Surely one should not overvalue a canonical standard such as *An Essay on Dramatic Poesy*, taking care to remember, as Finke has it, that such "essays' . . . status as self-evident and factual statements—are increased when they are reprinted as a succession of virtually oracular statements."[32] At the same time, one should not pretend that this important piece of writing did not exist or that it meant nothing to Behn, who very well may have regarded it as oracular. Dryden's Crites, in translating Velleius Paterculus (*Historia Romana*, 1.17), foretells and summarizes her career as a writer: "Emulation is the spur of wit; and sometimes envy, sometimes admiration, quickens our endeavours," (*An Essay* [K 1:37]).

III

I would not undervalue Poetry, so neither am I altogether of their judgement, who believe no wisdom in the world beyond it.
                                            —Preface to *The Dutch Lover*, 1673 (W 5:160)

however it will be imagin'd that Poetry (my Talent) has so greatly the Ascendant over me, that all I write must pass for Fiction, I now desire to have it understood, that this is Reality, and Matter of Fact, and acted in this our latter Age.
                                            —Preface to *The Fair Jilt*, 1688 (W 3:4)

Perhaps we should pause at two of Behn's attempts at oracular statement. Eleven years before the publication of *Poems upon Several Occasions*, the balanced sentence from her play preface reflects an even temperament about the genre she would later undertake with such effort and zeal. Her idea, which she very well may have intended to sound insolent, conflicts with the grand claims that many made (and make) for poetry. It was business for her, something to be neither undervalued nor overpraised. Four years after the printing of her collection, she makes a different pronouncement in a similar tone to justify her turn to prose narrative. Although she claims that her fiction reflects her skills more accurately, *"this is Reality,"* she considers herself a poet first of all (this passage the presumable source of Wagenknecht's dismissive comment cited above). Indeed, her insertion of *"Poetry (my Talent)"* in her defense of fiction-writing and her understated praise of poetry in justifying herself as an aspiring playwright both signify the relative esteem in which her readership held the three genres. Poetry obviously came first to this literary culture and to Behn. One could even say that it bridges her dramatic career to her tenure as a novelist. Since her own poetic practice suggests that she was in some ways traditional, in keeping with Augustan literary theory, one should attempt to define its outlines and boundaries, if only to determine Behn's place in it. Although this section cannot hope to be comprehensive in its coverage of late seventeenth-century poetics or recent accounts of it, a few representative samples from Restoration literary culture and late twentieth-century criticism of it may serve.

During the Restoration and in most recent criticism of the literature of the period, it is relatively rare to encounter a discussion of poetic theory without reference to the drama. Reasons for this phenomenon are fairly simple. Carolean theorists use "poet" to describe makers of verse and playwrights interchangeably in the capacious Sidneyan sense. Distinctions between dramatists and nondramatic poets were only just beginning to be made. Indeed, *The Oxford English Dictionary* records the first usages of "dramatist" and "playwright" in 1678 and 1687, respectively.[33] Also, the most important Restoration critic, Dryden, almost never writes about poetry without reference to the larger context of the discussion of drama. As James Engell reminds us, the age features the inception of the poet-critic-dramatist, so that genres easily overlap: *MacFlecknoe* and *Absalom and Achitophel* feature strongly dramatic elements, for example.[34] Finke stresses that Behn's own poetic prologues and epilogues to her plays qualify as criticism just as much as her prose prefaces to them do, so that she also fulfills the three writerly functions.[35] Michael Werth Gelber explains that Carolean theory held "no essential difference between the two major kinds of narrative verse, the epic and the drama:

they both . . . must conform to a strict verisimilitude and the rules of classical decorum."[36] Such factors may explain why contemporary scholarship does not often make the generic distinction, or tends to subordinate poetry to drama. Few book-length studies are devoted to Augustan poetry alone or to its poetic theory.[37]

Late seventeenth-century poets were in the process of re-evaluating the genre they practiced and the forms they practiced in, just as contemporary criticism seeks to account for a coherent view of the period, even squabbling over the propriety of adjectives such as "Augustan," "Carolean," "neoclassical," and "Restoration."[38] What is good poetry? What should one try to do? Gelber champions Dryden as the developer and arbiter of a twofold poetical theory made up of the "just" (formal, classical, Jonsonian) and the "lively" (imaginative, transgressive, Shakespearean), concepts that correspond roughly to my own articulation of Behn's wish to be understood and admired.[39] Sir Robert Howard's definition of a poem is probably something that his brother-in-law Dryden or Behn would not have disputed: "a premeditated form of Thoughts upon design'd Occasions" (Preface to Four New Plays, 1665 [CE 2:101]), as bloodless and cut-and-dried as this may seem to modern readers whose poetics have unconsciously been molded by Romantic, Arnoldian, and High Modernist theory.[40] So Hobbes fifteen years earlier: "the subject of a Poem is the manners of men, not natural causes; manners presented, not dictated; and manners feigned, as the name of Poesy imports, not found in men" ("The Answer of Mr. Hobbes to Sr. Will. D'Avenant's Preface before Gondibert," 1650 [CE 2:56]). Although we may feel, in many respects, that to look at one poem is to look at them all, this is to misread them. Eric Rothstein's concept of "positional poetry" applies here. Poets of Behn's time create a persona "as a kind of dramatic chorus or spokesman." They "rarely seek to complicate this speaking figure by giving him (or themselves, through him) a sharply individual voice, an 'authentic' expression of a singular psyche."[41] Augustan poets valued clarity and force of argument, attempting to tame all extravagances and excrescencies, striving not to violate neoclassical notions of decorum: good sense, ease, and regularity, the importance of natural wit. One can see these normative prescriptions at virtually every turn, such as the acerbic Thomas Rymer's savaging of the language of *Othello*: "here we see a known Language does wofully encumber and clog the operation, as either forc'd, or heavy, or trifling, or incoherent, or improper, or most what improbable" (*A Short View of Tragedy*, 1693 [CE 2:239]). Behn spends most of her poetical time trying to avoid having these six adjectives applied to her poetry.

The poets of midcentury, Cowley, Waller, Denham, not much read now, were simply crucial for the formation of Restoration poetics and the more "Augustan" theory that follows in the next century. Dryden praises his predecessors for what he chooses to practice himself: "every one was willing to acknowledge how much our poesy is improved by the happiness of some writers yet living; who first taught us to mould our thoughts into easy and significant words; to retrench the superfluities of expression, and to make our rime so properly a part of the verse, that it should never mislead the sense, but itself be led and governed by it" (*An Essay of Dramatic Poesy*, 1668 [K 1:135]). These "superfluities" are of course the practice of poets such as Donne and his ilk, whom Davenant disavows fifteen years earlier in the time of Oliver: "From the esteem of speaking they proceed to the admiration of what are commonly call'd *Conceits*, things that sound like the knacks or toyes of ordinary *Epigrammists*, and from thence, after more conversation and variety of objects, grow up to some force of *Fancy*; Yet even then, like young Hawks, they stray and fly farr off, using their liberty as if they would ne're return to the Lure, and often goe at check ere they can make a stedy view and know their game" (CE 2:22). Dryden, once himself such a young hawk (see his elegy on the death of Hastings), is less kind in *MacFlecknoe*, when Flecknoe urges Shadwell,

> Leave writing Plays, and chuse for thy command
> Some peaceful Province in Acrostick Land.
> There thou maist wings display and Altars raise,
> And torture one poor word Ten thousand ways.

(205–8)[42]

So much for Herbert, Vaughan, Crashaw, Cleveland, Donne, and, in some cases, Herrick.[43] They fail to understand true wit, as Davenant defines it: "*Wit* is not only the luck and labour, but also the dexterity of thought, rounding the world, like the Sun, with unimaginable motion, and bringing swiftly home to the memory universal surveys" (Preface to *Gondibert*, 1650 [CE 2:20]). Dryden does not disagree, but simply retrenches his predecessor. His words are worth citing again: "Wit . . . is a propriety of thoughts and words; or, in other terms, thoughts and words elegantly adapted to the subject" (*The Author's Apology for Heroic Poetry and Poetic Licence*, 1677 [K 1:190]). In one of her last poems, Behn says much the same thing:

> Wit is no more than *Nature* well exprest;
> And he fatigues and toyles in vain
> With *Rigid Labours*, breaks his Brain,
> That has *Familiar Thought* in lofty Numbers drest.
> ("To *Henry Higden, Esq*; on his Translation of the *Tenth Satyr* of
> *Juvenal*," 30–33 [W 1:229])

The key term, overdetermined then as now, becomes so broadly defined that it tends to resist definition except implicitly in practice.[44] Wentworth Dillon, Earl of Roscommon, in praising Virgil, anticipates the language of Pope in defining wit in terms of poetical music, a kind of mimesis:

> The Delicacy of the nicest Ear
> Finds nothing *harsh* or out of *Order* There.
> *Sublime* or *Low*, *unbended* or *Intense*,
> The *sound* is still a *Comment* to the *Sense*.
> ("An Essay on Translated Verse," 1684 [CE 2:307])

John Sheffield, Earl of Mulgrave, delineates the term according to the propriety of metaphor:

> *Figures of Speech*, which Poets think so fine,
> Art's needless Varnish to make Nature shine,
> Are all but Paint upon a beauteous Face,
> And in Descriptions only claim a place.
> ("An Essay upon Poetry," 1682 [CE 2:291])

One could even say that much of the foregoing matter, the avoidance of extravagant figurative language and the pursuit of natural wit and good sense, is reflected in Dr. Daniel Kendrick's praise of Behn's poetry the year before her death: "How soft and fine your manly numbers flow, / Soft as your Lips, and smooth as is your brow" ("To Mrs. *B*. on Her Poems," 1688 [S 6:296]). Although intellects such as Sir William Temple worried that such strictures would be confining (and, perhaps, produce the very "dissociation of sensibility" that Eliot notoriously finds in poetry of this type), his opinion is definitely in the minority: "The Truth is, there is something in the *Genius* of Poetry too Libertine to be confined to so many Rules; and whoever goes about to subject it to such Constraints loses both its Spirit and Grace, which are ever Native, and never learnt, even of the best Masters" (*Of Poetry*, 1690 [CE 3:83–84]). Poetry was not thought of as ephemeral, but constant, eternal, of infinite value, therefore in need of regulation, rules, theory. Behn challenges herself to make her verse worthy of these standards while defining her own poetic subjectivity.

IV

a warlike, various, and a tragical age is best to *write of*,
but worst to *write in*.
　　　　　　　—Abraham Cowley, Preface to *Poems*, 1656 (CE 2:80)

In describing his own time, Behn's hero and model foretells hers and our own, especially the year of publication of *Poems upon Several Occasions*.[45] In 1684, Shakespeare's Fourth Folio (like Vivaldi, Bach, and Handel) was being conceived and would be born the next year, the last anonymous editing of this playwright's works before Nicholas Rowe's edition of 1709 began the great procession of eighteenth-century editors that would culminate in the work of Edmund Malone in 1790. William Wycherley had long before stopped writing for the theater but amused himself with a succession of women, including Charles's Barbara Villiers, Duchess of Cleveland. He also wrote poetry, some of it most unkind to Behn, mocking her for pregnancy, love-sickness, bad reviews, and venereal disease: "lately you Lay-In, (but as they say,) / Because, you had been Clap'd another Way" ("To the *Sappho* of the Age, suppos'd to Ly-In of a *Love-Distemper*, or a *Play*").[46] Sir George Etherege had also several years since stopped writing plays and taken a diplomatic post in Germany, where he continued to debauch himself enough to arouse public comment. John Dryden, Poet Laureate, was less active in the theater and had turned primarily to poetry, translation, and criticism, and was working intently on an opera, *Albion and Albanius*, which was rehearsed before the King.[47] Thomas Otway had declined into alcoholism, Nathaniel Lee into madness. John Crowne, Edward Ravenscroft, and Thomas Shadwell were still writing plays and having them produced. William Congreve was a boy of fourteen who was attending Trinity College in Dublin along with his seventeen-year-old cousin, Jonathan Swift, who struggled to master the intricacies of Aristotelian logic and metaphysics. John Milton had been dead for ten years, Andrew Marvell for six, John Wilmot, Earl of Rochester, for four. Henry Vaughan and Edmund Waller were very much alive.

John Evelyn, to whom I will turn in a moment, busied himself as a socialite and diary-keeper; Anthony à Wood continued collecting anecdotes and working on his monumental tome on Oxford. Samuel Pepys had stopped keeping his diary fourteen years earlier and, after having resurrected the Royal Navy during his secretaryship at the Admiralty, began a two-year stint as president of the Royal Society. Henry Purcell was appointed Keeper of the King's Instruments at a salary of £60, in addition to composing dozens of songs and anthems for the Choristers at the Chapel Royal and the theater. One composition, "From those serene and rapturous joys," was a collaboration with Behn's friend, the poet Thomas Flatman, to celebrate Charles's return from his summer recess in September.[48] *The Voyages of Capt. Barth. Sharp* was published, featuring its racy account of Henry Morgan the buccaneer, surely an influence on the writers of fiction in the next century such as Defoe. Roscommon printed *An Essay on Translated Verse*, which in some respects mirrors Behn's own practice of translation. Thomas Creech's elegant renderings of Horace and Theocritus also saw print, the latter containing a fine translation of René Rapin's *De Carmine Pastorali,* which reflects much of Behn's understanding of the genre, as we shall see. Jacob Tonson's *Miscellany Poems* contained several translations by Dryden and others of ancient authors. Also appearing were John Bunyan's second volume of *The Pilgrim's Progress* and Thomas Burnet's *Theory of the Earth,* this latter volume yet one more significant astronomical work to appear during the year. Just as prominent were the treatises of Giovanni Cassini, best known for his works on the parallax of the sun and the divisions of the rings of Saturn, which announced the discovery of two more of the seventh planet's moons, which he named Dione and Tethys. Addison and Steele had their first meeting at school (Charterhouse). The year 1684 was also John Locke's first full year of exile. He had lost his position at Oxford, fled to Holland after Shaftesbury's disgrace the previous year, and there assumed the alias of Dr. Van Der Linden. He would not publish his first article for two more years, although he had been at work intermittently on *An Essay concerning Human Understanding* (pub. 1690) for more than a decade. In contrast, his friend Isaac Newton, happily ensconced at Cambridge and a member of the Royal Society over which Pepys presided, was at work on his *Mathematical Principles of Natural Philosophy* (pub. 1687), attempting, perhaps, to stay ahead of his rival Leibniz, who was busily composing his *Discourse of Metaphysics.* Watteau, whose paintings could illustrate Behn's pastorals, was born. Corneille, whose dramatic theory and corpus had done so much to shape the practice of Restoration playwrights such as Behn, died, as did Bishop George Morley and Henry Jermyn, Earl of St. Albans, both longtime servants of the King.

1684 was, for practical purposes, the last year of Charles II's life. This monarch, whose reign had given such shape to Behn's existence, including the issuance of a warrant for her arrest two years earlier for her criticism of his eldest natural son, James Scott, Duke of Monmouth,[49] had a busy twelvemonth. He depended heavily on two chief advisors— Laurence Hyde, Earl of Rochester, along with George Savile, Marquis of Halifax—to help him make many major decisions involving foreign and domestic policy. Also prom-

inent as advisors were the Duke of York and Louise de Kéroualle, Duchess of Portsmouth, now chief mistress to
Charles, with Nell Gwyn, Hortense Mancini, Duchess of Mazarin, and Barbara Palmer, Duchess of Cleveland, rele-
gated to background positions. (Louise had been made a
Duchesse by Charles's cousin, former protector, and deadly
rival Louis XIV and was in some senses a diplomatic liaison
between the kings, some speculating that it extended to
pleasure as well as business.) It is said that Charles fondled
Louise in public and was content to take his postprandial
diversions with her. He commissioned a yacht to which he
gave his nickname for her, "Fubbs" (kinder than Nell's
moniker for Louise, "Squintabella"). She was always an ad-
vocate for her religion, sometimes without the requisite tact
for a mistress whose master was the head of the Church of
England, and sought to win the approval and favor of her
co-religionist the Duke of York. In some ways, she functioned as an alternative queen to Catherine of Braganza
and did not hesitate to upstage her when she felt the urge.
In May of 1684, she took the place of one of Catherine's
maids and waited on the queen at dinner, which did not
amuse Her Majesty.

The consequences of the bizarre Rye House Plot of the
previous year, which planned the assassination of both
royal brothers, continued to unfold. The King came to accept the horrible possibility that Monmouth had been
somehow involved, or at least cognizant of the existence of
the Plot. After yet another failed reconciliation with his
angry father, who had called him "a beast and a block-
head," and hoping to avoid the malice of his uncle, Duke of
York (smarting from his nephew's roles in the Popish Plot,
the Exclusion Crisis, and several obstreperous refusals to
submit to his authority—and who would give this malice
full vent with a dull ax the next year), Monmouth exiled
himself to Holland under the aegis of his cousin Wilhelm.
Although Charles even believed for a time that Wilhelm
had been involved in the Plot, he received agents from Holland who came over to negotiate succession issues. Wilhelm, of course, would become William III three years later
and rule England jointly with Charles's niece, Mary. (Locke
would sail on the same ship with her in the triumphant re-

turn to England; Purcell would compose magnificent music for her funeral.) Her father, whom she would help depose after his stint as James II, was still very much Duke of York in 1684 and spent much of this year at the Admiralty and in Scotland. The Duke was active on the behalf of several prominent Catholics who had been languishing in prison since the time of the Popish Plot. At James's urging, Thomas Osborne, Earl of Danby, was released from captivity, along with other prominent Catholic peers. James must have also been pleased when his nephew Wilhelm somewhat unceremoniously booted his hated nephew from his country later in the autumn of the year.

Although Charles was as dependent on advisors as any other ruler, he was at the same time remarkably activist as a monarch in 1684, involving himself in any number of his country's problems, not always delegating to Hyde, Halifax, Louise, and his brother. He continued to defy his own Triennial Act, which dictated that the king summon Parliament every three years. With the help of Sidney Godolphin, head of the treasury, he sought to reduce the national debt and succeeded in eliminating £500,000 from it, reducing governmental expenditures to £1,175,000, the annual income showing a modest profit of almost £200,000, £1,370,000 in total. His long efforts to consolidate his prerogative in the city of London finally came to fruition, as well. In order to purge city offices held by religious dissenters, Charles had writs of *quo warranto* issued against all livery companies, be they Whig or Tory, and then replaced them with his own people, who were assuredly not of the Whiggish persuasion. He made a show of force to this faction by parading a standing army in London, actually a group of Irish units who had served in Tangier and who were conveniently on hand. Arguably, for the first time in his reign, he paid some attention to England's North American colonies and Bermuda, having writs served against them to assert the royal prerogative in these distant lands as well, the idea of empire finally beginning to take the shape it would assume in the next century under the Hanoverian monarchs. Charles took a particular interest in the troubles that erupted in Massachusetts and Maryland, where some of his royal customs collectors had been murdered. He was also aware of, and complicit in, the purges in Scotland, the so-called Killing Time, where all who denied royal authority were to be executed, as well as similar attempts to repress nonconformity in Ulster. In an unusual gesture for an English monarch, Charles consulted the Irish Privy Council to propose a way to settle difficulties in land settlement in that country rather than simply dictating policy to this governing body (although Hyde was dispatched to oversee the matter). After a few exchanges, the chief officers of the Irish government were empowered to check titles to land and issue new patents to it—this would also have consequences for future relations between Ireland and England.

For the most part, Charles avoided involving himself in Continental affairs. The Turks continued their advance to Vienna; the treaties of Ratisbon created a truce between Austria, France, and Spain; Pope Innocent XI oversaw the establishment of the Holy Alliance between Austria, Poland, and Venice at Linz. Louis XIV, no friend of Spain or Austria, did not support this alliance, much to the Pope's chagrin. He demanded that the Republic of Genoa stop building galleys for Spain and threatened dire results for noncompliance. He also finally captured the Spanish city of Luxembourg without much protest from Charles, after a few years of private negotiations for a different solution had failed, one of which included an offer of £77,000 from Louis to Charles if the latter would let it go without a fight. This busy year, 1684, may well have contributed to the stress that led to Charles's spectacular and sudden Sunday morning collapse on 2 February 1685 in front of an astonished court, as well as his four-day illness, and eventual death on 6 February. His legs had been bothering him for most of the year so that he was unable to take his accustomed three-mile walks, pamper the spaniels named for him, spend much time at the theater, or enjoy the cockfights, part of the carnival of life that he so loved.

The reader of *Poems upon Several Occasions* will note that virtually none of this political matter works its way into Behn's book—no polite poems in Waller's mode on the four mistresses, no Drydenesque Biblical allegory to comment on Monmouth, no Rochesterian insolence concerning Louis's absolutism, Charles's private parts, or Barbara's sexual escapades among the demi-monde. There are only the two slaps at the beautiful and stupid Monmouth, an easy target, and they barely connect. It is as if Behn's volume deliberately seeks to avoid all of those weightier matters, in defiance of the ferociously politicized modes of her age, dating to the revolutionary decade of her birth.[50] Why? She demonstrates during the brief reign of her beloved James II that she was more than willing to write political poetry to the point of hackwork, impassioned, furious, screaming to be read. Perhaps it is not tautological to suggest that this is simply not the way she wished to present herself. It may be that *Poems upon Several Occasions* was meant to represent a space apart, a place where no grime from the "real world" would be allowed to intrude, a veritable Grecian Urn. In this she had ample precedent in Cowley, whose *The Mistress* (1647) is a similarly unravished bride of quietude, apolitical.

As a letter Behn wrote to Tonson indicates (cited in the first chapter of the present study), 1683–84 was a very difficult time for her: physical hardship, financial deprivation, professional failure. Still she kept writing, revising, thinking of her place as a poet in relationship to Cowley and Orinda. Evelyn's diary entries for the first eight months of 1684 suggest another reason for difficulty and despair. The weather was ghastly, unseasonable in every season. He first notes the "extreame hard weather" on 6 January, and wonders at its continuance a week later. On 14 January it was so cold that the Thames froze solid and "was filled with people & tents selling all sorts of Wares as in the Citty it selfe," memorably recorded by the Dutch immigrant painter Abraham Hondius (c. 1638–91), whose landscape, *A Frost on the Thames at Temple Stairs* (1684), emphasizes the black sky more than the carnivalesque atmosphere on the river.[51] Evelyn marvels ten days later on 24 January, "The frost still continuing more & more severe, the *Thames* before London was planted with bothes in formal streetes, as in a Citty, or Continual faire."[52] This could not have been pleasant in a time with no central heating, no sewage disposal, no paved streets and roads, no easily shipped and stored fresh fruit and vegetables: a monarch whose legs hurt him, his mistresses who had to dress elaborately and then undress again in freezing rooms, a middle-aged poetess who may have fallen on the ice at least once, who had no place to go, and about whom no one much cared. Evelyn, it seems, made the best of it along with everyone else, but speculated on its causes, again, in his entry for 24 January:

> it was a severe Judgement upon the Land: the Trees not onely splitting as if lightning-strock, but Men & Cattell perishing in divers places, and the very seas so locked up with yce, that no vessells could stirr out, or come in: The Fish & birds, & all our exotique Plants and Greenes universaly perishing; many Parks of deere destroied, & all sorts of fuell so deare that there were greate Contributions to preserve the poore alive; nor was this severe weather much lesse intense in most parts of *Europe* even as far as *Spaine*, & the most southern tracts: London, by reason of the excessive coldnesse of the aire, hindring the ascent of the smoake, was so full with the fulginous steame of the Sea-Coale, that hardly could one see crosse the streete, & this filling the lungs with its grosse particles exceedingly obstructed the breast, so as one could scarce breath.

One wonders if the royal brothers viewed these events in the same way that they had seen the disaster of 1666, when they had felt compelled to go out wigless and fight the Great Fire themselves, or if they took consolation in the theory that their cousin and rival Louis was undoubtedly as cold as they were. (James may well have wished frostbite on Monmouth, who shivered with Wilhelm in Holland.) The great frost lasted until 8 February, until an equally great thaw and rain made London a quagmire, although the Thames stayed frozen for another week, chunks of floating ice damaging the hulls of ships that had already undergone enough stress from their winter prison. Behn's own "A Letter to Mr. *Creech* at *Oxford*: Written in the Last Great Frost" alludes to the treacherousness of walking about, "When melted Snow and Ice confound one, / Whether to break ones neck, or drown one" (32–33 [W 1:166]). But January and February were not the half of it. Evelyn's next reference to the weather is on 19 May, reporting "An excessive hot & dry Spring" with one brief rainstorm. It did not rain again until July, and then only a thimbleful. On 2 July, Evelyn despairs, "So greate a drowth still continu'd, as never was since my memorie." Ten days later, leaves fell from the trees as if it were autumn. Six weeks later (24 August), he remarks at the large number of people perishing. Needless to say, the crop failures drove food prices to preposterous heights. Surely Behn saw (and smelled) all of this, as well: the stink of corpses and raw sewage, the dead trees, the smoke that never departed, hanging over London so that the sun made the sky into a hot gray dome. It made her struggle in the "Toils of Sickness," as she recounted in the following year ("On the Death of *E. Waller*, Esq.," 3 [W 1:289], 1685). We should not be surprised, then, that Behn kept the hugger-mugger of events and the grime of the world out of *Poems upon Several Occasions*, and that its pastoral world reflects the opposite of the London in which she struggled: her "Groves appear'd all drest with Wreaths of Flowers, / And from their Leaves dropt Aromatick Showers" ("The Golden Age," 9–10), her lovers as she must have wished that she herself were, "The Brave and Witty" who "know no Fear or Sorrow" ("A Paraphrase on the Eleventh *Ode* Out of the first Book of *Horace*," 18). Not only was the book a mode of public discourse in which she would present herself as a poet; it was also something for herself, perhaps even, to cite a *bon mot* by Milton's nephew that I will use to begin the first chapter, a "small Memorial."

1

"A Fancy strong may do the Feat": The Structure of *Poems upon Several Occasions*

there is no Poetical Volume, be it never so small, but it requires some pains to bring it forth, or else a notable fluent knack of Riming or Versifying; and how small a matter is it for never so trivial a Work, before it comes to be condemn'd to the drudgery of the *Chandler* or *Tobacco Man*, after the double expence of Brain to bring it forth and of purse to publish it to the World, to have this small Memorial, *Such a one wrote such a thing.*
> —Edward Phillips, Preface to *Theatrum Poetarum*, 1675 (2:262–63)

What monstrous, leud, and irreligious Books of Poems, as they are call'd, have been of late days published, and what is the greater wonder, receiv'd in a Civiliz'd and Christian Kingdom with *Applause* and *Reputation*? The sweetness of the Wit makes the *Poison* go down with Pleasure, and the Contagion spreads without Opposition. Young Gentlemen and Ladies are generally pleas'd and diverted with *Poetry* more than by any other way of Writing; but there are few Poems they can fix on but they are like to pay too dear for their Entertainment. Their Fancies are like to be fill'd with impure *Ideas*, and their Minds engag'd in *hurtful* Passions, which are the more lasting by being convey'd in lively Expressions and all the Address of an artful Poet.
> —Sir Richard Blackmore, Preface to *Prince Arthur*, 1695 (CE 3:233–34)

MILTON'S NEPHEW AND BIOGRAPHER, PERHAPS MINDFUL OF the stress under which his uncle produced *Paradise Lost* (as well as its initial cool reception), aptly describes the agonies of authorship for someone such as Behn, who would say that her poems "like Transitory *Flowers*, decay" ("On the Death of *E. Waller*, Esq.," 21 [W 1:289], 1685). His plaintive last phrase may well have described her intentions. Two decades later, Blackmore's diatribe suggests how one segment of the reading public may have perceived such intentions, appalled by the corruption that artful poets spread among the young. The author of *Prince Arthur* appears to have cared little for the double expense of brain and purse to which Phillips alludes, one incurred by the irreligious as well as by those professing to be as pious as he. To him, a text such as *Poems upon Several Occasions*, with its powers to poison by its sweet wit, celebrating impure ideas and hurtful passions in lively expressions, was too dear a price to pay for mere entertainment.

That a woman equipped with a notable fluent knack for versifying produced this text would have seemed all the worse. Robert Gould, writing in Blackmore's vein, argues that all women by nature write loosely: "If any vain, lewd, loose-writ thing you see, / You may be sure the Author is a She" ("Prologue Design'd for my Play of the *Rival Sisters*").[1] And, although the polemics of Blackmore and Gould do not touch on Behn directly, their spirit makes explicit what is implicit in Anne Finch's somewhat arch appreciation of her colleague:

> A summons sent out, was obey'd but by four,
> When Phebus, afflicted, to meet with no more,
> And standing, where sadly, he now might descry,
> From the banks of the Stoure the desolate Wye,
> He lamented for Behn o're that place of her birth,
> And said amongst Femens was not on the earth
> Her superiour in fancy, in language, or witt,
> Yet own't that a little too loosly she writt;
> Since the art of the Muse is to stirr up soft thoughts,
> Yett to make all hearts beat, without blushes or faults.
> ("The Circuit of Appollo," 1713, 7–16)[2]

Finch anticipates Dryden's criticism of writing loosely (again, incautiously as well as unchastely) and evokes the same type of imaginative power that good poetry, erotic or not, can exercise over the minds of its auditors, especially a poet with Behn's facility in language, wit, and fancy. I seek here not to agree with Blackmore, whose own poetry a recent commentator has labeled "turgid doggerel,"[3] but to explain that this power, hardly accidental on Behn's part, results in part from her careful structuring of her collection. One poem leads very deliberately to another, becomes a unit in the design, a line, a word, a phrase sending the mind back to a jewel in the corona. Phillips's appreciation of poetical effort and art in spite of the general indifference of the world applies doubly to Behn, she who expended mightily in brain and purse to bring *Poems upon Several Occasions* to light, her small memorial, as she intended. There is nothing loose about this collection of lively expressions by this artful poet.

I

counterfeit *Astrea's* lustful Rage
Joyns to Debauch the too Effem'nate Age
　　　　—William Atwood, *The Idea of Christian Love*, 1688[4]

Custom is unkind to our Sex, not to allow us free choice
　　　　—Behn, *Sir Patient Fancy* 1. 1.14, 1678

Behn's heroine Isabella laments the position of women, which we can apply in turn to Behn as an author, whose critics would hysterically deny her free choice in their ironically titled compositions. In many ways, these covert comments by women in her plays, if taken together, constitute an introduction to *Poems upon Several Occasions* as well as an answer to the tribe of Atwood, Blackmore, and Gould. For, unfortunately, her collection contains no beautifully crafted preface in Dryden's mode, no pithy comments on writing, women, and professionalism, merely a dedication to James, Earl of Salisbury, who may have subsidized the publication along with Tonson. Only scattered comments throughout this rather fulsome encomium to gain "symbolic capital" may be said to describe some of her poetics.[5] The first line of the dedication is a recipe for panegyric: "Who should one celibrate with Verse and Song, but the Great, the Noble, and the Brave?" A few sentences later, she probably refers to the somewhat distant Popish Plot and Exclusion Crisis that would return the following year during Monmouth's Rebellion, anticipating her two mocking songs on Jemmy: "The violent storms of Sedition and Rebellion are hush'd and calm'd; black Treason is retir'd to its old abode, the dark Abyss of Hell."[6]

Again, probably the best introduction to the themes of the collection can be found in the 235-line Pindaric discussed in the Introduction, "Upon these and other Excellent Works of the Incomparable *Astraea*," anonymous but good enough to have been written by Behn herself. And again, it not only describes what the commender values in Behn, but what Behn herself values in poetry: the avoidance of "Barbarous and inexplicable Terms" (7) and "foreign aid" (25); the cultivation of "Learning, Sense, or wit" (39); the importance of feminine pastoral, with the evocation of "tunefull Shepherds" (54), "tender Reeds" (56), and the excellence of "her softer Pipe" (57); her formidable intelligence, a "Heaven-born Soul with intellectual fire" (70) and "large capacious Brain" (85); and her own physical beauty and seductiveness, a selling-point, it seems, for the collection. Ovid himself, whom the Restoration transcribed into its own culture as a rakehell, would have been "Pleas'd with her Form, and ravish'd with her voice" (160). This excellent résumé foretells the importance of Cowley, Rochester, and Creech's fine English transformation of classical, albeit foreign, authors to her poetics. Her idea of circular linkage seems to have been her own, perhaps buttressed by the previous century's sonnet sequences as well as Cowley's collection *The Mistress*, not to mention Paul Tallemant's *Le Voyage de l'Isle d'Amour*, which would become *A Voyage*. In her later elegy for Waller, she imagines him as the sun, and associates circles with almost Apollonian power: "in thy *Circulary Course*, didst see / The very *Life* and *Death* of Poetry" ("On the Death of *E. Waller*, Esq.," 52–53 [W 1:290], 1685). One might also recall Sir William Harvey's treatise on the circulation of the blood earlier in the century (1618), itself a kind of corona. There were many circulations of energy, as Stephen Greenblatt might say.[7]

One should not mistake the common foretitle, *Poems upon Several Occasions*, as lackadaisical or accidental. It reflects

Behn's attempts to fit in. It was in the title of her hero Rochester's posthumous collection of verses (1680) in which some of her poetry appeared under his name, as well as the famous collection, *Female Poems on Several Occasions: Written by Ephelia* (London: William Downing, 1679). In fact, the publishers apply it to the collected works of virtually every significant poet of the age: Samuel Pordage (1660); Edmund Waller (1664); Charles Cotton (1689); Thomas Fletcher (1692); Buckingham, Sir John Denham, Sir George Etherege, Charles Gildon, and Sir Robert Howard (1696); William Broome (1727); Matthew Prior (1729); William Congreve (1752); John Dryden (1773). The volumes of verse written by women who followed Behn also use this title: Mary, Lady Chudleigh (1703); Sarah Fyge Egerton (1706); Anne Finch (1713); Mary Barber (1735); Elizabeth Carter (1762). Given such august company, it is not fanciful to say that she places herself and her book in a different kind of circular linkage, just as Dante waggishly sets himself in the company of his classical betters.[8]

No direct theoretical statement of intent for the structuring of *Poems upon Several Occasions* exists. Only a letter to Tonson remains, first published in the nineteenth century. It overtly reveals the same desperation about money that Behn implicitly betrays in her hands-and-knees praise of Salisbury, as well as the one implicit reference to structural purpose:

As for ye verses of mine, I shou'd really have thought 'em worth thirty pound; and I hope you will find it worth 25l.; not that I shou'd dispute at any other time for 5 pound wher I am not so obleg'd; but you can not think wt a preety thing ye Island will be, and wt a deale of labor I shall have yet with it: and if that pleases, I will do the 2nd voyage, wch will compose a little book as big as a novel by it self. But pray speake to yor brothr to advance the price to one 5 lb more, 'twill at this time be more than given me, and I vow I wou'd not aske it if I did not really believe it worth more. Alas I wou'd not loose my time in such low gettings, but only since I am about it I am resolv'd to go throw wth it tho I shou'd give it. I pray go about it as soone as you please, for I shall finish as fast as you can go on. Methinks ye Voyage sho'd come last, as being ye largest volume. You know Mr Cowley's David is last, because a large poem, and Mrs. Philips her

plays for ye same reason. I wish I had more time, I wou'd ad
something to ye verses yet I have a mind too, but good deare Mr.
Tonson, let it be 5 lb more, for I may safly sweare I have lost ye
getting of 50 lb by it, tho that's nothing to you, or my satisfaction
and humour; but I have been without getting so long yt I am just
on ye poynt of breaking, espesiall since a boyd has no creditt at
ye play house for money as we usd to have, fifty or 60 deepe, or
more; I want extreamly or I would not urge this.[9]

Unhandsome, certainly, unless one considers the poverty
and the resulting circumstances that surely lay behind
these "low gettings," not the least of which were the horrible winter of 1683–84, the inflation of the currency, and,
most tellingly, the collapse of her main source of income,
the King's Company, whose contraction into the Duke's
meant the severe constriction of the market for new plays
and dictated that she write in other genres to make money.[10]
As she wrote this, she reserved the right to revise most of
the forty-five poems preceding her magnum opus: "I wou'd
ad something to ye verses yet I have a mind too." Her "preety thing ye Island," with the sequel already planned (*Lycidus*, 1688), should come last because her great predecessors,
Cowley and Philips, had done the same. The result, however, hardly as haphazard as this letter, suggests that she
added a good bit to what she had completed by the time of
this writing, a pretty thing surely worth the extra £5, especially when one considers that the same publisher may
have paid Dryden as much as £1400 over a decade later for
his translation of the *Aeneid* (1697).[11]

II

the whole chain of them was with such due order linked
together, that the first accident would naturally beget
the second, till they all rendered the conclusion necessary.

—John Dryden, Epistle Dedicatory of
The Rival Ladies, 1664 (K 1:2)

He only proves he *Vnderstands* a Text,
Whose *Exposition* leaves it *unperplex'd*.
—Wentworth Dillon, Earl of Roscommon,
"An Essay on Translated Verse," 1684 (CE 2:303)

Dryden's comment, although concerning the proper ordering of plots in plays, describes the idea of sequence that
Behn may have had in mind when conceiving the design of
Poems upon Several Occasions. Roscommon's couplet explains the perceived duty of the author and her critics as
well as of the garden-variety translator in a poem that Behn
herself read and spoke approvingly of in later work (see W
4:73). Her subtle linkages represent an effort to unperplex
her readers as she makes her conclusion seem necessary in
the linkage of her chain. To this end, her structure is ingenious in its simplicity. The end of one poem foretells the
next, from "The Golden Age" to *A Voyage*. In addition,
groups of poems tend to form clusters on related themes
and with similar forms. At times, poems answer each other,
not just those in proximity but across the collection, what
one might call auto-intertextuality, or even intratextuality.
The first six form a distinct unit: "The Golden Age," "A Farewel to *Celladon*, On his Going into *Ireland*," "On a *Juniper-
Tree*," "On the Death of Mr. *Grinhil*, the Famous Painter," "A
Ballad on Mr. *J. H.* to *Amoret*," and "Our Cabal," all pastoral-
infused, three of the poems irregular pindaric odes. For
some examples of mechanical linkage, "The Golden Age"
ends with the paraphrase of Catullus 5, "sleep brings an
Eternal Night" (198), which foretells the first word of the
valedictory "A Farewel to *Celladon*," "Farewell the Great,
the Brave and Good" (1), the poem itself an injunction to
Celladon to remember to prize "the Gay hasty minutes" that
the preceding Pindaric warns are fleeting ("The Golden
Age," 196), not to "Toyl, be Dull, and to be Great" ("*Celladon*," 45).[12] A line near the end of this poem, "Pitty our
Swaines, pitty our Virgins more" ("*Celladon*," 125) reminds
us that the next poem, "On a *Juniper-Tree*," concerns the
erotic congress of the swain Philocles and the virgin Cloris,
who enjoy the country pleasures in which Behn would have
Celladon luxuriate "With some dear Shee, whom Nature
made, / To be possest by him alone" ("*Celladon*," 89). Accordingly, the "death" and transfiguration of the tree into the
busks that will guard the door of Cloris's bodily temple naturally introduces the theme of the next poem, "*On the Death
of Mr. Grinhil*, the Famous Painter," he whose "eternis'd
Name" will be "Admir'd to all Posteritie" (65–66), just as the

tree intimates it will be, just as Behn hopes the poem, itself a piece of art, will be. "Mr. *Grinhil*" ends on a mordant note, imagining the virgins who will, as they were at the departure of Celladon to Ireland, "for a while become / Sad" (78). This provides a conjunction with the title of the next piece, "A *Ballad* on Mr. *J. H.* to *Amoret*, asking why I was so sad." This advice poem ends with an injunction to Amoret to "Fly from the Baits" that Mr. J. H. (John Hoyle, the man Behn is said to have loved) has set for her as well as for other shepherdesses, all of which the ensuing "Our Cabal" describes, which concerns Amoret, Mr. J. H., and all the pastoral intrigues of the poet's circle.[13] Behn links these six poems in many other ways and carefully orders them by slight contrasts, as well. "The Golden Age" demonstrates Behn's skill in translation/paraphrase and lays out her Edenic pastoral theme in an impersonal address. "*Celladon*," also Pindaric, is reflective and personal and anonymous; "*Juniper-Tree*" displays Behn's facility with tetrameter couplets and the narrative form; "Mr. *Grinhil*" returns to Pindarics, but is occasional, discussing a man whom her readership knows; "A Ballad" demonstrates the author's skill in yet another form, discussing some members of this readership, yet under the guise of pastoral names; "Our Cabal" strives for completeness by describing virtually all readers in the circle, but in the tetrameter couplets of "*Juniper-Tree*."

Behn's next five poems follow from "Our Cabal" and create a distinct unit, in form as well as in motif. Her series of songs demonstrates her skill in this musical cavalier mode: "The Willing Mistriss," "Love Arm'd," "The Complaint," "The Invitation," and "Song [When *Jemmy* first began to love]." And again, the ligatures are mechanical as well as integral. All songs are sung by a female persona. "Our Cabal" ends with an injunction to Cloris to give herself to Lycidas, to "attend . . . / What Love and Musick calls us to" (227–28): in short, to be willing. Aptly, "The Willing Mistriss" ensues, a monologue by a woman such as Cloris who happily bestows herself on a swain. The coy ending, that the shepherd "lay'd me gently on the Ground; / Ah who can guess the rest?" (23–24), is then probed and questioned by "Love Arm'd," which describes the possible consequences of such a bestowal, the fearful god sitting in "Fantastique

Triumph" (1) over the foolish lover on the ground looking up at her seducer. At the conclusion of this poem, the young woman who narrates it complains that "my poor Heart alone is harm'd, / Whilst thine the Victor is, and free" (15–16). The next poem, "The Complaint," provides contrast, imagining a victor who harms no hearts, "Amyntas that true hearted Swaine" (1), the "false Charming Maid" Silvia (4), and the speaker. This benign triangle leads to the more treacherous tripartite relationship in "The Invitation," featuring the speaker, the capricious Silvia, and now a certain Damon, who seems to prefer this "cruel Shepherdess" (12). Its concluding lines, "I'le Crown thee with the pride o'th'Spring, / When thou art Lord of *May*," (17–18), foretell the final song in the set, "When *Jemmy* first began to Love," a somewhat subtle and comic jab at Charles's eldest illegitimate son. Jemmy-Monmouth, that "Gayest Swaine" (2), is indeed the Lord of May.

The next two poems, Pindarics addressed to Creech and Anne Wharton, Rochester's niece, follow from the song sequence and dictate the ordering of the six poems that ensue: "The sense of a Letter sent me, made into Verse," "The Return," "On a Copy of Verses made in a Dream and sent to me in a Morning before I was awake," "To My Lady *Morland* at *Tunbridge*," "Song to *Ceres*, in the wavering Nymph or *Mad Amyntas*," and "A Song in the same Play by the wavering Nymph." The opening address to Creech, "Thou great Young Man!" ("To Mr. *Creech*," 1), provides a linked contrast with the great young man Monmouth who seduces shepherdesses who cry "what becomes of me?" ("Song [When *Jemmy* first began to Love]," 32). The ending, an assurance to her friend that "We," Creech's readership, "are content to know and to admire thee in thy Sacred Verse" (143), foretells the purpose of the poem to Mrs. Wharton, praise of another great young man who makes sacred verses, "The Great, the God-like *Rochester*" ("To Mrs. W.," 31). One should not miss the droll self-advertisement of the poem, that the spirit of Rochester would deign to visit Behn, its purpose to raise and cheer her "Drooping Soul" (28), anxious to pass on its wisdom to the flagging Aphra and even to criticize her: "Obligingly it School'd my loose Neglect" (38). The last line of this poem, assuring Wharton that all would pay Rochester the debt of "humble Adoration, humble Praise" ("To Mrs. W," 72), glances back at "To Mr. *Creech*" and creates a link with the next two poems, "The sence of a Letter" and "The Answer," a type of dialogue between a man and a woman, his admiration and praise of her appropriately humble. The conclusion of "The Answer" chides the male letter writer and reminds him that, in spite of his protestations and tricks, "Some hard-hearted Nymph may return you your own" (18) in return for his "proudly you aim, / New conquests to gain" ("The sence of a Letter," 16–17).

This pair segues into "On a Copy of Verses made in a Dream," in which another nymph, not hard-hearted, relates how she has been conquered by poetical blandishments sent in epistolary form. That this letter-writing poet resembles "an unwearied Conqueror day and night" ("On a Copy of Verses," 39), connects to the first line of the next poem, "As when a Conqu'rour does in Triumph come" ("To My Lady *Morland* at *Tunbridge*," 1). This verse epistle, in which Behn amusingly chides her better for stealing her man (who is unworthy of them both), ends with the suggestion that her ladyship deserves "A Virgin-Heart" (47). The two songs that follow, which Behn had written for a revival of Thomas Randolph's *The Wavering Nymph: Or, Mad Amyntas* (1638), feature a real virgin, "Chaste *Urania*" ("Song to *Ceres*," 11), albeit heartless, and her answer to her swain, scornfully dismissing him and all his kind: "I the whining Fools despise, / That pay their Homage to my Eyes" ("Song in the same Play, by the *Wavering Nymph*," 9–10). One could even say that Lady Morland is a wavering nymph herself.

Again, Behn provides linkages by subtle contrasts. "The Disappointment," her most widely read poem in modern times, belies the alleged capriciousness of Lady Morland and her sex. The poem's virginal heroine, Cloris, only runs away from the confusion that Lysander's snake, soft to the touch, created for her expectations, she who had prepared herself to stay the course. At the same time, Behn's fine narrative expands on the cynicism of the two preceding pieces, an authorial technique of playing the jilt. The Nymph's scorn for the "Amorous *Swains*" who resign their hearts to her ("*Wavering Nymph*," 5–6) speaks to the fate of the unfor-

tunately detumescent Lysander, unable to perform the virgin sacrifice. "The Disappointment," like others of its
stature in the collection, stands alone as a bravura set piece
but is at the same time intimately connected to everything
it follows and precedes. Just as "*Juniper-Tree*" demonstrates
the possibility of Edenic bliss that "The Golden Age"
evokes, "The Disappointment" suggests the opposite: inexperience, fumbling, fear, a lack of fruition, and finally, a
flight followed by cursing. Its concluding phrase (with a
touch of scorn), "the Hell of *Impotence*" (140), foretells the
first phrase of the ensuing "On a Locket of Hair Wove in a
True-Loves Knot," "What means this Knot, in Mystick Order
Ty'd, / And which no Humane Knowledge can divide?" (1–2).
Lysander's impotence is itself a kind of true-love's knot,
blocking his natural functions, confusing, unanswerable,
unutterable except by Behn the observer, who is not a juniper tree happy to be sacrificed to keep the door of love's
temple. The couplets that fuel "On a Locket of Hair" pose a
series of questions about the object, concluding that it is "a
Quiver for the God of Love" (21), the hairs themselves Cupid's "subt'lest surest Darts" (24) that convey "tender Passions" (26). These constitute the subject of the next poem,
"The Dream," the story of Astrae, who finds Cupid weeping
and who is then tricked into loving: "waking found my
Dream too true, / Alas I was a Slave" (35–36). The following
piece, Behn's sole example of truly personal satire in the
collection, "A letter to a Brother of the Pen in *Tribulation*,"
begins "Art thou caught?" (1), a different kind of slavery
since the poem describes the unfortunate Damon, his bout
with venereal disease, and his blaming of the woman who
infected him. In heroic couplets, the same form she uses to
address Lady Morland, Behn mockingly encourages Damon
to "Curse till thou hast undone the Race" of women (47)—
just as Lysander does at the end of "Disappointment,"
contemplating his true-love's knot. All of these poems concerned with love and its consequences suggest that this
emotional state is cyclical, subject to constant recalibra-
tions, not only for the participants evoked within, but for
the reader, who may reevaluate the echoing verbiage, linkage, meanings.

Behn's next song sequence, an interrelated series of six

lyrics, follows Damon in his sweating-tub and suggests, as Shakespeare does in the last line of his Sonnets, that water cools not love. The first poem, ingeniously titled "The Reflection," reflects a distorted image of the brother of the pen in tribulation. While in that poem an unusually jocular Behn facetiously encourages Damon to complain and curse her sex, the figure of Serena in "Reflection" suggests that one ought not to do this—that women have enough grief. Although Serena is no more possessed of a sense of culpability than her ranting male predecessor, she is as meek as Damon is arrogant, in mental rather than physical distress, and "In Silent Tears a while declar'd / The Sense of all her wrong" (7–8). She laments that her "Rifled Joys no more can Please" (47) and addresses such a swain as Damon as well as "ye Springs, ye Meads and Groves" (49). She then descends to a river, on whose "Melancholy Shore" she declares, "I lay me down and dye" (55–56), presumably studying her image in the water. She reflects on her state just as Lysander does in *A Voyage*. Two Pindarics in this longer work present an image of Lysander's subjective distortions of his experience and his beloved (469–506; 1260–80). Serena's "Reflection" of course reflects the next poem, "Song: To *Pesibles* Tune," which features a man, Amyntas, lamenting the "cold Disdain" of a woman named Silvia. The prescience of Amyntas's wounded cry, "Some One, my Perjur'd Fair, / Revenging my Despair, / Will prove as false to thee" (29–31), ought to be noted, resembling Damon's as it does, approximating the despairing Serena's condition on the melancholy shore. The next lyric, "On her Loving Two Equally," is spoken by a young woman such as Serena, who is faced with the choice of two men, Alexis and Damon, and who cannot make up her mind, suffering from a "restless Feaver in my Blood" (14) for both men. One might observe here that this line could serve as an epigraph for Behn's poetry and the furious activity within it. The ensuing "The Counsel" then scolds such a woman, in this case the capricious Silvia, for her wavering and jilting: "for shame the Cheat give o'er" (2). It imagines pastoral heaven again, "embracing . . . / Loosly in Shades on Beds of Flow'rs" (21–22), the same flora, perhaps, used in simile to describe the "Unconfin'd" heart of Phillis, "free as Flow'rs on Meads and

Plains" in the next song, "The Surprize" (1–2). Phillis's astonishment is her discovery of her own unknown carnal stirrings, her awakening, as it were, typical of the collection. Behn's droll last line, "For Modesty to speak denies" (18), is undercut by the next poem, simply entitled "Song," in which Phillis refuses to be denied by modesty and speaks anyway, explaining to Strephon the shepherd that "A Softness does invade each Part" (6). The following song, "The Invitation," addressed to Phillis by, it seems, Strephon, encourages her to slake her desires, to "throw away this Coy Disguise, / And by the vigor of thy Eyes, / Declare thy Youth and Fire" (30–32), which the preceding "The Surprize" and "Song" clearly reveal her to have done already. And the last song in the sub-sequence, "Silvio's Complaint," another stab at Monmouth (cf. "When *Jemmy* first began to Love"), is related to the previous five in language, tone, form. It, like its predecessors, is set in tetrameter; it is a kind of pastoral; its speaker undercuts his own reliability; he is infected with love, whose fires water cannot cool.

The fine "In Imitation of *Horace*," the first of two such poems in the collection, songlike and bucolic, naturally follows its predecessors. It is also the first of several poems in which Behn imagines a woman's disappointment or grief regarding men, an expansion of Serena's earlier lament: "To *Lysander*, who made some Verses on a Discourse of Loves Fire," "A Dialogue for an Entertainment at Court," "On Mr. *J. H.* in a fit of sickness," and "To *Lysander* on some Verses he writ." One might also note that Behn recalls the Monmouthian "*Silvio's* Complaint" in the first line of the Horatian imitation. She addresses a man rather than Horace's nymph, but one nonetheless in possession of "Amorous Curles of Jet" ("Imitation," 1), undulating tresses that Monmouth was most famous for sporting. The poem ends with imagining the man's "Sighs and Touches" metaphorically as "the Gods of Loves Artillery" (23–24), the approximate subject of the next poem, linked in title as well as in theme: "To *Lysander*, who made some Verses on a Discourse of Loves Fire." This puzzling poem in Cowley's late metaphysical mode—each stanza elliptical and related enigmatically, even tenuously, to the next—finishes with the complaint of a woman scorned: "if such Rivals in your Heart

I find, / Tis in My Power to die, but not be kind" (35–36). One will find that "A Dialogue" concerns a man scorned, who then wins the woman over, in the manner that the woman in "To *Lysander*" wishes to be won over. In "A Dialogue," Damon, presumably recovered from the ordeal in the sweating-tub, promises his "constant Faith, and tender Love" (49). The speaker in the ensuing "On Mr. *J. H.* In a Fit of Sickness," probably Aphra herself, demonstrates precisely such constancy to Hoyle in his time of need, what she must have wished that he would have shown to her, she who sought to avoid the charge of Silviadom. This exuberant and grieving Pindaric ends with an image of total loyalty as well as the sense of the deprivation that must ensue for the speaker on the parting of the couple. The numbered quatrains that follow, "To *Lysander*, on some Verses he writ," also concerns deprivation, in this case Lysander's withholding of his heart from the speaker, who complains of the same triangular double-dealing evoked in the "Loves Fire" poem: "For the sly Gamester, who ne'er plays me fair, / Must Trick for Trick expect to find" (51–52). The six lyrics are about nothing if not men's gamesmanship, trickery, and jealousy, the nausea of love for women, at least for women in Restoration comedies, if their complaints can be read as editorials.

Appropriately, and jiltingly, the next four poems, also a set, answer or present a distorted reflection of the previous six songs that criticize men and their ways. "To the Honourable *Edward Howard*, on his Comedy called *The New Utopia*," exorcises the disappointment and grief of its predecessors. Behn's poem to the brother of Dryden's brother-in-law (i.e., the aforementioned Sir Robert Howard, a more distinguished playwright) suggests, in its paradigm of writerly reciprocity, her ideal of male behavior, personally as well as professionally.[14] In "To *Lysander*, on some Verses he writ," Behn longs for personal reciprocity; in "To the Honourable *Edward Howard*," she demonstrates that she herself is capable of it. It encourages Howard to give full rein to his muse, to "let her lowdly Sing in every Ear" (94). The next piece, not surprisingly, concerns music, "To *Lysander* at the *Musick-Meeting*." (Just as the poem to Howard will remind some of Jonson's "Come, leave the loathed

stage," the poem to Lysander will remind others of Marvell's "The Fair Singer.") *"Musick-Meeting"* explains that
"Musick prepares and warms the Soul to Love" (36). The ensuing "An *Ode* to *Love*" also concerns Lysander, and reha-
bilitates him from his earlier incarnation as a writer of
insincere verses. The line from *"Musick-Meeting"* explains,
in essence, how Behn's songs were supposed to affect their
hearers, as this poem does, more of love's "Artillery" (18)
that will work itself on "the next Fair and Yeilding She"
(26), the subject of the next poem, "Love Reveng'd," about
such a she.

These poems foretell the political pair that follows: "Song
[Young *Jemmy* was a Lad]" on Monmouth and the satirical
"The Cabal at *Nickey Nackeys*" on Shaftesbury, as well as
the translations that follow these, "A Paraphrase on the
Eleventh *Ode* Out of the first Book of *Horace*" and "A Translation." "Love Reveng'd" ends with "in her Eyes she reads
her Fate" (18); the song to Jemmy-Monmouth is also about
fate; the Nickey-Nackey poem on Shaftesbury is naturally
related, as these two men are in history and in *Absalom and
Achitophel:* "And tho' we are the Knaves, we know who's the
Fool" ("The Cabal," 16). The Horatian paraphrase, an apos-
trophe in the mode of Catullus to Silvia to avoid scorning
the present (evoked earlier at the end of "Golden Age"),
urges that only "Busy Gown-men search to know / Their
Fates above," (3–4), a linkage with the image of fate in the
Jemmy song and the catalogue of intriguing fools in the
brief burst of satire on Shaftesbury. Its companion piece,
"A Translation," also a Latin poem, is similarly carpe diem.

The major works that end the volume, "A Paraphrase on
Oenone to *Paris*" and *A Voyage*, encompass every motif in the
previous forty-four poems. The last chapter of the present
study will discuss the masterful way that *A Voyage* makes its
linkage with its predecessors (its last couplet, "Then I
shou'd take the Wing, and upwards fly, / And loose the Sight
of this dull World with Joy" [2195–96], connects back to the
soaring flight of "The Golden Age" above the dull world of
London and thus completes the corona). A few words on
"Oenone to *Paris*" on this score are necessary here. This fine
reimagining of *Heroides* 5 is on Behn's perennial erotic
theme, that of a woman complaining to the man who de-

serted her for another. Oenone alludes to "those Eyes" (17) of Paris that wounded her, much as Behn's speakers bitterly remember the masculine gaze and its power to flatter, control, and seduce. Oenone has a bit of the arrogant shepherdess in her: "Me all the Village Herdsmen strove to gain" (35). Many of Behn's Silvias think much the same thing, and then get their comeuppance. Oenone's frank appreciation of her physical joys with Paris, "Now uncontroll'd we meet, uncheck'd improve / Each happier minute" (66–67) will remind many readers of the praise of the Blessed Minute in *"Juniper-Tree"* and elsewhere. Even her fetishistic admission that she wears Paris's amorous curls of jet as "sacred Charms" and "Bracelets" reminds one of "On a Locket of Hair Wove in a True-Loves Knot." And the last line of *"Oenone,"* "And pierce that dear, that faithless Heart of thine" (313), speaks to every disappointed poem on Lysander and Hoyle, as well as the approximate theme of *A Voyage*—which some might note is really a long verse epistle, just as *"Oenone to Paris"* is. Dryden, for whose collection the Ovidian piece was first written, admired it very much: "I was desired to say that the author, who is of the fair sex, understood not Latin. But if she does not, I am afraid that she has given us occasion to be ashamed who do" (Preface to the Translation of *Ovid's Epistles*, 1680 [K 1:243]).

III

the frequent alteration of the Rhythm and Feet affects the mind with a more various delight, while it is soon apt to be tyr'd by the setled pace of any one constant measure.

—Thomas Sprat, *An Account of the Life and Writings of Mr. Abraham Cowley*, 1668 (CE 2:132)

Sprat's praise of Behn's poetical mentor nicely evokes her refusal to tire her reader with the settled pace of a constant measure. And, with this diversity, she provides prosodic as well as thematic linkages between poems, again anxious to show the world what she can do. (Perhaps her most bravura metrical performance is "A Dialogue for an Entertainment at Court, between *Damon* and *Sylvia*" in which she uses six different stanzaic forms.) What her age terms "Pindarick" or "Pindarique" is undoubtedly her most experimental form, in Cowley's mode rather than the Greek *auctor* who precedes them. As my next chapter will argue, the Pindaric has been neglected in the history of English poetry, dismissed as the stuff of Augustan poetasters whom Pope, Johnson, and Eliot skewer with glee (as if their own poetics had not profited from their reading of Dryden's exercises in the form). It should instead be praised as a vehicle of liberation for mid- and late-seventeenth-century poets, who used it to experiment with meter, line-length, tone—even the concept of "form" itself.[15] One need not be rigid or even numbingly consistent. Rhymes can accrue as they will; lines can change their length as it pleases their creator. The very couplets that "structurally replicated principles of social order and civic harmony," as Gerald MacLean puts it, need not confine one.[16] Hobbes, whose view of the possibilities of social order and civic harmony are dark indeed, suggests that couplets actually force poets to be delusory: "for a man to obstruct his own way with unprofitable difficulties is a great imprudence . . . to chuse a needlesse and difficult correspondence of Rime is but a difficult toy, and forces a man sometimes for the stopping of a chink to say somewhat he did never think" ("The Answer of Mr. Hobbes to Sr. Will. D'Avenant's Preface before *Gondibert*," 1650 [CE 2:57]). The popularity of the Pindaric could be read as an endorsement of such a statement, and implies that other types of harmony were possible. Or, as a noted commentator explains, the "Enraptured" poet can examine a subject "from all sides in the logical and chronological disorder that . . . is the truest order of the excited mind."[17] Behn's experiments with the form suggest that she was happy to avoid stopping chinks with what she did never think.

Since most Pindarics, Behn's especially, differ widely from one another, to describe and scan them individually would be somewhat pointless. Like Cowley's, hers are discursive, but unlike his, rarely on a focused theme such as wit or inconstancy. They tend to be more occasional (like Pindar's form itself), but always with the illusion of intimacy: "On the *Death* of Mr. *Grinhil*," "To the Honourable *Edward Howard*," "To Mrs. W. On her Excellent Verses," "To

Mr. *Creech*," "A Farewel to *Celladon*," and "On a Copy of
Verses made in a Dream," among others. These poems are
meditative and allusive, sometimes wrenchingly personal,
even anguished, as "On Mr. *J. H.* In a fit of Sickness." All deploy different line lengths: the expected pentameter and tetrameter, even sometimes hexameters and trimeters for
special effect. For each she uses a slightly different form,
sometimes from stanza to stanza. For example, "The Golden
Age" has as its first stanza a4 b3 a5 b5 c5 d5 c5 d5 e5 e5 f5 g5
f4 f4 f4 g5: two quatrains, one couplet, one triplet that splits
two rhyming lines, one line that rhymes with the triplet, the
a-rhyme unbalanced between tetrameter and pentameter,
the b-rhyme featuring a pairing of trimeter and pentameter.
Behn understood the distinguishing emphasis of a very long
or short line, something that she learned from Donne, Herbert, and Traherne, as well as Cowley. Her modulations
heighten the effect of the passions therein; the preceding
diagram of the first stanza of "Golden Age" provides the
template for the illusion of exuberance that the poem presents, the "truest order of the excited mind."

Not only does Behn have a favored form, but also has a
preferred line-length—tetrameter—one that Marvell before
her and Swift after her use for different effects, hypnotic
and comic in their couplets. Like her more distinguished
colleagues who practice it, she understands that it suits the
lighter touch, or the illusion of the rococo jeu d'esprit when
she has something more serious to say. Indeed, perhaps
"the most obvious joke is customarily in the rhyme itself."[18]
She also seems fearless in applying tetrameter to varying
forms. She chooses it for narrative in *"Juniper-Tree"* and deploys couplets for the incantatory effect in the mode of the
French romancers of the twelfth century such as Marie and
Chrétien, the witches in *Macbeth,* or Marvell's "Coy Mistress." In songs or thumbnail sketches of her friends, she
sometimes fuses tetrameter couplets into sestets, such as
"A Ballad on Mr. *J. H.* to *Amoret*" (i.e., aabbcc), or into quatrains (and much larger blocks) such as in "Our Cabal." For
lyrics, Behn also seems unafraid to forge tetrameter stanzas
that are not simply the result of compressing couplets. In
the alternately rhyming "Love Arm'd" (ababcdcd), she
makes an octet. In "The Invitation [*Damon* I cannot blame

your will]," she divides two couplets with a rhyme to make a sestet (aabccb). She even bifurcates two triplets in an octet with a rhyme to make a different kind of octet, such as the corresponding poem with the same title but a different addressee, "The Invitation: A Song [Come, my *Phillis*, let us improve]" (aaabcccb). And the masterfully crafted ten-line stanza of "The Disappointment," a narrative in the mode of "*Juniper-Tree*," features nine tetrameter lines with a finishing pentameter (i.e., abbacddce4e5). It glances at the Spenserian stanza that Keats would use so well in "The Eve of St. Agnes," with its eight pentameter lines and concluding alexandrine (ababbcbc5c6).

Just as Behn can make tetrameter into a great and supple thing, she is also capable of using even lighter lines and forms for diverse effects. "The Willing Mistriss," "The Dream, "The Reflection," and most notoriously, the satirical "Song [When *Jemmy* first began to Love]" reflect her deployment of English Common Meter. This quatrain of the Puritan hymn is really a fourteener that the poet breaks so that it rhymes in the middle (i.e., a4 b3 a4 b3), a form that Emily Dickinson uses in virtually every poem. Furthermore, Behn dares to experiment with anapestic meters, as well, which prove extremely difficult to manage and can sound ridiculous in the wrong hands. Both "The Sence of a Letter sent me" and the accompanying "The Return" are triumphant evidence of Behn's skills in this area, built in sestets of two couplets divided by a rhyme (a2 a2 b4 c2 c2 b4).

Surely Behn knew that pentameter was considered the greater and more esteemed form, the playground of Dryden, Milton, Shakespeare, Ben. Her choice of this meter reflects her other prosodic decisions—capricious, varied, and useful. She uses the heroic couplet where one would expect, in the verse epistle "To my Lady *Morland* at *Tunbridge*." The poem begins in a dignified and formal fashion, gently and slyly modulating to the satirical in which we see that Behn's comic point is that her ladyship is the object of a sly dig for her willingness to take on Aphra's leftover men, for whom both of them are far too good. The more avowedly satirical "A Letter to a Brother of the Pen in *Tribulation*" thereby constitutes the perfect medium for the heroic couplet, Behn surely having seen the usage to which Dryden put it in *MacFlecknoe*. It is perhaps not glib to note that a pentameter line allows for more material than a tetrameter one, more room for meditative and metaphysical thinking, such as is reflected in "On a Locket of Hair Wove in a True-Loves Knot" and "To *Lysander* at the *Musick-Meeting*," and, of course, the Ovidian verse epistle "*Oenone* to *Paris*." Behn also deploys pentameter in the non-couplet form: the sestets of "In Imitation of *Horace*" (ababcc), and the enigmatic "To *Lysander*, who made some Verses on a Discourse of Loves Fire," and in the alternating quatrains (abab) of Dryden's *Annus Mirabilis*, "To *Lysander*, on some Verses he writ." In form and meter, Behn demonstrates her desire to "tread in those successful Paths my Predecessors have so long thriv'd in, to take those Measures that both the Ancient and Modern Writers have set me" (Preface to *The Luckey Chance*, 1686–87 [W 7:217]). She wishes to be admired and understood.

IV

> What Man that does not boast of the Numbers he had thus ruin'd, and, who does not glory in the shameful Triumph? Nay, what Woman, almost, has not a pleasure in Deceiving, taught, perhaps, at first, by some dear false one, who had fatally instructed her Youth in an Art she ever after practis'd, in Revenge on all those she could could be too hard for, and conquer at their own Weapons?
>
> —"The History of the Nun; Or, the Fair
> ˙Vow Breaker," 1689 (W 3:211)

One of the last things Behn wrote, this rueful editorial on her own modern iron age in one of her prehistoric works of short fiction, helps account for the importance of the first poem in her collection. Reading "The Golden Age" against this outburst suggests that the nascent vein of pessimism one can discern in the passage above never leaves her, a sense that interactions between fallen people must always fail. (Even Ovid, the most celebrated evoker of golden ages, knows that he writes from the perspective of bronze or iron.) Yet, at the same time, the hope and optimism in "Golden Age" permeates everything that follows it and provides for a different kind of unity besides circular linkages, forms, and prosodic concatenations. In theory, the poem represents her pastoral Eden, "When no scorn'd Shepherds on your Banks were seen" (3), which Behn puts into practice in *"Juniper-Tree"* and *"Celladon,"* whose swains achieve the blessed minute. Its pleasantly "artificial" world represents the very opposite of the Kent from which she had escaped and the London that she endured. No filth, dead animals, rotten teeth, or putrid water can be discerned in the poem and its successors, in keeping with other cavalier notions of pastoral, such as Lovelace's "Love Made in the First Age: To *Cloris.*"[19] It has no particular smell, but it is "Aromatick" (10), a word that permeates the poem, and to which she returns in *"Juniper-Tree"* (3). Flowers, naturally, provide much latent sexual imagery, male and female: "Whose fragrant Heads in Mystick Twines above" (11); "still young opening Buds each moment grew" (42). Behn's complicated figure of the serpent (not nocent yet, as Milton would say) and detumescent penis also makes its first appearance in "Golden Age": "No spightful Venom in the wantons lay; / But to the touch were Soft" (47–48). She will pick this up again, so to speak, in "Disappointment" (110), and "Fair *Clarinda*" (15–17). It represents her Eden, happily populated by baroque "young wanton Gods of Love" (15) or "little Gay-wing'd Loves" (85) that flutter through the rest of the collection, even in *A Voyage*, where Lysander notes "A little *Cupid* waiting by my side" (384). The appropriately irregular, free Pindaric form of "The Golden Age" demonstrates her comfort and ease not only with lines of all lengths, but with poetry itself.

Again, although Behn proves herself a committed polemical poet in her later work,[20] the political has little function in this collection, unless one chooses to read the following as dangerous topical statement: "Monarchs were uncreated then, / Those Arbitrary Rulers over men" ("Golden Age," 51–52); "Ambition was not known" (55). It might also be possible to read such comments as the pastoral urge toward the Horatian cultivation of ease, a theme to which she returns in much of what follows. Man was better off "Till false Ambition made him range" ("A Farewel to *Celladon*,"16). "Business" is "the Check to Mirth and Wit, / . . . the Rival of the Fair" (37–38). Her strongest attack in the poem is on Honour, "the Error and the Cheat / Of the Ill-natur'd Bus'ey Great" ("Golden Age," 74–75), "thou who first did damn, / A Woman to the Sin of shame" (117–18), a villain she actually personifies in *A Voyage* who snatches Aminta from her beloved not once, but twice (1310, 1840). Hardly a necessary virtue to cultivate in a golden world, Honour causes men to boast and women to deceive as they calibrate the odds against one another, an idea to which Behn returns constantly, as in her shepherdess's outburst against the deceitful and boastful Lysander, who wishes to plight his troth to more than one: "Honour does your Wish deny, / Honour! the Foe to your Repose" ("*Lysander* . . . Loves Fire," 25–26). The libertinism of her contemporaries constitutes an empty parody of the freedom in the golden world. "Then it was glory to pursue delight, / And that was lawful all, that Pleasure did invite" ("Golden Age," 80–81). Here, shepherds should avoid being "uninspir'd" (96) and maids should yield: "Trembling and blushing are not marks of shame, / But the Effect of kindling Flame" (100–101). Much kindling is effected in subsequent verses: "Her new desire she could not hide: / Nor wou'd the Shepherd be deny'd" ("On a *Juniper-Tree*," 49–50).

Honour is the consequence of living in an iron age. "Miser Honour, hord'st the sacred store" ("Golden Age," 136), the "base Debaucher of the generous heart" (140), something that should "Be gone!" (166), but which we see cannot be gone even from the collection itself, its allegorical personification abducting Aminta as it does in *A Voyage:* "*Honour* I call him: *Tyrant* of the Wood" (1422). Many of these sentiments can be found in Cowley, Behn's poetical mentor, who entertained her mind and in whose works she found every pair entwined. We shall see how she reads and reconstitutes Cowley, who gives her license to express herself frankly on matters of sexual love.

2

Notions of the Lyric and Pindaric: The Debt to Cowley

Books give me no content at all;
Unless soft *Cowly* entertain my Mind,
  Then every pair in Love I find
                    —*A Voyage to the Isle of Love* (486–88)

whoever would do him right should not only equal him
to the Principal Ancient Writers of our own Nation, but
should also rank his name amongst the Authors of the
true Antiquity, the best of the *Greeks* and *Romans*.
          —Thomas Sprat, *An Account of the Life and
          Writings of Mr. Abraham Cowley*, 1668 (CE 2:145)

IT MAY SEEM INCOMPREHENSIBLE TO MODERNS THAT A POET OF
Behn's type or that an intellect of Sprat's stature would
value Cowley, whose reputation has been in eclipse ever
since Dr. Johnson's somewhat magisterial condemnation of
him and his ilk in *The Lives of the Poets* (1781). He did not
benefit from the revaluation of the "metaphysical" style in
T. S. Eliot's famous essay named for this group of English
baroque writers (1921), itself required reading for countless
university survey courses in seventeenth-century literature
whose syllabi seldom include even a stanza of Cowley. However, in keeping with her time, Behn thought this poet magnificent, fully worthy of burial in Westminster Abbey near
Chaucer and Spenser, clearly deserving of the ecstatic
praise of the historian of the Royal Society, an organization
not known for its endorsement of figurative language of any
kind.[1] Her hero Rochester would certainly agree, he also a
poet of an entirely different type, not given to the elaborate
conceits that Cowley spins in his lyrics and odes. Behn, like

65

Rochester, refashions this important predecessor, using as foundation something that Sprat takes scant interest in, his "soft" (romantic) subject matter. Once one understands how she receives and reconfigures him, her debt to him becomes apparent.

I

> a further misconception of [Cowley's] talents is seen in the so-called Pindaric Odes, the ungainly parents of much of the worst verse of the subsequent hundred years.
>
> —Helen Gardner, 1958[2]

> The Reader will perceive that Mrs. *Behn* had no Notion of a Pindarick Poem, any farther than it consisted of ir-regular Numbers, and sav'd the Writer the Trouble of even Measure; which indeed is all our common Pindar-ick Poets know of the Matter.
>
> —*Muses Mercury*, 1707 (S 6:427)

We should discount the archness of Gardner and her anony-mous eighteenth-century predecessor concerning writers of "Pindaricks" during the Restoration. They do not appreci-ate how the form "demands that the speaker's fervor bubble up through irregular meter, jumps of thought, exclama-tions, and the profusion of imagery that a heated imagina-tion naturally employs."[3] In order to create such effects on her own readers, Behn studied Cowley to learn how the an-cient Greek ode worked so that she could imitate and emu-late it, thereby refashioning it for her own time.[4] When Swift describes Pindar's defeat of "*Afra*, the *Amazon* light of foot," in *The Battel of the Books* (1697), he surely means to imply that Behn fails in this activity, just as the ancient au-thor's previous vanquishing of Cowley suggests that her pre-decessor falls short, as well.[5] Yet Sprat would not agree. He defines his friend's heuristical processing of the classical past as "this imitating of *Pindar*, which may perhaps be thought rather a new sort of Writing than a restoring of an Ancient" (*An Account* [CE 2: 145]). He appreciates (and fore-tells) these poets' exuberance, wit, and daring experimen-tation with line-length and rhyme, their approximation of

how Pindar would have sounded in the court of Charles II
and his brother James. What did Behn value in Cowley besides "softness"? Sprat's continued praise provides several
clues:

> If his Verses in some places seem not as soft and flowing as
> some would have them, it was his choice, not his fault. He knew
> that in diverting mens minds there should be the same variety
> observ'd as in the prospects of their Eyes, where a Rock, a Prec-
> ipice, or a rising Wave is often more delightful than a smooth,
> even ground or calm Sea. . . . He never runs his Reader nor his
> Argument out of Breath. He perfectly practices the hardest se-
> cret of good Writing, to know when he has done enough. He al-
> ways leaves off in such a manner that it appears it was in his
> power to have said much more. (*An Account* [CE 2:129–30])

He appreciates exactly what Johnson would later condemn,
the irregular, jagged stanzas, the roughness of the diction
and rhyme, the mutant metaphors. Curiously, his encomium
also claims that Cowley's poetry exemplifies restraint and
tension, even brevity, precisely the opposite of Johnson's
judgment that the extravagances of *The Mistress* (1647)
surely do not reflect an understanding of when one has
done enough, the opposite of good sense and natural wit.
Perhaps even Eliot would not have wished the collection
longer than it is. Yet Behn's poetry implies that she would
have, and that she read Cowley with almost exactly the
same reverence as Sprat did, albeit in a different spirit.
Poetry should not always be smooth and flowing; an argument or reader should not be run out of breath; one should
leave off even though there is more to say. Thomas Rymer,
that notorious mocker of *Othello* and deflator of extravagant
metaphors, also suggests what Behn took away from her
reading of Cowley: "He understood the purity, the *perspecu-
ity*, the *majesty* of stile and the vertue of *numbers*. He could
discerne what was beautiful and pleasant in Nature, and
could express his Thoughts without the least difficulty or
constraint. He understood to dispose of the matters, and to
manage his Digressions" (Preface to the Translation of *Rapin's Reflections on Aristotle's Treatise of Poesie*, 1674 [CE
2:171]). A poet need not always present a harmonious surface. He should avoid blandness yet express the beautiful

as accurately and as decorously as he can help his reader to discern it, avoiding digressions and taking care to imply, not to declaim.

Cowley, self-aware to the point of self-depreciation, despaired that his readers would understand his poetic experiments. He may have seen that the prehistoric Augustan mode adopted by Waller and other Sons of Ben would trump the style of Donne from which his own descends. He knew that his poetry taxed the patience of his readers and that those who navigated it wished to see fewer rocks and rising waves, calmer seas, and even a less majestic style:

> as for the *Pindarick Odes* . . . I am in great doubt whether they will be understood by most *Readers* . . . The digressions are many and sudden, and sometimes long, according to the fashion of all *Lyriques*, and of *Pindar* above all men living. The figures are unusual and even bold, even to *Temeritie*, and such as I durst not have to do withal in any other kinde of *Poetry*. The *Numbers* are various and irregular, and sometimes (especially some of the long ones) seem harsh and uncouth, if the just measures and cadencies be not observed in the *Pronounciation*. So that almost all their *Sweetness* and *Numerosity* . . . lies in a maner wholly at the *Mercy* of the *Reader*. (Preface to *Poems*, 1656 [CE 2:86])

Behn learns from this, as well, discerning that she risked the scorn of her readership as a consequence of her own experiments. One must trust the reader to be merciful. She seems to have memorized Cowley's *Pindarique Odes* in the 1656 *Poems:* the neoclassical solemnity of the first, "On the Praise of Poetry," as well as the stoicism of the fourth, "On the Uncertainty of Fortune." The fifth ode, "In Commendation of the Time We Live Under, the Reign of Our Gracious *King Charles*," conceives of the very Golden Age that Behn would evoke to commence *Poems upon Several Occasions*. Her other Pindaric odes in the collection, "A Farewel to *Celladon*," "On the Death of Mr. *Grinhil*," "To the Honourable *Edward Howard*," "On Mr. *J. H.* In a Fit of Sickness," reflect Cowley also, with their stately paces and controlled exuberance tempering the public voice with private, even intimate, reflection.

Elizabeth Spearing stresses the importance of the 1656

preface and edition for Behn, a text that "must have contributed powerfully to an association of translation with poetic innovation and creativity" so that, in forming her own
"politics of translation" she could transcend the political
and negotiate a "distinctive, and distinctively feminine,
participation in power-relationships involving text and
reader."[6] I suggest that there are other, more prosaic negotiations. Behn's poems seem relatively unencumbered by digressions, bold and extravagant figures, and certainly of
harsh and uncouth meter. But her line-length is equally various and irregular when it suits her in her Pindarics, her
formal inheritance from her model. Free from the tyranny
of a rigidly set form such as the pentameter couplet, a poet
can modulate one's line-length to suit the phrase or situation for emphasis and, in effect, un-corset her verses. She
appreciates the opportunity to lay "stiff Heroicks by," and
to pursue "this more *Gay*, more *Airy* Path" ("To *Henry Higden, Esq*; on his Translation of the *Tenth Satyr* of *Juvenal*," 28
[W 1: 229]). One could even say that her prosody and diction
approximate the encomiums of Sprat and Rymer for Cowley
more than his own writing could ever fulfill such praise.
Sprat's enthusiasm for his late friend's poetry also hints at
another freedom that Behn allows herself:

> never yet so much was written on a subject so Delicate, that can
> less offend the severest rules of Morality. The whole passion of
> Love is inimitably describ'd, with all its mighty Train of Hopes,
> and Joys, and Disquiets. Besides this amorous tenderness, I
> know not how in every Copy there is something of more useful
> Knowledge very naturally and gracefully insinuated, and every
> where there may be something found to inform the minds of
> wise Men as well as to move the hearts of young Men or Women.
> (*An Account* [CE 2:131])

Sprat's droll last sentence implies that the eroticism of
Cowley's collection provided the offensively delicate subject. The next century would turn such drollery into mock-
ery of the author. Johnson dismisses Cowley's love verses as
insincere and insipid: "The compositions are such as might
have been written for penance by a hermit, or for hire by a
philosophical rhymer who had only heard of another sex."[7]

However, in Cowley's own time, the venerable Edmund Elys castigated him for concupiscence in preface to his *Divine Poems* (1659), and would do so again in the ingeniously titled *An Exclamation to All those that love the Lord Jesus in sincerity, against an apology written by an ingenious person for Mr. Cowley's lascivious and prophane verses* (1670). Although Behn's more hostile readers found little in her verse that they would have labeled useful knowledge, her escort of commenders at the beginning of *Poems upon Several Occasions* champions her inimitable descriptions of love and the situations in which it arises, as well as the power that such descriptions have to move the hearts of the young. Behn, a quick study, did not need more justification than this to be free in her quest for universal approbation. Although a detailed study of Cowley's oeuvre is not possible or necessary here, some examples from it, read against Behn, will reveal that she was an avid reader of *The Mistress;* it gave her a license to write.

II

Till now, my careless Muse no higher strove
T'inlarge her Glory, and extend her Wings;
   Than underneath *Parnassus* Grove,
To sing of Shepherds, and their humble Love;
But never durst, like *Cowly,* tune her Strings,
   To sing of Heroes and of Kings
          —Behn, "A Pindaric Poem to the Reverend
          Doctor *Burnet,*" 33–38 (W 1:308), 1688

This excerpt from Behn's sarcastic poem to Rochester's first biographer (and William of Orange's most ardent clerical supporter) suggests not similarity between her mentor and herself but the most apparent difference between them. She wrote no (strangled) epic such as the *Davideis.* There are no poems in extremely bad taste such as "Maidenhead," whose most amusing and unbearable couplet runs, "Thou thing of subtil, slippery kind, / Which *Women lose,* and yet no *Man* can *find!*" (23–24).[8] There are no religious lyrics in *Poems upon Several Occasions*, no intricate musings on abstract philosophical themes. She refuses to be fettered in the metaphorical logic of the more desiccated metaphysical style in which Cowley sometimes tangles himself. Another difference may be discerned from Graham Parry's comment on *The Mistress* as a collection: "What is striking is the absence of social setting in these poems: Cowley has dispensed with the courtly or pastoral backgrounds that gave Cavalier love-poetry much of its character and appeal, writing instead of unlocalized love—and unerotic love as well—in a way that was immediately successful."[9] One could say that *Poems upon Several Occasions* is entirely "social setting," completely derivative from (if not dependent on) Cavalier tradition. However, another idea lurks beneath the surface of the critic's observation: the absolutely apolitical nature of *The Mistress*. And this absence of the political constitutes Behn's general inheritance from Cowley for her own volume. If this paragon of poetry felt free to dispense with panegyrics and other verses on contemporary events and affairs of state, she had permission to do the same. Cowley's fervent wish to excise the urban and embrace the rural constitutes a license for Aphra to create her pastoral world: "Who . . . can endure the stings, / The *Crowd*, and *Buz*, and *Murmurings* / Of this great *Hive*, the *City*[?]" ("The Wish," 6–8). Shepherds and the shepherdesses who love them require a rural milieu. Celladon will fare better in Ireland; lovers will reach their consummations under juniper trees in the country.

Behn attached importance to the surface details in *The Mistress*, its poetical forms and rhetorical habits, its aesthetic of variation and multiplicity, for which Sprat praises Cowley: "For certainly, in all Ancient or Modern Times, there can scarce any Authour be found, that has handled so many different Matters in such various sorts of Style" (*An Account* [CE 2:119]). The tetrameter of "My Heart Discovered"; the echoing and emotive choruses of "The Despair": "*Ah wretched youth!* twice did I sadly cry: / *Ah wretched youth!* the fields and floods reply" (8–9); the mellifluously songlike nature of what is already a musical form, the lyric. Indeed, seventeenth-century composers set most of *The Mistress* to music, as the most recent modern edition of the collection extensively documents in over three hundred pages.[10] Accordingly, twenty-two of Behn's compositions in

Poems upon Several Occasions are songs or are labeled as such. And, as we have seen, she employs Cowley's tetrameters extensively in these verses. She knew that "Beauty and *Musick* must the Soul disarme" ("To *Lysander*, at the *Musick-Meeting*," 32), as her mentor did. Whence Behn's constant use of abstractions, such as in "The Golden Age"?

> *Lust*, the scorching *Dog-star*, here
> Rages with immoderate *heat*;
> Whil'st *Pride* the rugged *Northern Bear*
> In others makes the *Cold* too great
> ("The Welcome," 19–22)

One could say that the foregoing quatrain explains, in its extremity, precisely the conflict that occupies most of Behn's poetry, albeit from her more restrained point of view. Allegory, it seems, was safest for Cowley to make his moral arguments, to explain the systole and diastole of courtship. Here Behn found precedent to do the same, to delineate in pastoral code the ravages of Honour in the hypocrisy of an Iron Age. *A Voyage*, of course, provides her most extended use of this form, and may reflect Cowley's influence even more than the Gallic personifications that she anglicizes from Tallemant.

A theme in *The Mistress* that may have been of immense significance to Behn, one that the greater part of a masculine readership (however enlightened) may not have noticed at the end of the seventeenth century (or discern at the beginning of the twenty-first): Cowley is remarkably kind and courtly to women. One may note a touch of misogyny in *The Mistress*, but it is remarkably free from Gould's savagery, Rochester's violent prurience, Wycherley's sniggering contempt. Its author does not rehearse the Petrarchan trope of passive-aggressive servitude to his addressee. Instead, his pose of sincerity suggests an appreciation, even a gratitude for any attention he might receive, not anger at a perceived failure on the woman's part for not loving him: "Let me but *love*, what ere she be, / Shee cannot seem *deform'd to me*" ("The Request," 10–11). He exorcises Donne's rage as he attempts to reinvigorate the trope of the woman as all: "Men strait shall cast their eyes on Thee / And know at first that *Thou art Shee*" ("The Given Love," 71–72). The focus does not seem to be exclusively on a frustrated or enraged male speaker, but "*She* who is all the world" ("The Wish," 35) because she bestows the gift of Love, which "like a *God* by pow'rful Art, / 'Twas *all* in *all*, and *all* in *every Part*" ("All-over, Love," 9–10). Janet Todd's imaginative reconstruction of Behn's psyche suggests why such sentiments may have been attractive to her. She "opposed arranged unions and felt temperamentally at odds with marriage in general. Yet, what else was there for a young woman? To turn from idealised love and marriage was to enter the libertine world with its misogyny and lonely pregnancies."[11] Cowley provides an antidote to such libertinism, its male-centered ethos of inconstancy, as well as an alternative to the prison that patriarchal marriage structures created for women. He does not wish to be subtle, reserved, distant, ironic, but to create the illusion that the woman addressed possesses an indescribable singularity, one that a reader might feel free to re-create in herself as vicarious beneficiary.

Perhaps Behn noticed that sometimes the attachment between Cowley's lovers extends to androgyny, a step further than his predecessor Donne's idea of unity in "The Extasie" and "A Valediction: Forbidding Mourning," he who sharply and ironically separates the genders elsewhere in his corpus. In this concluding conceit, Cowley's notion argues that by exchanging hearts, "So powerful is this change, it render can, / My *outside Woman*, and your *inside Man*" ("The Change," 23–24). However, this exchange transcends the surface. He demands that a reader rethink the traditional binaries of gender in order to confront or even dissolve them in the interest of mutuality. In another poem, he achieves unity more drastically: "I Thee, both as a *man*, and *woman* prize; / For a perfect *Love* implies / Love in *all Capacities*" ("Platonick Love," 12–14). Here, the binaries still exist, but their dichotomous nature creates, paradoxically, even stronger unity for the lovers, within themselves and toward each other. Again, Cowley seems to have served as a significant precedent for Behn. Androgyny surely informs her notion of self-presentation, the woman who defines writing as her masculine part, who solicits praise from male commenders not just for conventional feminine beauty but for her manly pen, who writes poems such as "To the fair *Clarinda*, who made Love to me, imagin'd more than Woman" (1688), whose arboreal speaker in *"Juniper-Tree"* keeps its gender indefinite so that the reader cannot discern whether it robs a kiss from the shepherd or the shepherdess (36), who praises a member of her circle, "His Beauty Maid; but Man, his Mein" ("Our Cabal," 190)—this an apt description of the way she wished to be perceived, seeking poetical love in all capacities, to be prized as both man and woman, just as Cowley dared to do before her.

Johnson (and probably Eliot) could not stomach the extremity of Cowley's ideas about love, unsurprising for a person of his tastes at the end of the eighteenth century. In contrast, Behn found herself so powerfully attracted to these ideas that she, in a sense, answers them with her own notions, equally unsurprising for a person of her tastes at the end of the seventeenth century. She also shows an awareness of what is conventional about *The Mistress*. As with virtually all serial addressees of the Renaissance, the male poet shows little interest in fashioning a subjectivity for his female object—like Shakespeare's Man Right Fair and Woman Colored Ill, the Mistress has no name—yet shows much more interest in defining his own perspective toward her. Still, Cowley subtly recalibrates the parameters of the conventions that he inherits, just as Behn will refashion him. The Mistress's singularity lies in the poet's appreciation of her centrality and her androgyny. She does not in herself necessarily reflect corporate masculine poetical perspectives:

> I would not have *her know* the pain,
> The Torments for her I sustain:
> Lest too much *goodness* make her throw
> Her *Love* upon a *Fate* too low.
>
> ("Love undiscovered," 9–12)

He does not grovel, but attempts to recapture the sense of gratitude for the possibility of being loved. Who would not want to hear this, or something like it? The position transcends the hoary dynamic of lover as vassal and lady as lord by the intensity of sentiment and the sense of unworthiness. The concept of devotion should be all the more notable when one considers the libertine milieu in which Cowley lived and wrote, in Charles's court, exiled and restored. "*Variety* I ask not; give me One / To live perpetually upon" ("Resolved to be Beloved," 21–22) answers all poems about inconstancy. Cowley never mentions even the most basic physical characteristics of his Mistress, not the beamy black eyes of Sidney's Stella. Furthermore, in absolute defiance of convention, youth is not a prerequisite for either speaker or beloved: "Nay *Age* it self does me to rage encline, / And strength to *Women* gives, as well as *Wine*" ("The Inconstant," 23–24). One need not be a psychologist or a savant to understand how much a middle-aged poetess might have appreciated this couplet. Furthermore, she may have become more resolute in attempting to forge a female poetic consciousness from reading such poetry. If the great Cowley considered it worthwhile to describe a man's desire to fulfill a woman's wishes in so altruistic a fashion, then perhaps women themselves could describe their own wishes in poetical form. Surely a being worthy of such deference should be allowed to express herself.

Behn, like Sprat and Elys, would not have agreed with Johnson's notorious dismissal of Cowley's love poetry as the ravings of a penitential hermit who had never as much as smelled a woman. He understands and privileges desire, perhaps Behn's most significant inheritance from him. It "takes wings and strait does fly, / It stays not *dully* to inquire the *Why*" ("The Request," 13–14), an idea that informs Lysander's quest in *A Voyage* as well as her most extended shorter poem on the subject, "On Desire: A Pindarick" ([W 1:282], 1688). To her, it is "a malicious spright" (24) that "dost dilate / Thy mighty force thrô every part" (58–59). Yet Cowley is perhaps yet more frank on the subject than his successor. The urge he describes is its own entity: "I'le *enjoy* the very *Love*, / And make a *Mistress* of mine own *Desire*" ("The Request," 19–20). If it lacks intensity, it does not exist, a failure in the lover rather than in the beloved: "*Lukewarmness* I account a sin, / As great in *Love*, as in *Religion*" ("The Request," 27–28). One thinks here of Behn's mischievously vigilant Cupids prodding inattentive shepherds and shep-

herdesses in "The Golden Age" and *A Voyage*. And, with
Cowley, the urge is avowedly, unabashedly physical, as with
Donne: "When *Souls* mix, 'tis an *Happiness*; / But not compleat till *Bodies* too do joyne" ("Platonick Love," 2–3). Similarly, in the bluntly titled "The Injoyment," he explains to
his addressee that his "full" love "never *dry* or *low* can
prove, / Whilst thy unwasted *Fountain* feeds my Love" (11–
12). Joined with such obvious physicality is the constant insistence on "*Loving*, and *Enjoying* thee" ("The Given Love,"
7–8) and even nakedness: "Wouldst thou a *white* most perfect show, / Thou must at all *no garment* wear" ("Clad all in
White," 3–4). Cowley ponders the habits of the animal kingdom on the subject and does not distinguish between
human beings and the lower orders as sharply as Milton's
Raphael does to Adam in Eden (see *Paradise Lost* 8.581–82;
593–94). Cowley's beasts

> taste those pleasures, as they do their food;
> *Undrest* they tak't, devour it *raw*, and *crude*:
> But to us *Men*, *Love Cooks* it at his fire,
> And adds the *poignant sawce* of sharp desire.
>   ("Answer to the Platonicks," 9–12)

What some mislabel lust, Cowley snorts, "is *Loves* noblest
and divinest heat, / That *warms* like his, and does, like his,
beget" (23–24). In the universe of *The Mistress* as in the ancient world, love and sex are not distinguishable: "I have
Love, and *Love* is *all*" ("The Passions," 5). There is even the
Biblical precedent of Solomon to support his general argument: "*Pleasures* he chose, and plac'd them all in *Love*"
("Wisdom," 12). Behn could not have a clearer precedent to
justify her practice. Her female speaker unashamedly recounts her own desire for a shepherd swain: "Your Body
easey and all tempting lay, / Inspiring wishes which the
Eyes betray" ("To *Lysander* at the *Musick-Meeting*," 21–22).
Her Oenone fondly recalls her raptures with Paris: "Now
uncontroll'd we meet, uncheck'd improve / Each happier
Minute in new Joys of Love!" ("*Oenone* to *Paris*," 66–67). And
in *A Voyage*, the regulation by female abstractions of Lysander's pursuit of consummation with Aminta resembles
an erotic Stations of the Cross. They make him stop and reflect.

III

Such limits to the progress of every thing, even of worthi-
ness as well as defect, doth Imitation give; for whilst we
imitate others, we can no more excel them, then he that
sailes by others Mapps can make a new discovery.
            —Davenant, Preface to *Gondibert*, 1650 (CE 2:7)

exact *Imitation* . . . a vile and unworthy kind of *Servitude*,
is incapable of producing any thing good or noble.
            —Cowley, Preface to *Pindarique Odes*, 1656[12]

The composition of *Poems upon Several Occasions* coincides
with the late-seventeenth-century anxiety regarding issues
of imitation, emulation, and translation, as well as the nebulous concepts of "originality" and plagiarism, all of which
would climax in the First Copyright Act (1709).[13] The Dave-
nant-Cowley criticism of imitation represents a familiar position in the long debate on the merits of the enterprise that
began in antiquity and continued into Dante's time. Hu-
manists such as Petrarch and Ascham reinvigorated the
issue, championing various types of imitation as the only
way for writers to learn their craft, reminding their readers
that the novice should also distance himself from his
source-text once the essential essence of it had been di-
gested and reformed in his own work.[14] However, other theorists disdained such modes of thinking. Debates on the
aesthetics of actual translation (most notably by Dryden)
complicated the matter further.[15] Surely all writers learn
from models, as Cicero explains, and as he exemplifies in
his emulation of Demosthenes. As the scholarship of Howard D. Weinbrot and Harold Love invites us to ask: when
one translates, does not one attempt to emulate as well as
imitate the source-text? What are the differences between
metaphrase, paraphrase, and imitation? Can one always
distinguish between them as one translates? Is the imitation or emulation of a poet not a type of translation?[16]

Copyrights make very little difference to poets, who have
always imitated, emulated, and stolen from each other. As
Dryden diplomatically explains, "great contemporaries
whet and cultivate each other; and mutual borrowing, and
commerce, makes the common riches of learning" (*Dis-*

course Concerning the Original and Progress of Satire, 1693 [K
2:25–26]). Along similar lines, Carol Barash argues that
Behn thought "translation and paraphrase were sites for re-
visionary poetics, places where she could expose the cultural codes at work in poetry and the world that produces
and consumes it."[17] I would extend this argument to Behn's
emulation of Cowley. For a statement of purpose roughly
contemporaneous with her time, one need only turn to Sir
John Denham, who sounds much like Petrarch or Ascham
as he says of the emulative or translating poet, "it is not his
busines [sic] alone to translate Language into Language, but
Poesie into Poesie; & Poesie is of so subtile a spirit, that in
pouring out of one Language into another, it will all evapo-
rate; and if a new spirit be not added in the transfusion,
there will remain nothing but a *Caput mortuum*" (Preface
to *The Destruction of Troy*, 1668).[18] So Behn with Cowley. Her
imitation-emulation of him tends to be heuristical or dialectical, in competition with her model. Gerard Langbaine,
in praising Behn's translations from French, suggests that
this was her general practice.[19] Her endorsement of Roscommon's *Essay on Translated Verse* (1684) in her preface to
her translation of Fontenelle confirms this suggestion (W
4:73).

We have already seen how Behn appropriates Cowley's
prosody, structure, attitudes to love, concepts of androgyny
and eroticism. At this point it would be most useful to compare a fairly typical poem of Cowley's, "Ode: Of Wit,"[20] with
Behn's closest approximation of his poetics in a concen-
trated place, her own skilled and difficult "To *Lysander*, who
made some Verses on a Discourse of Loves Fire." Cowley's
ode warrants a brief summary and explanation of its technique, especially its most distinguishing and typical feature, its enigmatic tendency to forego obvious ligatures in
thought and to keep such connections very subtle—if you
will, a trick in which one begins with knots and ends with
straight rope, causing the observer to wonder not how the
rope became straight but how the trickster tied the knots.

Cowley's poem consists of the cabalistic number of nine
octets rhyming a5a4b5b5c4c4d5d5. These jagged and modulated stanzas, with their slant rhymes for bounce and ballast, create the illusion of freedom and irregularity within

a carefully controlled form (in this case, four couplets of slightly uneven lengths), an effect that Behn produces in her own poetry. Cowley addresses "Of Wit" to an *adversarius* who presumes to understand the chief term, just as Behn does to Lysander, who professes fidelity. Wit, as discussed previously, is a highly fraught term in the Enlightenment, as elusive as love's fire, which Cowley's poem acknowledges by its very existence.[21] Naturally, then, after its first use at the end of the first line of the poem, it becomes an abstract quality, indeed vaguely defined by the pronoun "it" in the rest of the first stanza (lines 2, 4, 5, 7), as well as in the rest of the poem (21, 25, 33, 41, 47, 49, 55, 72). The end of the first octet, "Yonder we saw it plain; and here 'tis now, / Like *Spirits* in *a Place*, we know not How" (7–8), explains the aesthetic of the poem as well as the nature of the subject, ephemeral and chimerical. Wit is multiplex, abstract: "Some things do through our Judgment pass / As through a *Multiplying Glass*" (13–14). Cowley does not deploy his key term again until the third stanza, and then redefines it as a common rather than a proper noun, imitative of its frustrating vagueness: "a *Wit* ... / Grows such a common Name" (17–18). His next strategy is to use negative definition ("'Tis not") through the next four stanzas, turning back to the use of common noun by pronoun (25). He then returns to his agenda, poetry. Neither meter nor images should be contrived or flashy, "not to adorn, and gild each part" (26, 33). Similarly, wit should not be coarse fare, "Jests for *Dutch Men*, and *English Boys*" (42), "*Bombast*" (51), or "the dry chips of short lung'd *Seneca*" (52). Cowley answers his ultimate question, "What is it then, which like the *Power Divine* / We only can by *Negatives* define?" (55–56), with the end of the poem, in which he draws all parts together, "all things must be, / Yet all things there *agree*" (57–58), and then returns to the *adversarius:* "What thing right *Wit*, and height of *Genius* is, / I'll onely shew your *Lines*, and say, '*Tis This*" (71–72). He appropriately abjures a definite answer. Wit cannot be ultimately defined, dependent for its meaning on a given readerly community with its own agenda, as Stanley Fish would tell us.[22]

Behn's poem, on an entirely different subject, uses similar techniques as well as an ode-like form: six seemingly irregular but carefully modulated sestets (a4b4a4b4c5c5); the

address to an *adversarius;* negative definition; vaguely anal-
ogous thinking in which the reader must struggle to fasten
the metaphorical ligatures between stanzas in her own
mind. The speaker channels her hurt and rage into a metaphor comparing love to fire in order to discuss an obscure
triangle between herself, her faithless Lysander, and a je-
june rival. The poem's form and technique exemplify, in
some ways, the wit that Cowley struggles to define. Behn
transforms her predecessor's *adversarius* from a fairly neu-
tral receptor of information to a person with whom she is
emotionally and enigmatically involved:

> In vain, dear Youth, you say you love,
> And yet my Marks of Passion blame:
> Since Jealousie alone can prove,
> The surest Witness of my Flame:
> And she who without that, a Love can vow,
> Believe me, *Shepherd,* does not merit you.
>
> (1–6)

The two words that begin the poem cut both ways; Lysander
says he loves in vain; Aphra implies that his declaration of
love is useless, prideful, foolish. And, rather than focusing
on one vague term such as "wit," she extends her inquiry to
another highly charged and nebulous word, "love," demonstrating, perhaps, what "wit" really means: to define the un-
definable by persuasive example. The speaker makes it
apparent that the addressee not only possesses a profound
ignorance of love, but also lacks the proper empathy for the
woman for whom he claims to own his "Passion," since he
misreads and disdains its "Marks" in her. Her jealousy, for
her the surest sign of her love, merely confuses and angers
him. The false "she" who lacks it, her rival Amynta, therefore does not deserve him as much as she herself does. This
meditation, like Cowley's on wit, constitutes a lesson from a
master to a presumptuous novice, in this case an experienced woman to a callow young man, which creates the impression of a deeply held and long-considered position.
Cowley's technique of slant rhyme surfaces in the pentameter couplet, in which "vow" and "you" appropriately do not
chime in twain.

Now, with the destabilization of the chief concepts and their markers, the speaker makes her first attempt at recasting them by a type of negative definition:

> Then give me leave to doubt, that Fire
> I kindle, may another warm:
> A Face that cannot move Desire,
> May serve at least to end the Charm:
> Love else were Witchcraft, that on malice bent,
> Denies ye Joys, or makes ye Impotent.
>
> (7–12)

The "Flame" (4) now becomes "Fire" (7), an extension of motif that mimetically explains the extent of the speaker's passion, which has blazed and spread to the second stanza. And Behn, demonstrating true wit, uses another word that cuts both ways for the first two lines, "doubt," which can mean "suspect" as well as "be uncertain." It is not even clear who "another" is, the rival, the addressee, or herself. How are the first two lines to be read? "Let me suspect that the fire I kindle in you warms Amynta?" "Let me doubt that the fire I kindle in me warms you?" These readings and echoes complicate a phrase from earlier in the collection, "the Effect of kindling Flame: / Which from the sighing burning Swain she takes" ("The Golden Age," 101–2). In that poem, the transmission of fire is clear and unambiguous, from male to female. In "Loves Fire," one cannot finally discern the source of the flame or its destination, much less its intended recipient, which precisely constitutes the speaker's critique of Lysander's shallow notions of love. The next two lines are also enigmatic because of the ambiguity of the word "Charm," which could refer to the speaker's love for Lysander, his for her, or her love for him surreptitiously warming Amynta. And, in Cowley's mode, it is difficult to discern how this thought follows logically from its predecessor. If we read lines 7–8 as "I suspect that you have transferred my love for you to Amynta," it is possible to gloss 9–10 as "since I ('A Face') cannot make you love me ('move Desire'), I will tactfully staunch my humiliation by ceasing to love you ('end the Charm')." If this reading is plausible, the following couplet may make best sense as: "Otherwise, I would translate my passion (the 'Charm') into vengeful 'Witchcraft' that would poison your new relationship," as it seems to for Lysander in "The Disappointment," where Cloris's "soft bewitching Influence / Had Damn'd him to the *Hell* of Impotence" (139–40). Cowley is simply content to explain what wit is not. Behn struggles to demonstrate the ambiguity of love itself without defining it, hinting that, in any case, Lysander has no idea what it means, and should fear the "malice" that a certain witch can possess if she chooses, the disclaimer aside. As for the concluding pentameter couplet, it seems most appropriate that "bent" and "Impotent" rhyme perfectly, for fairly obvious reasons.

The fire spreads to the third stanza, as does the ambiguity. Rather than present another negative definition, the speaker anticipates what may be another argument of Lysander's, who has perhaps protested, in his half of the conversation that Behn does not report, that he understands what love means. The speaker refuses to listen. His passion is not even honest lust, but simple, fiery expediency that she empathizes with in spite of herself:

> 'Tis true, when Cities are on Fire,
> Men never wait for Christal Springs;
> But to the Neighb'ring Pools retire;
> Which nearest, best Assistance brings;
> And serves as well to quench the raging Flame,
> As if from God-delighting Streams it came.
>
> (13–18)

She, by analogy, is the "Christal Springs" and the "God-delighting Streams"; Amynta is, condescendingly, "the Neighb'ring Pools" that can "quench" as well as she, if this is all that is required, merely a convenience. It might also be noted that Behn's evocation of this analogy of dousing water on Lysander's "raging Flame" coincides with her disavowal of him in the midpoint of the poem, and that she, in effect, "douses" the love-passion-fire metaphor until the last line of the next stanza (24), when she rekindles it, a mark of her own passion that she cannot hide. The poem demonstrates by its existence that the speaker understands true passion as well as unpoetical Lysander's hollowness. First, how-

ever, she must continue to conduct his humiliating education:

> A Fancy strong may do the Feat
>   Yet this to Love a Riddle is,
>   And shows that Passion but a Cheat;
>   Which Men but with their Tongues Confess.
> For 'tis a Maxime in Loves learned School,
> Who blows the Fire, the flame can only Rule.
>
> (19–24)

The exact meaning of "the Feat" seems enigmatic. By liga-
ture, it should refer to the matter of the previous stanza, but
given the three lines that follow, it more likely refers to the
initial charge of the first, that Lysander loves in vain. One
cannot love by the imagination alone or coerce by words
only. They become vacuous as they betray the hollowness of
the professed passion. In contrast, her "Fire," genuine and
unquenchable, is not subject to the wishes of its catalyst,
who can only foment it.

Behn now concludes her lesson and draws all disparate
elements together in her final stanzas, much as Cowley does
in "Of Wit." First she invokes an old enemy to her side:

> Though Honour does your Wish deny,
>   Honour! the Foe to your Repose;
>   Yet 'tis more Noble far to dye,
>   Then break Loves known and Sacred Laws:
> What Lover wou'd pursue a single Game,
> That cou'd amongst the Fair deal out his flame?
>
> (25–30)

Elsewhere, Honour is one "that hindred mankind first, / At
Loves Eternal Spring to squench his amorous thirst," a
"Miser" and "base Debaucher of the generous heart / That
teachest all our Looks and Actions Art" ("The Golden Age,"
120–21, 136, 140–41), the demon of *A Voyage*. It is death in the
pastoral netherworld, but in a post-Arcadian setting, simple and necessary self-esteem. To grant Lysander's wish
would be more humiliating than loving him in vain—one of
love's sacred laws is fidelity, the bane of all libertines in
training. She is also no wanton coquette. As Behn's Ovidian

heroine puts it, "Not my fair Rival wou'd I wish to be, / To come prophan'd by others Joys to thee" ("*Oenone* to *Paris*," 248–49), a subtle nod in the direction of the tactless Amynta in the poem presently under discussion. The concluding question is sarcastic and ambiguous, depending on the referent of "That" (i.e., "Lover" or "Game"): what lover (Lysander) would love just one person? Or, what lover (herself) would waste her love on one person who perfidiously loves others? But the "flame" (30) still blazes. And then Behn concludes, simply, unambiguously:

> Since then, *Lysander*, you desire,
> *Amynta* only to adore;
> Take in no Partners to your Fire,
> For who well Loves, that Loves one more?
> And if such Rivals in your Heart I find,
> 'Tis in My Power to die, but not be kind.
>
> (31–36)

To love "one more" is to "break Loves known and Sacred Laws," which, as Cowley has it, include melding into one another to the point of androgyny or to convince one that she is all the world, all in all, not to change partners as in a dance. The speaker will not be a stooge or stalking-horse for the Lysanders and Amyntas of the world. In some ways, the stanza exemplifies two recent theories concerning patterns in Behn's poetry: intense emotional involvement and an equally studied detachment. Judith Kegan Gardiner suggests, "The woman always wants reciprocity, as does the lover of either sex; the man or the beloved wants freedom."[23] And, to repeat Ballaster's comment from the Introduction, Behn "repeatedly inscribes herself into her tales of love, compulsively turning her reader's gaze from the amorous couple to the amatory narrator, who then uncannily retreats or withholds herself from view."[24] Indeed, even though Behn makes herself a character in the poem, one is always aware of her distance as speaker as well, creating the dual effect of studied neutrality and fierce empathetic participation in the events therein. As the practical lesson concludes ("who well Loves, that Loves one more?"), her amorous "Fire," since her Honour allows no "Partners," is definitely out.

Dryden's authoritative statement exemplifies Behn's emulative recasting of Cowley: "to imitate well is a poet's work; but to affect the soul, and excite the passions, and, above all, to move admiration . . . a bare imitation will not serve" (*A Defence of An Essay of Dramatic Poesy*, 1668 [K 1:113]). In "Loves Fire," she attempts to be admired and understood by exciting the passions in a display of "right *Wit*," lines that Cowley might have shown and said, "'*Tis This*." He might well have made the same observation of other compositions in *Poems upon Several Occasions* that partake of his poetics but then demonstrate a studied difference. Again, a reader could observe that her experiments in prosody, diction, form, style, and erotic subject matter fulfill the praises of Cowley's contemporaries for his work more completely than his own writing does. Behn competes with her model and achieves a modest victory. Dryden, in the mode of the medieval and Renaissance theorists before him, argues that this is the motivation of all imitative-emulative writerly activity: "We ought not to regard a good imitation as a theft, but as a beautiful idea of him who undertakes to imitate, by forming himself on the invention and the work of another man; for he enters into the lists like a new wrestler, to dispute the prize with the former champion" (Preface to *Troilus and Cressida*, 1679 [K 1:206]). In the next chapter, we will see how the poetess wrestles with three of the most significant writers of antiquity with the aid of her young friend Thomas Creech, who made Horace, Lucretius, and Theocritus available to her so that she could, in effect, create her own pastoral space.

3

The Debt to Daphnis: Theocritus, Horace, Lucretius

> thou hast taught me more,
> Then all the mighty Bards that went before.
> Others long since have Pal'd the vast delight;
> In duller Greek and Latin satisfy'd the Appetite:
> But I unlearn'd in Schools, disdain that mine
> Should treated be at any Feast but thine.
> > —"To Mr. *Creech* [under the Name of *Daphnis*],
> > on his Excellent Translation of *Lucretius*," (19–24)

> You Nymphs, who deaf to Love's soft lays have been,
> Reade here, and suck the sweet destruction in:
> Smooth is the stream and clear is every thought,
> And yet you cannot see with what you're caught
> > —T[homas] C[reech], "To the Authour, on her
> > Voyage to the Island of Love," (27–30)

THE RELATIONSHIP BETWEEN THE EXCELLENT CLASSICIST (1659–1700) and his admirer is difficult to decode. In some passages of her tribute to him, she addresses him as though he were too young to have experienced the passions that he renders into English: "mayst thou prove / Still sacred in thy Poetry and Love" ("To Mr. *Creech*," 127–28). At other junctures in the same poem, she describes him in terms so laudatory that they approach the heroic, even bombastic: the champion of women everywhere because his translations make the ancients accessible to them.[1] Along with Cowley's model of (neo-)classicism, Behn appropriates the work of the fellow of All Souls' who would write occasional verses, edit a classical text, and translate Plutarch, Marcus Manilius, Juvenal, Theocritus, Horace, and Lucretius (the libertine *locus amoenus*)—and then somewhat mysteriously hang

86

himself at the turn of the century, eleven years after her own death.[2] Unashamed to admit that her reading of Creech's work helps her form her golden world, Behn does not allow her lack of proficiency in classical languages, the basic admission requirement to the ferociously male academic literary culture, deter her. Her friend provides her with access. Perhaps her rather brazen admission of this lack of credentials in her exuberant, "Pindarique" praise of Creech signifies her recognition that even if she were "fluent" in Latin and Greek (as St. Augustine, Petrarch, and Pope were not in the latter language), her gender would preclude such acceptance. No corset-wearers were allowed, a division of experience that Behn herself appears to have endorsed. In one play, she depicts a woman learned in classical languages as a hypocrite and a fool.[3] Even Creech thinks of Behn's own translation of the Abbé Paul Tallemant's *Le Voyage de l'Isle d'Amour* (1663), *A Voyage to the Isle of Love*, as an aphrodisiac for women readers who would suck the sweet destruction in, not so much a model for them to emulate should they wish to write.[4] But Behn clearly considered Creech's Lucretius as a model, even a classical precedent for her type of poetry. This great paean to a materialist universe informs her stress on the sensual as well as the sensuous, and influences her conception of libertinism. And her friend's translations from a contemporary theorist of pastoral and its two celebrated ancient practitioners were crucial to her understanding of the genre and its forms.

I

As for the *Manners* of your *Shepherds*, they must be such as theirs who liv'd in the Islands of the Happy or Golden Age: They must be candid, simple, and ingenuous; lovers of Goodness, and Justice, affable, and kind; strangers to all fraud, contrivance, and deceit; in their Love modest, and chast, not one suspitious word, no loose expression is to be allowed: and in this part *Theocritus* is faulty, *Virgil* never; and this difference perhaps is to be ascrib'd to their Ages, the times in which the latter liv'd being more polite, civil, and gentile. And therefore those who make wanton Love-stories the subject of Pastorals, are in my

opinion very unadvis'd; for all sort of lewdness or debauchery are directly contrary to the *Innocence* of the
golden Age.
                    —*A Treatise de Carmine Pastorali, Written by Rapin*, 67[5]

Although several useful studies of pastoral, ancient and
modern, exist for the general reader, it would be most productive at this point to understand how Behn's culture appropriated the genre.[6] René Rapin (1621–87), best known for
his vernacular translation of and commentary on Aristotle's
Poetics, *Réflexions sur la Poétique d'Aristote* (1674), which
Thomas Rymer faithfully translated into English,[7] also
wrote the Latin treatise *De Carmine Pastorali*. This was considered to be the ultimate authority on the subject in the
seventeenth century. Creech's translation of the tract,
which he uses as a preface to his Theocritus, provided Behn
with access to contemporary theory as well as to the *auctor*
himself. A reading of her poetry in conjunction with Rapin
suggests a relationship between them. Her reconfiguration
of the familiar conventions enumerated in the preceding
quotation from Creech's translation would suggest as
much.[8] Her shepherdesses and shepherds are no more candid, simple, and ingenuous than those whom Marie Antoi-
nette and her court would portray for their amusement at
the end of the following century. And what Rapin describes
as wantonness is not contrary to but typical of the Golden
Age, as Behn sketches it. It is not wantonness at all.

Rapin primarily envisions pastoral as didactic, "so that
our Humors and Conversations may be better'd, and im-
prov'd" (47). Therefore, a writer should emulate this form of
classicism to move and teach rather than delight the
reader: "its design in drawing the image of a Country and
Shepherd's life, is to teach Honesty, Candor, and Simplicity,
which are the vertues of *private* men; as *Epicks* teach the
highest fortitude, and Prudence, and Conduct, which are
the vertues of *Generals*, and *Kings*" (47). Private men, subject
to the decadence of contemporary society, require instruction in virtue, so Rapin prescribes the bucolic mode as an
antidote: "we ought to prefer before the gaity of a great and
shining State, that Idol of the Crowd, the lowly simplicity of
a Sheapards Life: for what is that but a perfect image of the

state of Innocence, of that golden Age, that blessed time, when Sincerity and Innocence, Peace, Ease, and Plenty inhabited the Plains?" (5). A writer could even inculcate this Edenic goodness into the subjects themselves: "why may not *Pastoral* . . . be admitted to regulate and improve a *Shepherd's* life by its *Bucolicks*?" (47). One can recognize Behn's Golden Age in some of the foregoing, but her poetry could never be labeled didactic. Her shepherds and shepherdesses, creatures of their urban culture, cannot recover prelapsarian honesty, candor, and simplicity. She would not presume to teach us through them any more than she would recommend that shepherds read pastoral to alleviate the difficult, lonely, and tedious labor of tending their sheep.

Rapin constructs his theory of pastoral much as Aristotle does for tragedy in the *Poetics*. He extracts prescriptive examples from the best writers he knows to serve as exempla for novice practitioners. Here he follows Julius Caesar Scaliger in subject and method: "*Pastoral* is the imitation of a *Pastoral* action either by bare narration, as in *Virgil's Alexis*, and *Theocritus's* 7th Idyllium, in which the Poet speaks all along in his own Person: or by action as in *Virgil's Tityrus* and the first of *Theocritus*, or by both mixt, as in the Second and Eleventh *Idylliums*, in which the Poet partly speaks in his own Person, and partly makes others speak" (29). At the same time, like his great predecessors, Rapin must negotiate between the vague and the strict and avoid overburdening his reader with rules—and, like Aristotle, he cannot always be successful. If a writer of tragedy follows every nuance of the *Poetics*, he or she will simply reproduce *Oedipus Rex*. If a pastoral poet were to ingest *De Carmine Pastorali*, he or she would construct low-grade vernacular Theocritus and Virgil. To Rapin's credit, he recognizes the problem: "since *Pastoral* is of that nature, that it cannot endure too much negligence, nor too scrupulous diligence, it must be very difficult to be compos'd, especially since the expression must be neat, but not too exquisite, and fine: It must have a simple native beauty, but not too mean; it must have all sorts of delicacies, and surprizing fancies, yet not be flowing, and luxuriant" (51). It demands a decorum that must be observed: "the manners might not be too Clownish nor too Courtly" (33). One should also attend to more specific kinds of propriety: "let *Pastoral* never venture upon a lofty subject, let it not recede one jot from its proper matter, but be employ'd about Rustick affairs: such as are mean and humble in themselves; and such are the affairs of Shepherds, especially their Loves, but those must be pure and innocent; not disturb'd by vain suspitious jealousy, nor polluted by Rapes; The Rivals must not fight, and their emulations must be without quarrelings" (51–52). Yet Rapin, recognizing that Virgil approaches the sublime in the *Eclogues* with regard to style and meter, qualifies the first pronouncement: "for tho *Pastoral* is simple, and bashful, yet it will entertain lofty subjects, if it can be permitted to turn and fashion them to its own proper Circumstances, and Humor" (53). Some of Behn's subjects are lofty indeed. Yet her approaches to love are far too sophisticated for the constraints he imposes. Her relationships between her subjects, unpolluted by rapes, feature quarrels and vain suspicious jealousies in great quantity. This is precisely their charm.

Yet Behn's disarming simplicity with regard to style follows Rapin's mode, which probably provides a better explanation of her method than the theory that she, as poetess, must cloak her skill "as if disavowing competition with men."[9] Rapin repeats the dictum that pastorals appear artless more than any other prescription: "all things must appear delightful and easy, nothing vitious and rough" (25), "chiefly simple, and ingenuous" (56). Behn follows it. The writer should be clear: "The Sense must not be long, copious, and continued" (35); "as Simplicity was the principal vertue of that Age, so it ought to be the peculiar Grace, and as it were *Character* of *Bucolicks*" (37); "that it might not be uncomely, ought sometimes to be negligent, or the fineness of its ornaments ought not to appear and lye open to every bodies view" (44). He or she should be brief: "let him that writes *Pastorals* think brevity, if it doth not obscure his sense, to be the greatest grace which he can attain" (41); "tis properly requisite to a *Pastoral* that there should be a great deal coucht in a few words, and every thing it says should be so short, and so close, as if its chiefest excellence was to be spareing in Expression" (39). And the pastoral poet must be measured and decorous: "Let the Expression be plain and easy, but elegant and neat, and the purest which the language will afford" (35), "bright and simply clean, not filthy and disgustful, but such as is varnisht with Wit and Fancy" (44); "without gawdy trappings, and all those little fineries of Art, which are us'd to set off and varnish a discourse: But let an ingenuous Simplicity, and unaffected pleasing Neatness appear in every part" (59). Clearly, Behn informs her own poetry with such theories in the mode of her male contemporaries, and her friend Creech allows her to do so in her quest to be admired and understood.

II

παρθένος ἔνθα βέβηκα γυνὴ δ᾽ εἰς οἶκον ἀφέρπω
—Theocritus, *Idylls* 27.65[10]

I'me Woman grown that was a Maid before.
—Creech, *The Idylliums of Theocritus* 24 (126)

In Acrotime's admission to Daphnis, Theocritus (third century BCE) invents a pastoral convention that Creech observes, the initiation into womanhood, which Behn reenacts with great frequency in her poetry.[11] "*Oenone to Paris*," "The Disappointment," "The Willing Mistriss," and "On a *Juniper-Tree*" reflect it, the intended conclusion to countless carpe diem lyrics by the masters of the early seventeenth century: Herrick, Waller, Lovelace. Similarly, her Arcadia teems with sex or references to it in her farewell to Celladon, elegy to Grinhil, tributes to Rochester, advice to lovelorn shepherdesses, and stories of stolen moments in the grass and under trees. All gather rosebuds while they may. That Behn uses "Daphnis" as a moniker for Creech suggests an interesting inversion of their relationship. Instead of the man twenty years her junior of indeterminate sexuality, the slightly fuzzy academic in need of a night of love, this Daphnis is the learned one, not the initiate. Or, if one reads sex as the poetic appropriation of classical culture, Aphra is indeed the novice.

Some readers may draw speculative life parallels between classicist and poetess because of their use of the aforesaid moniker. In the preface to the first *Idyllium*,

Creech mentions one of its speakers, Thyrsis, who will "bewail *Daphnis* who dy'd for Love" (1 [1]). Near the end of the collection, the translator again identifies Daphnis in another preface in similar terms, as "A scorn'd *Shepherd* [who] hangs himself" (*Idyllium* 22 [111]). This Daphnis, unlucky in love as he is not in *Idyllium* 24, threatens to go "Where certain Cures for Love, as Stories tell, / Where dismal shades, and dark *Oblivion* dwell" (*Idyllium* 22 [112]). By fate or irony, Behn's young colleague indeed committed suicide in this fashion, and reputedly for this reason. Another complication might tempt further speculation. In her poetry, Daphnis is one of the few shepherds who does not engage in some form of heterosexual activity, nary a mournful lament to a Sylvia or Phyllis. Even more unusual, she does not flirt with him, poetically speaking, as she does with Hoyle and the others. Unrequited love for "a cruel fair" later justly "kill'd by the Statue of *Cupid*," causes the suicide of Theocritus's Daphnis, this unworthy beloved "An *Angells* body with a *Fury's* mind" (22 [111]). This person is fair and male. Earlier on, Daphnis not only attempts to seduce the aforementioned Acrotime, but also shows his ardor for a young man similarly particularized as angelic and furious. He "kisst, and clasp't the lovely Boy" (*Idyllium* 6 [40]). If Creech were gay (or even bisexual, like Theocritus's Daphnis), it could explain his boldness in faithfully rendering the ancient author's evocation of man-on-man love, Behn's sexual distance, their happily intense friendship (because uncluttered by eros), and what appears to have been his extreme unhappiness and mysterious end.

Behn's rapturous praise of her friend suggests that he functioned as the classics department in her liberal education and taught her to write pastoral. This seems to be true even in the most incidental fashion, such as Behn's use of some of the approved conventions. She had few other avenues for learning them, as she directly states in her Pindaric to him. Since the patriarchal academic system had closed "duller *Greek* and *Latin*" to women and she could therefore not satisfy her "Appetite" for the material, she, "unlearn'd in Schools, disdain that mine / Should treated be at any Feast but thine" ("To Mr. *Creech*," 22–24). In *Poems upon Several Occasions*, she reproduces the custom of alternating speakers in non-engaged dialogue that Creech's Theocritus demonstrates in *Idyllium* 1 between Thyrsis and the Goatherd. We can see this in "A Dialogue for an Entertainment at Court, between *Damon* and *Sylvia*," and in paired poems such as "The Sence of a Letter sent me, made into Verse" and its companion "The Return," which function in approximately this way. Behn's favored prosody has its precedent in Creech's tetrameter rendition of *Idyllium* 26. Her songlike refrains have numerous parallels in Creech, such as his *"Pan raise my voice, Pan move my learned tongue, / Begin sweet Muse, begin the rural song"* (*Idyllium* 1 [9]). Similarly, the stock figure of anaphora, such as Creech's "As much as" (*Idyllium* 12), is deployed at numerous junctures by Behn, although generally for two lines, not eleven or twelve: "Charming he is . . . / Charming without" ("Our Cabal," 21–22). The language, sometimes deliberately "bland" as Rapin would have it, makes its way through Creech to Aphra: "sweeter Notes thy Pipe do fill / Than murmuring springs" (*Idyllium* 1 [2]); "I live by pleasant Brooks, and purling Streams, / And have as much as e're you saw in dreams" (*Idyllium* 9 [56]). In *Peri Bathous* (1727), Pope would later castigate Behn for using similar diction in "The Golden Age" (9–14) without understanding, perhaps, that the poet who was more than capable of sharp, clear, and original language simply followed her betters. Her evocation of this Age also has its pastoral precedent in Theocritus: "The Farmer fearless ploughs his fruitful soil, / No Hostile Navies press the quiet *Nile*" (*Idyllium* 17 [97]).

At the same time, regardless of Pope's scorn, one cannot label Behn as a wooden reproducer of the conventions that Rapin enumerates. His ideal of pastoral "is either *Alternate*, or hath but one *Person*, or is *mixt* of both: yet 'tis properly and chiefly *Alternate*" (*A Treatise de Carmine Pastorali* [55]). There are no such singing contests in *Poems upon Several Occasions*, as one finds in Theocritus 5 and in some of Virgil's *Eclogues*. The non-engaged dialogue may also have been a product of her musical aptitude, a popular form practiced most notably by Purcell in his songs.[12] She avoids stichomythia altogether, a favorite of both *auctores*. Perhaps Behn thought such customs foolish or overly artificial. Maybe she saw no need for this masculine competitiveness in her idealized feminine Arcadia. Or it could be posited that she had no desire for poetical competitions. As the only singer in her pastoral landscape, she assures her victory:

> For I can sing, and by our *flattering* Youth
> I'me prais'd, and call'd the charming *Muses* mouth;
> They say I pipe the best, and would deceive
> By praise; but I'me not easy to believe:
> My Songs are mean, my Pipe claims no repute
> Compar'd to *Sceli*'s or *Phileta*'s Flute
>
> (*Idyllium* 7 [44])

Creech's handsome rendition of Theocritus's humble description of his technique approximates Behn's deceptively understated vision of herself as pastoral poet. Her songs were also accounted "mean" and inferior to those of her contemporaries, but she was also praised. "I'me not easy to believe" may fit her best, especially as she plays the humble shepherdess with the modest pride of Milton's Eve. Her light, almost teasing humor, the banter of Restoration comedy, has no parallel in Creech's Theocritus. The dearth of women therein demands scurrilous jests instead. Nor are there the complications of modern love one finds in Behn, the triangles doubled and even tripled between members of various genders. However, her constant demand for fidelity finds its precedent in Cupid's stern warning on the flesh of the scornful boy who breaks Daphnis's heart: "*Be kind, and Love for mutual Love return, / For see the God takes vengeance on my scorn*" (*Idyllium* 22 [114]). This yearning for mutuality, present also in Creech's Horace and Lucretius, fertilizes the green space of Behn's Arcadia.

Just as Cowley's Pindarics and lyrics had licensed Behn to evoke the erotic, so, apparently, did Creech's Theocritus, whose rustic sexuality has no analogue in Virgil or the neoclassical pastoral tradition that follows. (The Roman author's alleged proto-Christianity and ensuing incorporation into school curricula in the west from the fifth century onwards, as well as Theocritus's absence from it until the late fifteenth century when the serious study of Greek began, would also explain the primacy of the Virgilian mode.) Of course, the sexuality that one finds in *Poems upon Several*

Occasions is never coarse. Behn redacts and reconfigures the matter in Theocritus-Creech, delicately refining it so that her subtlety of feeling and description results. One cannot accuse his Daphnis of subtlety, as in the blatant physicality of the boar describing his assault on Adonis's groin:

> But when I saw his naked Thigh
> As white as polisht Ivory,
> How did my *Flame* and *Fury* rise!
> How was I *fir'd* at the surprize!
> At last unable to resist
> Ah me! too *furiously* I kisst.
>
> (*Idyllium* 27 [133])

Creech's clarity and attention to detail blossom when he imagines the enjoyment of masculine charms and beauty, here and in his Horace. Behn does not particularize in precisely this fashion, but she pictures the equally intense ardor of Lysander's attack on Cloris's "Unguarded Beauties" as he "Kisses her Mouth, her Neck, her Hair," and then takes further liberties ("The Disappointment," 39, 34; see 36–37). Neither boar nor boor, his impotent fate nonetheless results from the precipitous rising of his flame and fury, the former extinguished and the latter exacerbated by kissing somewhat too furiously. Furthermore, Theocritus-Creech may have given Behn license for the primacy of male sexuality (albeit dysfunctional) in her comic narrative. The rustic Corydon remarks to Battus on the collision between a "brave old lusty Goat" and his dear: "in yonder grove / I trac'd, and found them in a Scene of Love" (*Idyllium* 4 [29]). Even the fertility god Priapus, whom Behn also finds in Creech's Horace (*Satyrs* 1.8 [408–10]), makes an appearance, inquiring of a sad shepherd, "Poor *Daphnis*, why dost pine? why hang thy head?" (*Idyllium* 1 [6]). Lysander, although no old goat, certainly has much to hang his head about because of his failure in his scene of love, one that Behn reproduces and refashions in "On a *Juniper-Tree*," to celebrate successful and rapturous heterosexual congress—there, love for mutual love is returned, as Creech's Cupid would have it.

Behn appears to have read *Idylliums* 2 and 24 with particular care. Of the thirty poems that Creech translates, these are two of the three in which women speak or are primary. In the first, the grieving and lovelorn Samoetha, forsaken by young Delphis after enthusiastically obliging him, resolves "to try the force of Charms to recover his affection" (*Idyllium* 2 [11]). Behn uses a speaker much like her in many poems, especially those to the man she is alleged to have loved, John Hoyle. Perhaps Theocritus-Creech gave her warrant for creating pastoral female personae who discuss their erotic feelings with such candor, something entirely absent in Virgil. The second Idyllium recounts a dialogue already mentioned here between Daphnis and Acrotime (whom Creech labels "Shepherdess"), in which the shepherd attempts to persuade the young woman to enjoy physical love. Given Creech's ambiguous sexuality and Behn's strictly poetical relationship with him, it would be unwise to read *Idyllium* 24 as wish-fulfillment for the translator or his admirer, even as a truly amusing inside joke. But if we interpret Behn's appropriation of classical culture from Creech as a type of sex, we might read the Daphnis-Acrotime congress as simply a different type of intercourse, joke or no. Her "On a *Juniper-Tree*," among other poems, appears to have been the progeny of this *Idyllium*, just as "The Disappointment" refracts Samoetha's.

Theocritus's deserted shepherdess, whom Creech transforms in his Restoration Arcadia, serves as precedent for Behn's many unhappy young women who bemoan the shepherds who scorn them. Samoetha resolves on the supernatural so that "I might charm my false, my perjur'd Swain, / And force him back into my arms again" (*Idyllium* 2 [11]). She will make use of a moon-infused aphrodisiac: "*Hippomanes* a Plant *Arcadia* bears, / This makes Steeds mad, and this excites the Mares" ([14]). Behn invokes virtually the same phrasing as she hopes to make her beloved Hoyle well and thereby to bring him back to her arms: "By all thy Charms I do Conjure thee, live" ("On Mr. *J. H.* In a Fit of Sickness," 59). One of her personae uses a necromantic subtext to warn her straying shepherd: "A Face that cannot move Desire, / May serve at least to end the Charm: / Love else were Witchcraft" ("To *Lysander* . . . Loves Fire," 9–11). A remarkable number of poems recount the dynamic of perjured swain and lovelorn shepherdess, Creech's Samoetha and the perfidious Delphis. In her own person, Behn warns young Amoret of the delicious seductions of Amyntas-Hoyle:

> Each Smile he us'd, had got the force,
> To Conquer more than soft Discourse:
> Which when it serv'd his Ends he'd use,
> And subtilly thro' a heart infuse.
>
> ("A *Ballad* on Mr. *J. H.* to *Amoret*, asking why I was so sad," 45–48)

Having served his ends through deception, "ere the Night our Revels crost, / I was intirely won and lost" (65–66). Behn, as Samoetha, warns her junior that she may share her fate, just as in the person of another shepherdess, she asks the conventional postcoital question. When one's lover leaves for other climes, "what becomes of me?" ("Song [When *Jemmy* first began to love]," 32). This person, like Serena in another Behn song, regrets that she was "By such dear Perjuries won" because "'twas as easie to Prevail, / As after to Betray" ("The Reflection," 42, 27–28). Behn complicates the scenario by introducing a third person to create a triangle, as in "The Return" and "*Oenone* to *Paris*." Her Lysander exhibits similar rogue male behavior, his inamorata somehow not as guilty as he: "From me she Ravishes those silent hours, / That are by Sacred Love my due" ("To *Lysander*, on some Verses he writ," 29–30). In "The Invitation," Damon prefers Silvia to Behn's speaker. She finds her love unrequited although she intercepts Cupid's arrows. Similarly, the love god tricks her into being wounded in "The Dream," perhaps the same sort of phantasm that causes her to lament Hoyle's flirtatious and teasing nature in "On a Copy of Verses made in a Dream." Creech's Samoetha lives throughout Behn's corpus, her situation a prototype of what women must endure. In furnishing Cupid with his arrows, women find themselves undone by cooperation, the desire to please: "Thus thou and I, the God have arm'd, / And sett him up a Deity; / But my poor Heart alone is harm'd, / Whilst thine the Victor is, and free" ("Love Arm'd," 13–16).

Creech's Theocritan shepherdess recounts her seduction with remarkable candor and detail, which Behn reproduces in the blandishments of Amyntas against which her

Astraea warns Amoret in the ballad about Hoyle. She summarizes and analyzes the behavior of the faithless shepherd
in the force of his smiles to conquer her speaker, in conjunction with his discourse that subtly infused itself into
this person's heart. Such summary partakes of Creech's dra-
matization of the same situation. His Samoetha remembers
Delphis preparing his assault: "Then *cruel* he sate down, he
prest my bed, / His eyes were fixt" (*Idyllium* 2 [18]). Is this the
(mute) discourse that infuses itself into her heart? Love, she
remembers him saying, "Young tender *Maids* to unknown
Madness drives, / And from warm *Husbands* Arms it forces
Wives," which "*heedless I* believ'd too soon" ([19]). This was
his lucky minute. Samoetha continues:

> He prest *My* hand in *His*, and laid me down
> On the soft bed, when streight lock't Arm in Arm
> In strickt embraces both grew *gently* warm;
> Our *breath* was hot and short, we panting lay,
> We look't, we *murmur'd*, and we dy'd away:
> Our Cheeks did *glow*, and *fainting* vertue strove,
> At last it yielded to the force of Love:
> But what need all this talk? bright sacred Moon,
> *Both were well pleas'd, and some strange thing was done*:
> And ever since we lov'd, and liv'd at ease,
> No sullen Minutes broke our Happiness
>
> (19–20)

Here is a precedent for the intimacies and detail of Behn's
"On a *Juniper-Tree*," "The Disappointment," and "*Oenone* to
Paris." We have the initial words, the faint stirrings, the
foreplay, the sweet nothings, the transformation of "*fainting*
vertue" to another plane, and the assurance that all was
well until the faithless shepherd made an untimely and un-
looked-for departure. After all, "*Both were well pleas'd, and
some strange thing was done*," is written in the same vague
and naïve language of Behn's own virginal shepherdesses,
especially that of Cloris, who must not seem to enjoy what
she has enjoined her swain to attempt: "Her Bright Eyes
sweet, and yet severe, / Where Love and Shame confus'dly
strive" ("The Disappointment," 21–22). Behn's transforma-
tions of her predecessors, what she disingenuously dismisses as "What in strong manly Verse I would express, /

Turns all to Womannish Tenderness within" ("To Mr. *Creech*," 13–14), simply represents another more measured perspective, courtesy of her female pen, her peculiar view of similar proceedings. Behn summarizes what Creech represents in dialogue, which intensifies the crucial moment of experience for her shepherdess, who then laments its passing and fallout.

"On a *Juniper-Tree*" and "The Disappointment" dramatize the issue of mutual sexuality and the problems inherent in attaining this state. Philocles does not "force" Cloris, nor does he wrestle her into the desired position. In fact, in the former poem, Behn relates, "Kind was the force on every side" ("On a *Juniper-Tree*," 47). Here, "Kind" means "natural" rather than "courteous." And "every side" implies that Cloris not only participates but serves at times as aggressor. They simply behave as couples in this state tend to behave, naturally speaking. "The Disappointment" seems somewhat murkier on the subject. Even the description of the thicket in which the encounter takes place, "Silent as yielding Maids consent" (12), is ambiguous, and appropriately foreshadows the character of the tryst to come. Here Cloris, far from silent, makes a great show of protesting to preserve her reputation (as Aminta does in *A Voyage*): "*My Dearer Honour ev'n to You / I cannot, must not give*" (27–28). She cannot seem willing, even as she enjoys Lysander's relentless advance to the "Altar," where "Gods of Love do sacrifice" (45–46). And this behavior after she "Permits his Force, yet gently strove" (14) and meets his breast with her hands, "not to put him back design'd, / Rather to draw 'em on inclin'd" (16–17) so that he could not possibly misinterpret her intentions. Small wonder, Behn implies, that Lysander, inexperienced and agitated by lust, implodes into impotence. Cloris's clearer signals to Philocles ensure no such misfiring under the juniper.

Behn's precedent for these love matches is *Idyllium* 24, the previously mentioned dialogue between the libidinous Daphnis and the reluctant Shepherdess (Theocritus's Acrotime), who does not fear for her honor, but for the possibility of undergoing the dangers and physical agonies of pregnancy and childbirth. Creech's Arcadians blurt out what Behn (more worldly, experienced, and subtle, surely) conveys by tacitly noted action:

> S[*hepherdess*]. Rude Swain, what means your hand
> upon my breast?
> D[*aphnis*]. The Cluster's ripe, and sueing to be presst:
> Those I must pluck; oh! with what Heat they move!
> And how they rise at every touch of Love!
>
> (*Idyllium* 24 [125])

Again, Behn's Cloris does not object in this flatfooted manner. To Lysander she must appear unwilling, whispering the cliché resistance of the romance novel heroine to her swain's undue friskiness while practically pulling him on top of her into position: "*What would you do?*" ("The Disappointment," 26). Creech's Shepherdess can only state the obvious: "You will deceive, *you Men* are all deceit, / And *we* so willing to believe the cheat" (*Idyllium* 24 [126]). Nor can the silent swain, beside himself with excitement, stop to admire her physical charms and their transformation at his touch. Instead, with what could be properly described as realism, "His burning trembling Hand he prest / Upon her swelling Snowy Brest" ("The Disappointment," 36–37). Behn encapsulates Creech's awkward (and faithfully translated) exchange into two lines that evoke great nervousness and excitement, the clumsiness of inexperience, and the unhappy conflation of these entities in Lysander's hot, shaky, and undoubtedly moist grasp of the rising cluster, ripe and suing to be pressed.

Yet the end of the encounter in Creech's translation does not result in any physiological disasters, even after the verbal sparring. As plainly as primitive Arcadians would, the author implies, they "went, and knew the Mystery of Love" (*Idyllium* 24 [126]). Behn, of course, insists on more detail. And, with the matter happily concluded in Theocritus, the postcoital description suggests the simple reemergence of equilibrium:

> She rose, and smil'd, and *banisht* Modesty
> Regain'd her Seat, and sate upon her Eye:
> Yet secret Pleasure thro her looks appear'd;
> And joyful *Daphnis* went, and fed his Herd.
>
> (24 [126])

Perhaps Behn knew that this would only be possible if the passing of these blessed minutes had been truly mutual, which it is certainly not in "The Disappointment," hence the dysfunctionality of the encounter. Behn does not need to describe any secret pleasure in Cloris's looks after her moments with Philocles under the juniper, nor does he sprint off to feed the sheep. Their (mutual) satisfaction is embodied in their attention to their arboreal sponsor and protector: "Their Gratitude to every Tree / They pay, but most to happy me" ("On a *Juniper-Tree*," 79–80). The hint of constancy and mutuality in Theocritus-Creech develops fully in Behn's English Arcadia, especially in the gratitude and altruism of her lovers.

Although Creech occasionally lapses into bathos, he is also capable of subtle humor in Behn's mode, a light touch without superficiality. "Even *empty* Kisses have a secret bliss" (*Idyllium* 3 [23]) epitomizes Lysander's psyche as he soldiers on in spite of Cloris's nonresponsiveness in "The Disappointment"; the unsuccessful blandishments of shepherds to scornful shepherdesses in numerous lyrics; Behn's own lovesick personae in the poems to Hoyle. On this last subject, Creech's rendering of Theocritus's ἔροτα . . . φάρμα-κον (11.1['érota . . . phármakon]), "There is no cure for the disease of Love / Besides the *Muses*" (*Idyllium* 11 [62]), suggests one function of poetry in Behn's collection. While she internalizes this precursor of the Ovidian concept, the *remedio Amoris*, she recognizes that no cures exist, yet another reason that Creech's "Weomen know all below, and all above" (*Idyllium* 15 [82]) may have served as a tribute to her. Surely she knew the precursor of the Virgilian concept of *omnia vincit Amor*: "Love seizes all; and doth all Minds controul" (26 [131]), as love does in her poetry, with great subtlety and humor.

III

Some underneath a Myrtle shade,
Or by smooth Springs supinely laid,
With Mirth, and Wine, and wanton Play,
Contract the business of the Day.
—*The Odes, Satyrs, and Epistles of Horace, Done into English*, Odes 1.1
("Maecenas atavis edite," 2)[13]

So the young classicist evokes *otium* in his excellent translation of the whole Horatian corpus, apparent on every
page of Behn's collection, itself redolent of myrtle shade,
smooth springs, and wanton play. In the very back of
Creech's volume, the Tonson brothers proudly list their recent publications, most of them concerning ancient culture
by the most esteemed authors of the age. An entry ensconced in this august company would appear, on the surface, to be out of place: "Poems upon several occasions with
A Voyage to the Island of *Love* by Mrs. A. *Behn*" (Nn6v). It
would also seem to discount the possibility of the influence
of Creech's translation on Behn's poetry, since her little
book appears to have been published first. However, this
fact may support the opposite premise. Given the Theocritan interconnectedness between poetess and classicist, one
may speculate that Behn also read versions of Creech's
Horatian translations in manuscript, even in conceiving of
her own versions of *Carmina* 1.5 ("Quis multa gracilis") and
1.11 ("Tu ne quaesieris"), the latter providing the west with
the *locus classicus* for the phrase, carpe diem. His rendition
of these two poems provides the most likely source in English for her access to them, although her versions do not
merely ape his. At the same time, his expert knowledge of
classical prosody may also have informed her attempts to
"imitate" Horace's metrics, since it is relatively impossible
for someone who cannot read Latin to approximate the language's meter in English without a great deal of assistance.
One must understand ancient vowel quantity very well indeed in order to re-create it with modern syllabic stress.
Behn would have needed supervision in negotiating this
jealously guarded area of masculine academic culture
whether or not she sought to debunk its authority.[14]

Creech's preface to his Horace enunciates theory that
Behn's poetry reflects, although he argues against Cowley's
free and enthusiastic method of translating Pindar, "thinking it better to convey down the Learning of the Antients,
than their empty sound suited to the present times, and
show the Age their whole substance, rather than their thin
Ghost imbody'd with some light Air of my own" (A7). At the
same time, Creech's Horace must by necessity reflect his
times—the ideal country gentleman expressing himself

with easy and natural wit. After all, "*Odes* are made only to delight and please" (A5v). And his versions of *Carmina* 1.5 and 1.11 serve as templates on which Behn can work her variations.[15] She does not, in effect, translate, but paraphrases and imitates what has already been translated for her, something that was not at all suspect to her masculine peers, but quite commendable and unexpected for a woman writer.[16] Her prefatory commender F. N. W. goes even further, placing her among the most esteemed classical poets as well as their midcentury interpreter. Neither "*Virgil's* Shade or *Ovid's* Ghost, / Of Ages past the pride and boast; / Or *Cowley* (first of ours) refuse / That thou shouldst be Companion of their Muse" ("To Madam *A. Behn* on the publication of her Poems," 136–39). Even Behn might have thought this a bit excessive.

Behn's debt to Creech's Horace exceeds the two loosely paraphrased lyrics in question. At the same time, her reinterpretation of what she learns from them makes the notion of debt superfluous. This paradox becomes less enigmatic as one examines her poetry in light of this solid Carolean Horace:

> Now Love to hear the hiding Maid,
> Whom Youth hath fir'd, and Beauty charms
> By her own tittering laugh betray'd,
> And forc'd into her Lover's Arms.
>
> (1.9 ["Vides ut alta," 15])

Behn's "yielding Maid" who "but kind [i.e., natural] Resistance makes" ("The Golden Age," 99) emanates from this, as do Philocles and Cloris, whom the juniper "saw . . . kindle to desire, / Whilst with soft sighs they blew the fire" ("On a *Juniper-Tree*," 41–42). Creech's Horatian evocations of ease also find their way into Behn's corpus. Dicta such as "Life's span forbids Thee to extend thy Cares" (1.4 ["Soluitur acris hiems," 8]) are offered to Celladon: "Mix thus your Toiles of Life with Joyes" ("A Farewel to *Celladon*," 97); Phillis: "let us improve / Both our Joyes of Equal Love" ("The Invitation," 1–2); and Silvia, in Behn's version of carpe diem: "Let us enjoy to day, we'll dye to Morrow" ("A Paraphrase," 19). Horace's dominant principle of the *aurea mediocritas* (or, precisely stated, "auream quisquis mediocritatem / diligit" [*Carmina* 2.10.5–6], "whoever values the golden mean") also underlies *Poems upon Several Occasions*, filtered through Creech: "To those that choose the golden Mean / The waves are smooth, the Skies serene" (2.10 ["Rectius vives, Licini," 65]). Or, more apposite to Behn's attempts to sift through the passions in her poetry:

> Let not too much of cloudy Fear,
> Nor too intemperate joys appear
> Or to contract, or to extend thy Brow.
>   (2.3 ["Aequam memento rebus," 56])

The speakers and subjects in her collection refute such apparent stoicism. Nor can she completely fulfill the ideal of moderation that she recommends to Celladon in his Irish sojourn or to Lady Morland in her love-intrigues, as we have seen in the poems to Lysander and Hoyle. One could also say that even in the most operatic poetry, such as Oenone's soliloquy to Paris, she never gives passion free rein, or if she seems to do so, it is illusory—and appropriately so. Augustan poetical theory requires that strictness of form must always leaven the emotional content, as Behn herself puts it in another context: "Soft ev'ry word, easie each Line, and true" ("On a Copy of Verses made in a Dream," 34). The conclusion of an ode to her beloved Hoyle provides the perfect example of the foregoing. Should he perish, "I will the Deaf and Angry Powers defie, / Curse thy Decease, Bless thee, and with thee die" ("On Mr. *J. H.* In a Fit of Sickness," 69–70). The first line, for all the talk of defiance, uses perfectly regular iambic pentameter. In spite of the rhythmic turbulence of the concluding line (trochees in the first and third feet ruffling the iambics), such minor disturbance is entirely fitting for the moment, and rhymes precisely with its metrically perfect predecessor, the alliterative "d's" linking the essential diction: "Deaf," "defie," "Decease," "die." A poet who seeks to be admired and understood, not stinted to singularity, could hardly give a better performance.

Minor confluences exist between Creech's Horace and Behn that suggest some type of collaboration or at least mutual thinking. The distinctive and ironic phrase, "Loves Artillery," in Creech's rendition of *Carmina* 3.26 ("Vixi puellis nuper," 121), fittingly finds its match in Behn's version of 1.5, "In Imitation of Horace" (24). Creech's version of this same poem that Behn obviously knew (i.e., "Quis multa gracilis") contains the word "rifles" (9), one that she uses to describe the unwarranted manual liberties that shepherds some-times take with shepherdesses: "The Rifled Joys no more can Please" ("The Reflection," 47); "all my Rifled Joy" ("To *Lysander*, on some Verses he writ," 24). Horace's many refer-ences to trees, especially the lyric "Ille et nefasto" (*Carmina* 2.13) concerning an old pine on his estate that nearly fell on him, may have helped inspire the soliloquy of Behn's juni-per. Creech's translation of one of Horace's pieces about Bacchus, with the description "harmless Snakes / In inno-cent folds twin round each drunken Head" (2.19 ["Bacchum in remotis," 81]), could well have inspired Behn's similar passage on "Snakes . . . / Not doing harm, nor harm from oth-ers felt" ("The Golden Age," 44–45). Speaking more gener-ally, Creech's "Thrice happy They, that free from strife / Maintain a Love as long as life" (1.13 ["Cum tu, Lydia," 14]), like similar sentiments in his Theocritus, reflects Behn's wish for mutual love in the poems to Lysander and Hoyle, a *locus classicus* for permanent fidelity. Perhaps the young classicist's version of the Horatian "ex humili potens" from the celebrated "Exegi monumentum" (3.30.12), "I, the great from mean descent" (126), voices another type of desire that Behn had for posterity's view of her poetical career, much like the aforementioned phrase of Creech's shepherd in the *Idylliums*: "I'me prais'd, and call'd the charming *Muses* mouth" (7 [44]).

Although Creech may have demurred from translating some of the odes for political reasons,[17] he seems quite fear-less in his accurate (and even accelerated) rendering of some homoerotic material therein, in keeping with his ver-sion of Theocritus. These passages serve another purpose. They provide Behn with classical precedent for the descrip-tion of masculine beauty. That the appreciation of this natu-ral phenomenon should be voiced by a woman provides a twist on convention, unprecedented in English literature produced by women.[18]

Creech is bold indeed in his depiction of alternative sexualities in the *Odes*, even more so than in his Theocritus, yet faithful to Horace, whose culture did not consider a "fair surprizing Boy, / Or to admire, or to enjoy" (1.4 ["Soluitur acris hiems," 8]) anything untoward. He could be quite useful in either capacity, a living *kouros*:

> What perfum'd Royal Boy
> To shoot in's Fathers Bow exactly skill'd,
>   Attend thy board;
> And serve Thy pleasure in another joy?
> (1.29 ["Icci, beatus nunc," 40])

Actually, in the event that a woman, such as Behn, should admire such a boy, or mean to enjoy him, Horace-Creech finds himself enraptured, besotted, aflame:

> When *Lydia* praises *Damon*'s Charms,
>   His rosy Neck, and waxen Arms
>   His Air, and rowling Ey;
> My Mind scarce thinks on what it does,
> My sickly Colour comes and goes;
>   I rage, I burn, I dy
> (1.13 ["Cum tu, Lydia," 20])

Concerning this subject, the cultivation of *aurea mediocritas* and the avoidance of intemperate joys do not apply, as we saw in the Theocritan description of the amorous boar mauling Adonis's flank (see *Idyllium* 27 [133], above). Creech's intensification of these Horatian passages suggests that he eschews mere translation and makes some kind of statement, one that the Tonson brothers felt no need to edit, censor, or excise. He addresses the boy Ligurine, wistfully and hungrily:

> Thee, Thee, my lovely Boy,
> Now now I clasp, and now in Dreams
>   Pursue o'er Fields, and Streams;
> Thee, Thee, my Dear, my flying Joy.
> (4.1 ["Intermissa, Venus, diu," 129])

Creech multiplies Horace's two uses of "te" (39–40) to four instances of "Thee" and almost precisely captures the mood of the repetition of "iam" (by adding a third "now") in the source-text: "iam captum teneo, iam volucrem sequor" (38). From these passages Behn learns how one praises, evokes, or addresses a man one loves. It should also be noted that she never attempts to reach this soaring, unguarded emotional pitch.

Behn's passion reflects heterosexuality rather than its opposite. She describes it as "This restless Feaver in my Blood" in her desires for Alexis and Damon, both male ("On her Loving Two Equally," 14). It does not often manifest itself in a direct way, but its presence is nevertheless felt. She appreciates the shepherd Philocles in strictly physical terms, not unworthy of Horace himself:

> If any thing can add a Grace
> To such a Shape, and such a Face,
> Whose Natural Ornaments impart
> Enough without the help of Art.
> His Shoulders cover'd with a Hair,
> The Sun-Beams are not half so fair
> ("Our Cabal," 95–100)

The hypnotic iambic tetrameter re-creates the Horatian poetical milieu. The often complained-of Lysander receives similar treatment, with the addition of a metrical foot:

> Your Body easey and all tempting lay,
> Inspiring wishes which the Eyes betray,
> In all that have the fate to glance that way:
> A careless and a lovely Negligence,
> Did a new Charm to every Limb dispence
> ("To *Lysander* at the *Musick-Meeting*," 21–25)

Behn focuses on sight, or, to be more precise, the eyes, whether those of the appraised or the appraiser, appropriate to the discussion of male sexuality, of which the visual is so important a factor, engendered in the eyes, which she underscores in the descriptive powers of Lysander in *A Voyage*. One must see to desire. It provides her primary means of attraction to the mysterious and heartbreaking Mr. Hoyle. Beware, Amoret:

His Eyes their best Attracts put on,
Designing some should be undone;
For he could at his pleasure move,
The Nymphs he lik'd to fall in Love
("A Ballad on Mr. *J. H.* to *Amoret*," 37–40)

Behn found herself undone, moved to fall in love:

His Eyes are Black, and do transcend
All Fancy e'er can comprehend;
And yet no Softness in 'em move.
They kill with Fierceness, not with Love
("Our Cabal," 159–62)

Creech, through Horace, describes what it is like to love a man. Behn, no less Horatian, makes us feel a man's fierce passion for her as well as her own for him. She describes Hoyle's power over her no less wistfully or hungrily than Horace-Creech does with Ligurine. She looks, she watches, but the penetrating and appraising male gaze unsettles, unnerves, and attracts her, inspiring wishes that her eyes betray. In this memorable fashion, along with her appropriation of Horatian themes and motifs, Behn shows her appropriation of Creech's translation for the formation of her own poetics.

IV

The *Males* and *Females* Seed agree to make
The tender *Young*, of both the Young partake;
But yet that Sex the *Young* resembles most,
That hath more *powerful* Seed, more *vigorous* Lust.
—T. Lucretius Carus, the Epicurean Philosopher, 4 (137)[19]

Methinks I should some wondrous thing rehearse,
Worthy Divine *Lucretius*, and Diviner Thou.
  But I of Feebler Seeds design'd,
  Whilst the slow moving Atomes strove,
  With careless heed to form my Mind:
  Compos'd it all of Softer Love.
—"To Mr. *Creech*," 5–10

Behn's witty appreciation of Creech's Lucretius appropriately invokes an important Epicurean idea to explain the influence of her friend's translation on her own creative processes, one that can be found in Edmund's "Thou, Nature, art my goddess" soliloquy in *King Lear* (1.2). Procreation is by necessity mutually accomplished, but the child partakes of the more powerful or vigorous parent, certainly in evidence if the child exhibits powerful or vigorous tendencies also, a folk belief that persists into our own day. Dryden makes precisely this point concerning Monmouth: "inspir'd by some diviner Lust, / His Father got him with a greater Gust" (*Absalom and Achitophel*, 19–20). Behn employs the concept as if the "Seeds" or "Atoms" of creation begat both herself and Creech, as they do for all things, but that she is inferior not only to the ancient *auctor* ("Divine"), but to her young friend, as well, who surpasses the master ("Diviner"). One might also note that she slyly praises herself by including herself in the same poetical pantheon as these eminent men. Behn's commendatory poem, although carefully censored by Creech's publisher, includes her as part of this controversial book, the first full translation of *De rerum natura* into English.[20] Its heretical nature accounts for its vexed presentation and mixed reception in Carolean England—an apt description of Behn and her own volume, as well.

The prefatory material provides the first of the contradictory impressions that Creech's translation makes on some readers. His eminent commenders (Behn, John Evelyn, Nahum Tate, Thomas Otway, Edmund Waller) praise him as *fides interpretor* foremost. For this, Tate explains that the country owes a debt to the great young man as ennobler of the English tongue: "With thine thy Countrys Fame thou here dost show, / What British Wit and British Speech can do" ("To His Ingenious Friend Mr. CREECH: On his Excellent Translation of *Lucretius*," c4v). At the same time, the dramatist adds, just as this liberating yet potentially heretical material must be treated with extreme caution, so must the praise of Creech for his achievement:

> Thy pains oblidge us on a double score,
> True to thy Author, to Religion more.

Whilst Learnedly his Errors thou dost note,
And for his Poyson Bringst an Antidote
("To His Ingenious Friend," d)

The translator renders Lucretius properly as well as accurately. He does not lapse into personal impiety. "True to" his "Religion," Creech notes the ancient author's "Errors": denying the immortality of the soul, suggesting that the universe is governed foremost by the mechanical laws of nature, asserting that various gods cannot or will not intervene in human affairs. Similarly, Dryden, whose own version of *De rerum natura* 4 owes much to Creech's, imitates his young predecessor by reminding his readers that Lucretius "was so much an atheist, that he forgot sometimes to be a poet" and apologizes for his "luscious English" in his frank rendering of the ancient author's theories on the physiology of sexuality (Preface to *Sylvae*, 1685 [K 1:262]). Creech also defends himself in his prefatory letter against his enemies, who would naturally equate him with the dangerous material he handles: "Let Hatred to my Person, or Envy to the Performance Biass them" (*T. Lucretius Carus*, A2v). And, after presenting such Lucretianisms as the promise to "loose men from *Religion's* grievous chains" (4 [102]) and the unvarnished assertion, "This World was made without the Powers above" (3 [69]) in the text of the poem, he then disclaims them in his Notes: "Authority will prevail litle with a proud *Epicurean,* whose Talent is to scoff at all beside his own Sect, and undervalue every man that is not delighted with the weeds of his Garden" (7). At the same time, he preserves a note of subversive defensiveness, as if he has a perfect right to partake of any doctrine he chooses and resents the intellectual contortions to which this scholarship necessarily stretches him. Valuable ideas can always be deliberately misinterpreted: "*Epicurus* knew this very well when he baited his hook with Pleasure, and appealed rather to the loose affections of the debauched, than the reason of the Sober" (A4). The translator, ultimately, should not shoulder the responsibility for the malicious misreadings of the material that he translates.

Lucretius (99–55 BCE) fashions his *De rerum natura* as a justification of Epicurus (340–270) as well a response to and synthesis of the atomist Democritus (460–352).[21] One can hardly overstate the importance of this text for Enlightenment thinking, especially for the development of rationalism, empiricism, and materialism. In translating it, Creech makes not only a poetical but a scientific contribution to his culture. His Rapin praises Lucretius as "that accurate Searcher into Nature" (*A Treatise de Carmine Pastorali* [14]). The Roman philosopher-poet, like his predecessors, bases his metaphysics on the principles of atoms (or "seeds"), motion, and the void: "proper Seeds on all things wait" (*T. Lucretius Carus*, 1 [7]). The world began from the chaos of atoms which eventually created its own order. Yet this continual ordering prevents stasis or permanence: "curious *Nature* joyns / The various Seed, and in one Mass combines / The jarring Principles" (1 [3]). Libertinism, as well as the Hobbesian metaphysics from which Restoration thinkers derive it, begins with this principle, hence the manifold references to the "lucky minute" in poetry and drama of the period. Atoms cannot be destroyed, and although they possess no secondary qualities, they have size, shape, and weight: "*Seeds* can never change their natural state, / They must endure free from the power of Fate" (1 [25]). Therefore, the mechanical laws of the universe govern all life in it:

> But because Things on certain Seeds depend
> For their Beginning, Continuance, and End.
> Therefore unfruitful *Nothing* nothing breeds,
> Since All things owe their life to proper Seeds.
>
> (1 [8])

This vexed idea is crucial to Hobbes as well as the libertine thinking that ensues (see, for instance, Rochester's celebrated "Upon Nothing").[22] It is also, at least for Creech and the audience for whom he translates, the ancient writer's most heretical (albeit Aristotelian) idea, because it denies the doctrine of *ex nihilo* creation in Genesis: "*Nothing* was by the Gods of *Nothing* made" (1 [6]). Nothing can come of nothing, as Lear admonishes Cordelia.

The implications of such metaphysics are immense for beings human and divine. If nothing comes of nothing, only "seeds" can be eternal. Lucretius posits that "*Death* dissolves, but not annihilates" (1 [9]). Furthermore, the soul or human psyche must also have a material origin and an atomic structure and cannot be immortal. It cannot even be the most important part of a human being. Since "the *Mind*, in which the *Reason* lies, / Is part of Man, as Hands, and Feet and Eyes," it follows that "the *Soul* / Is *part*, and not the *Harmony* of the Whole" (3 [72]). Indeed, if "*Souls* are born and grow, / And all by age decay as *Bodies* do," then "the *Soul* and *Mind* must die" (3 [81]). Lucretius, no atheist, believes in the gods, but insists on their independence from, even indifference to, mortal creatures. In a concept central to Newtonian Deism, the ancient writer reports that divinities are self-sufficient and do not intervene in human affairs:

> For every Deity must live in peace,
> In undisturb'd and everlasting ease:
> Not care for us, from fears and dangers free,
> Sufficient to his own felicity.
> Nought here below, Nought in our power he needs,
> Ne're smiles at good, ne're frowns at wicked deeds.
>
> (2 [53])

As Creech emphasizes in his translation, one should not fear this idea as unsettling but embrace it as liberating. If God is a gentleman and does not interfere in our lives, He also does not visit retribution on us for our earthly misdeeds in an afterlife because we have no immortality of soul. We return to seed, so to speak, and therefore need not suffer "that dread of Hell, those idle fears, / That spoil our lives with jealousies and cares" (3 [70]) while we live. Hence the beginning of wisdom lies not in mystical contemplation of godhead but in sensory perception: "From *Sense*, all *Truth* and *Certainty* infer" (4 [116]). And thereby follows Lucretius's most misunderstood idea. From the senses comes pleasure, our chief good, but the ultimate pleasure is the search for peace, a pure heart, and truth, something we possess the free will to do: "sure tis *Piety* to view the *Whole*, / And search *all Nature* with a *quiet* Soul" (5 [177]). One ought not, as libertinism and its critics have it, counterfeit a license to debauch oneself by claiming that a lack of free will compels us to descend into savage sensuality: "Moral Rules / And Arts do polish, and reform our Souls" (3 [77]). Morality is not only possible but essential, especially in a materialist universe.

Lucretius subjects love to the same materialist analysis in *De rerum natura* 4, hardly controversial in his own time but extremely so in Behn's, especially for his translators. The ancient author explains the purposes and processes of sexuality in a somewhat clinical fashion, which Creech avoids rendering in full. He prefers to concentrate on the origins of desire rather than the act itself. Desire for the beloved can be explained scientifically, as well, stimulated at root by *simulacra*, which Creech translates as "images":

> Love rises then, when from a *beauteous* face
> Some *pleasing* forms provoke us to embrace
> Those *Bawds to lust*, when with a *tickling* Art
> They gather turgent *seed* from every part,
> And then provoke it: Then rise *fierce* desires,
> The Lover burns with strong, but pleasing fires.
>
> (4 [132])

In an implicit metaphor that the reader may not have to strain to see as tumescence, Creech evokes the origin of the same "seed" that serves as provocative agent for all life and motion and personifies it in human terms. Desire, then, cannot merely be a phenomenon, nor the reassuring traditional phantasms of little quiver-hung Cupids. It is the life-force itself. It is also no laughing or joyous matter, but a source of distraction and even danger. Copulating couples compulsively exhaust themselves:

> In vain, fond Fools, they cannot mix their Souls,
> Altho they seem to try, in Amorous rolls
> So strictly twin'd, till all their *powers* decay,
> And the *loose airy pleasure* slips away:
> Then a short *pause* between, and then returns
> The same *fierce lust*, the same *fierce fury* burns;
> Whilst they *both* seek, whilst they *both* wish to have
> What e're their *wanton* fancies, *wanton* wishes crave.
> For *this* no cure, for *this* no help is found;
> They waste, and perish by a *secret* wound.
>
> (4 [134])

The act of love, albeit a natural process, arises from the unreasonable instinct to merge souls, exhausting, nasty, brutish, and short. Dryden's translation of parts of the same book of Lucretius, while owing much to Creech, were intended to be corrective.[23] Although it is possible that Behn saw parts of Dryden's translation before she published her own volume, Creech obviously influences her, who tactfully omits the Lucretian material that his distinguished colleague preserves in his own attempt to be *fides interpretor*— references to "th'erected furnace" and to the moment "when the gather'd bag has burst its way" (*Lucretius: The Fourth Book. Concerning the Nature of Love*, 88, 83), this last phrase the Laureate's English equivalent of Lucretius's "conlecta cupido" (*De rerum natura* 4.1115).

Behn's rapturous praise of Creech's Lucretius warranted her inclusion in his translation and placed her in the distinguished company of Tate, Otway, and the other commenders. If her enthusiasm owes less to altruistic considerations than her tone implies, so be it. This is how the book trade worked. Yet if we read her poetical emotion as genuine, she would have much for which to be genuinely thankful. If Creech advanced science for Tate, he also advanced it for women like Behn who "unlearn'd in Schools" ("To Mr. Creech," 23) had no Latin for understanding scientific texts. To re-cite the passage from the beginning of the current section:

> Methinks I should some wondrous thing rehearse,
> Worthy Divine *Lucretius*, and Diviner Thou.
>   But I of Feebler Seeds design'd,
>   Whilst the slow moving Atomes strove,
>   With careless heed to form my Mind:
> Compos'd it all of Softer Love.
>
>   (5–10)

Perhaps we can read Behn's underrating of herself as disingenuous, just as her reference to "worthless me" in the poem to Rochester's niece (in which she finds herself worthy enough to be visited by His Lordship's ghost) appears to be droll understatement in her own behalf, modest pride ("To *Mrs. W*, on her Excellent Verses," 26–43). Thinking herself worthy enough to write something "wondrous" that would be fit to praise Lucretius and Creech, her avowed comprehension of seeds-atoms suggests that there is nothing "Feebler" about her than the next (i.e., male) person. Nor can her audience dismiss her as a mere poetess whose mind is composed "all [entirely] of Softer Love." She considers herself an intellect, a believer in Lucretian metaphysics, the principles of atoms, motion, and the void, the interconnectedness of all things in nature. One could even posit that the linkages between poems in her collection owe something to this principle.

Creech's Lucretius appears frequently in *Poems upon Several Occasions* in occluded form. Although the ancient *auctor* does not discourse on poetry per se, his principles of expression can be said to be Behn's. He emphasizes simplicity, direct speech, especially for the explanation of abstract ideas:

> Fools regard
> What seems obscure, and intricate, and hard.
> Take that for *Truth*, whose *Phrases* smooth appear,
> And dancing Periods charm the wanton Ear.
> *(T. Lucretius Carus*, 1 [21])

Creech found a willing audience for such pronouncements as he translated them, especially in closed couplets, where "no hard Notion meets or stops its way" (1 [54]). So Behn, who strove to achieve "Soft ev'ry word, easie each Line, and true" ("On a Copy of Verses made in a Dream," 34), the epitome of the normative prescription that underlies the theory of Enlightenment poetics: Hobbes, Dryden, Mulgrave. One can detect more specific Lucretian influences throughout her collection, such as the doctrine of the materialist universe and its variety in her first poem's invocation of the "Virgin Earth," who

> yielded of her own accord her plentious Birth,
> Without the Aids of men;
> As if within her Teeming Womb,
> All Nature, and all Sexes lay,
> Whence new Creations every day
> Into the happy World did come
> ("The Golden Age," 33–38)

The earth, sufficient unto itself, needs no men to effect its processes—the gods, notably absent, appear to have no influence. Ever fertile, seeds are always in motion. Matter finds its own order from apparent chaos, deceptively so, even in the penetrating male gaze of Behn's bête noire, Mr. Hoyle: "so he order'd every Glance, / That still they seem'd but Wounds of Chance" (A Ballad on Mr. *J. H.* to *Amoret*," 41–42). Nothing comes of nothing. Behn's juniper tree alludes to this belief in its reference to the virginal Cloris, who "did translate, / My being to a happier state" ("On a *Juniper-Tree*," 98–99)—when the lovers choose it as a sponsor and symbol of their love and the young woman, without the aids of men, transforms it into an agent of personal protection in a lucky minute. Hence Behn's ambiguous and manifold references to this subsidiary idea. In "The Golden Age," one should "the Gay hasty minutes prize" (196); in "The Disappointment," Lysander proceeds to his unfortunate fate because "All things did with his Love conspire" (5); in "An *Ode* to *Love*," Behn forms her "Charming Youth" in "a *lucky* houre" (10).

Again, this earthly self-sufficiency does not give divine beings much of a role or, frankly, much to do, as Behn seems to have noted, which underlies several other ideas in Lucretian thinking. One could also observe that the absence of the conventionally religious in her poetry constitutes a tacit endorsement of the philosopher's thinking on the matter, although her epithet "dull Religion" ("To Mr. *Creech*," 76)[24] represents her closest approach to "Consider, that Religion did, and will / Contrive, promote, and act the greatest Ill" (*T. Lucretius Carus*, 1 [4]). Creech's translation reads, "For whatsoere's *Divine* must live in Peace, / In undisturb'd and everlasting Ease." Since the gods live in ease, they do not intervene: "Not care for Us, from fears and dangers free, / Sufficient to its own felicity" (1 [3]). Behn's many references to godlike young men (Rochester, Creech, Hoyle, Grinhil) partake of these ideas. For example, she urges "The great, the Godlike *Celladon*," appropriately "careless and delighted," to pursue "Glorious and Luxurious Ease" as an ideal, in the manner of the distant and pleasure-seeking Lucretian divinities ("*A Farewel to Celladon*, On his Going into Ireland*," 63, 13, 47). Human beings should emulate them, as they did in antiquity: "that was lawful all, that Pleasure did invite" ("The Golden Age," 81). This may also explain the stress on the senses in Behn's poetry, her endorsement of the pleasure principle, as easily misunderstood as it is in Lucretius, especially from a poetess who usurped the masculine prerogative by writing at all. Art also begins with the senses, especially the underrated one of touch:

> So bold, yet soft, his touches were;
> So round each part's so sweet and fair.
> That as his Pencil mov'd men thought it prest,
> The Lively imitating rising Breast,
> Which yield like Clouds, where little Angels rest
> ("On the *Death* of Mr. *Grinhil*, the Famous Painter," 35–39)

Art conceals and foments art at several removes. Grinhil's knowledge of the female anatomy informs his representation of it; Behn reproduces this idea in her own representation of the breast as she describes the artist's re-creation of it. His brush not only imitates the sense of touch that informs his work; the artistic touch is itself transformative and, in the words "rising" and "yield," erotic.

One can trace much of Behn's commendatory gratitude to her reading of Creech's politely inaccurate translation of *De rerum natura* 4. The powers of passionate love that she celebrates so avidly in her poetry have a sound philosophical basis in Lucretius as well as in the important precedent of Cowley. To cite a few examples: "On a Copy of Verses made in a Dream" depends on the idea of *simulacra*, or images, that Lucretius cites as primary as the genesis of erotic feeling. Eyes, sight, perception—all are crucial in Behn's discussion of the matter, as in "Love Arm'd": " 'twas from mine [eyes] he took desire, / Enough to undo the Amorous World" (7–8). Just as the senses are the beginning of wisdom, they also provide the inception of love, and not only the eyes, but the ears. Lucretius states, "when you hear your beloved's name / *Love enters with it at the Ear*" (*T. Lucretius Carus*, 4 [133]). Behn's manifold references to music as aphrodisiac approximate this idea, as in the metaphor, "No ravishing thoughts approach our *Ear*," which she appropriately includes in her poem praising the translation of Lucretius ("To Mr. *Creech*," 32). This is also at work in "To *Lysander, at the Musick-Meeting*": "Ravisht Lovers in each others Armes, / Faint with excess of Joy, excess of Charmes" (5–6). Behn also invokes the dangers of love, admittedly an old trope but certainly traceable to Lucretius: "Cure then, thou mighty winged God, / This restless Feaver in my Blood" ("On her Loving Two Equally," 13–14); "*Pan*, grant that I may never prove / So great a Slave to fall in love" ("Song in the same Play, by the Wavering Nymph," 1–2).

Behn, then, possesses a sound philosophical understanding of the basis of libertinism at its classical source, one perhaps even more profound than Rochester's, whose poetry she admires and, at the same time, answers. Libertinism holds that free will does not exist; Behn's writings, fueled by her understanding of Lucretius via Creech, state the opposite case. Again, the relationship between poetess and classicist is difficult to decode. Creech seems to have been master in some things initially: pastoral traditions at their source in Theocritus and Rapin, ease and urbanity in Horatian spaces. Yet Behn soon became master over Creech, as one of her commenders states, be it Dryden, Tonson, or herself: "her sweeter Muse did for him more, / Than he himself or all Apollo's sons before" ("Upon these and other Excellent Works of the Incomparable *ASTRAEA*," 117–18).[25]

4

Behn's Godlike Rochester and Libertinism

So rich a Prize the *Stygian* Gods ne're bore,
Such Wit, such Beauty, never grac'd their Shore.
He was but lent this duller World t'improve
In all the charms of Poetry, and Love;
Both were his gift, which freely he bestow'd,
And like a God, dealt to the wond'ring Crowd.
                        —Behn, "On the Death of the Late Earl
                                of *Rochester*" (5–10 [W 1: 161]), 1685

The Poetesse Afra, next shew'd her sweete face,
And swore by her Poetry, and her black Ace;
The Lawrell, by a double right was her owne,
For the Plays she had writ, and the Conquests she had
won.
                        —Rochester, "A Session of the Poets" (72–76), 1670s

THE DISCREPANCY IN TONE AND LENGTH BETWEEN THE EARNEST
flattery of Behn's long elegy on Rochester and his two
droll couplets about her in "A Session of the Poets" may
seem jarring. His utterance, emblematic of the scornful
male public that demonized her sexually the more forcefully she labored to gain its respect by writing well, implies that a supremely self-aware and mercenary erotic
prowess wins her the "Lawrell" twice over. Although
Behn also describes Rochester's "gift" as similarly twofold, she ingenuously depicts his delights as dolphinlike,
above their element, in keeping with the lavish praise
from this same public once it was assured that he was
safely dead. Yet her modern admirers, who might view
such a reading as hopelessly sentimental and ahistorical,
suggest that she may have been secretly pleased that the

119

earl included her in his roll call of poets along with Etherege and Wycherley and stress that her elegy was
printed in the standard mid-eighteenth-century edition of
his works, both facts constituting an imprimatur for her
as author.[1] Indeed, Behn's somewhat pedestrian piece, almost certainly a species of the competition for representation that marks so much Restoration poetry, provides
an occasion to showcase talent rather than to emote sin-
cerely in the post-Augustan way that moderns cherish.
And Rochester's coupling of "Poetry" and "black Ace"
may well constitute a tribute to her. His word placement
implies that he appreciates the literary more than the
erotic, strangely in keeping with Behn's own view of her
writing as her "Masculine Part" that competes against the
feminine within: "What in strong manly Verse I would
express, / Turns to all Womannish Tenderness within"
("To Mr. *Creech*," 13–14).[2] Truly scornful allusions to her,
such as Gould's, conflate the literary and erotic: "What
has this Age produc'd from Female Pens / But an Ob-
sceneness that out-strides the Men's? ("The Poetess: A
Satyr, Being a Reply to *Silvia's Revenge*").[3] The reasons for
this are simple to deduce. To such men, her act of writing
was the epitome of obscenity.

Yet even a perfunctory reading of Behn's prolegomena
to her works, bristling with anger at those who accuse her
of libertinism as a way of dismissing her writing, suggests
that she may not have been honored by Rochester's exercise in synecdoche either, regardless of the placement of
part or (w)hole. In her sarcastic preface to *The Dutch Lover*
(1673), an epistle to the "Good, Sweet, Honey, Sugar-Candied Reader,"[4] presumably male, she seeks to prove that
she is something more than the sum of her nether regions:

> For waving the examination, why women having equal education
> with men, were not as capable of knowledge, of whatsoever sort as
> well as they: I'll only say as I have touch'd before, that Plays have
> no great room for that which is mens great advantage over women,
> that is Learning; We all well know that the immortal Shakespears
> Playes (who was not guilty of much more of this than often falls to
> womens share) have better pleas'd the World than Johnsons works,
> though by the way 'tis said that Benjamin was no such Rabbi nei-

ther, for I am inform'd that his Learning was but Grammer high.
(W 5:162)

Her forceful argument in which she compares herself to
Shakespeare and Jonson must have seemed as impudent as
Lady Wishfort's big-bellied actress to this implied saccha-
rine-coated Reader. If a lack of formal education provides
no obstacle to male intellectual achievement, why should it
be a barrier to impede Behn's own, or that *in potentia* of any
other woman? Why should a woman's act of writing occasion sexual judgment? Ignorance, Aphra implies, does not
merely fail to recognize genius, but actively promotes and
endorses like ignorance.

How much of this radical thinking came up in her conversations with her friend Edward Ravenscroft, author of the
scurrilous city comedy *The London Cuckolds* (1681), or with
the wits, hangers-on, actors, performers, and other denizens
of the theater? Perhaps she discussed these matters with
Elizabeth Barry, who first distinguished herself by her
scandalous affair with Rochester and then made herself
into London's leading actress, playing virtually all of Behn's
leading female roles early in her career, including the virtuous breeches-part of Hellena in *1 Rover* and other significant characters such as Mrs. Loveit in *The Man of Mode* (1676)
and Mrs. Marwood in *The Way of the World* (1700).[5] Since their
professions forced them to work together closely, Behn and
Barry could well have confided in each other as women
characters in Carolean drama do, Mrs. Fainall's pronouncement having a certain currency for playwright and actress:
"Men are ever in Extremes; either doating or averse" (*The
Way of the World* 2.1.3–4). Although mere biographical gossip
provides most of the information about the Rochester-Barry
relationship, some of his letters to her survive, both doting
and averse. One angry and jealous missive to Barry vali-
dates Fainall and has a curious resonance for Behn: "I
thank God I can distinguish, I can see very woman in you,
and from yourself am convinced I have never been in the
wrong in my opinion of women. . . . You have a character and
you maintain it, but I am sorry you make me an example
to prove it."[6] Those acquainted with Rochester's lifelong
misogyny and infidelity to his wife will snort at such hypo-

critical pronouncements. Although none of Barry's correspondence to Rochester is extant, her colleague in the
theater seems to have responded for her, she who was also
a kind of actress and changed her shape as her milieu demanded, "whore" proving scarcely more reproachful than
"poetess."[7] Behn must have known what kind of man Rochester was, at his worst as well as at his best. Willmore (*1* and
2 Rover, 1677, 1681), reputed by legend to represent Rochester, suggests a kind of benign revenge on Behn's part, much
less the man of mode than his source, the title character of
Thomas Killigrew's *Thomaso* (1654), a real (if unproduced)
stage rake.[8] One of many interesting possible topical references occurs as Hellena-Barry in her breeches reforms
Willmore-Rochester and brings him to marriage. When the
lovers confront each other at play's end, Willmore's over-
tures to Hellena, dressed as a boy, may have had more resonance than we think, given Rochester's bisexual notoriety,
which he himself immortalizes in a song praising a sweet
soft page who does the trick worth forty wenches.[9]

Throughout Behn's works, her black ace trumps Rochester's charms of poetry and love before the wondering crowd,
making him an example of a character that she maintains
throughout her career as a writer. Although some recent
scholarship implies that she endorses or condones rakishness, I argue the opposite. Her study of Lucretius through
Creech armed her with real knowledge of his philosophy at
its root, and dictated that she criticize libertinism. Even
though Behn depends utterly on the libertine for the life of
her writing, she excoriates him in her plays, poems, and fiction.[10] The topic, central to Restoration literature, warrants
an investigation into her other genres and works besides
the collection that is the subject of this book. This broader
inquiry will aid in the understanding of some of the issues
in *Poems upon Several Occasions*.

I

Lovis: If you're resolv'd, I'll warrant you success.
Alonzo: I think I am resolv'd in spite of all my inclinations to libertinism.

—*The Dutch Lover* 2.7.81–83

As James Grantham Turner argues, those who discuss libertinism in English literature and culture seem reluctant to define it or to delineate its characteristics. This is not difficult to understand: the term has had a confused history in our language. The *Oxford English Dictionary* records that "libertine" surfaces in the sixteenth century as a word to describe (contemptuously) a person who professes a type of radical Protestant Christianity rumored to be associated with an unorthodox sect such as the Family of Love: the mechanical operation of the spirit includes sensual gratification. Milton always loads the word with such connotations: "those that may be justly number'd among the hinderers of *Reformation*, are Libertines, those suggest that the Discipline sought would be intolerable."[11] Some Ranters during the Revolutionary period such as Tobias Crisp appropriate it for themselves with pride and defiance: "To be called a libertine is the most glorious title under heaven."[12] Hence the eventual broadening of the term to include both religious-philosophical freethinking and sexual profligacy; the latter meaning is of course the one we now apply, particularly when we describe the "libertine literature" of Rochester and his circle.[13] Behn herself comically evokes all three concepts in this passage from *Love-Letters between a Nobleman and His Sister* (1684–87), when Philander begins his epistolary seduction of Silvia: "let us love like the first race of men, nearest allied to God, promiscuously they lov'd, and possess'st, Father and Daughter, Brother and Sister met, and reap'd the joys of Love without controul, and counted it Religious coupling, and 'twas encourag'd too by Heav'n it self" (W 2:12). Perhaps it would be best to say that the concept itself is rather nebulous and resists clarity, but that commentators know it when they see it. One could say the same of playwrights like Behn. In the epigraph that begins this section, her rakish Alonzo, spouting his conventional ideas about constancy, women, and Hobbes, makes his declaration to the brother of the woman to whom he intends to be uncharacteristically faithful, resolved to go no more a-roving. Turner himself does not offer a simple definition but explains that we should generate "a cautiously maximalist history of libertinism that nevertheless respects the paradoxes and shortcomings that nourish the minimalist view."[14]

Commentators on French literature are not as reluctant to define libertinism, nor are they troubled by its tendency to resist definition. Their work anticipates and, to some extent, answers Turner's call for a "maximalist history." Given their main figure of study, the scandalous Marquis de Sade, it is not surprising that literature on the subject is so developed and extensive. And, although Carolean libertinism—informed by Hobbes's materialism, Lucretius's Epicureanism, and La Rochefoucauld's cynicism—obviously precedes Sade's extreme version, the characteristics of the philosophy that commentators find in the Marquis apply in many cases to the behavior and sentiments of rakehells in Restoration plays.[15] In French scholarship, libertinism is primarily excess, the championing of self-gratification in all of its forms over mutuality and altruistic love. This hedonism is engendered in part by the materialistic view of frenzied and destructive nature, rife with the busy and voluptuous atoms that make us man. If God is not dead, He is certainly ailing, so conventional morality does not apply; libertinism is not so much immoral as amoral. Sentiment is a sign of weakness and must be overcome by writing nihilistic poetry and prose or engaging in sadomasochistic sex, both of which are intended to violate the compassionate impulse and finally overcome it, rendering it moribund. Hence the glorification of physical endurance and excess in all of its forms, sexual and otherwise. Since nature is ferocious, so are we, truly free when we relinquish our self-control: taboos against incest, sodomy, torture, and even murder are therefore of no consequence.[16] Lucretius seems deliberately misunderstood in this case, a great distance from the pious, ascetic champion of Epicurus: "honour, wealth, and nobleness of bloud; / Tis plain they likewise do our *mind* no good" (Creech, trans., *T. Lucretius Carus*, 2 [36]).

Turner wisely observes that a libertine is an elitist, a member of an aristocratic counterculture who rebels against "the rules of upper-class civility even though it is precisely these rules that give [him] the license to be uncivil," full of respect for the codes he violates.[17] He also argues in his later work that, predictably, Charles himself served as the paradigm for such behavior. Disorder in his court created a Hobbesian "general state of warfare, both verbal and physical, in which sexuality and disease are the weapons." The king saw it as his prerogative to assert his private sexuality in the public sphere, installing mistresses such as Barbara, Nell, Hortense, and Louise in the face of his queen, zealous in his attacks on those who lampooned them, clearly violating the established norms of his society, especially those his own father had set in his pattern of un-wavering (and touching) fidelity to his mother. Turner con-cludes: "This arbitrary mix of hedonism and repression generated confusion, social tension, and hostility towards displays of libertinism."[18] Bourgeois culture then as now did not approve of such behavior. Such anti-values reach their zenith (or nadir) in the next century courtesy of Sade's *L'Ecole du Libertinage*, better known as *Les 120 Journées de Sodome*, but are nascent in the poetry of Rochester with its "Buggeries, Rapes, and Incests" (*A Ramble in Saint James Parke*, 24).

These highly fraught social, political, and literary issues concerning libertinism trickle down in diluted form through Carolean drama and translations of Lucretius by Dryden and Creech—eventually, they reach Behn, whose profession placed her on the fringe of court life and thereby forced her to negotiate them. Even though the occasional character praises "divine *Hobs*" as late as 1682 (*The Round-heads* 2.1.369), "pure" Hobbism is no easier to discern in Behn's plays, poems, and fiction than in the work of her con-temporaries. Actually, in the preceding quotation, the play-wright shows her two satirical Puritan characters, Lady Desbro and Freeman, misinterpreting the philosopher's definition of power as "a great Pleasure to cheat the World" (368). Nor does she seem to have misread *De rerum natura* or *Leviathan* as a license to debauch oneself, as Rochester is alleged to have done. In her *Dutch Lover* preface, she mocks those who misunderstand Hobbes or accuse her of the same fault. If she

> had presented you with two or three of the worst principles trans-crib'd out of the peremptory and ill natur'd, (though prettily inge-nious) Doctor of Malmsbury undigested, and ill manag'd by a silly,

fancy, ignorant, impertinent, ill educated Chaplain, I were then suf-
ficiently in fault. (W 5:160)

The excesses of libertinism, in fact, seem distasteful to her, although not to the disgusted extent apparent in Shadwell's farce *The Libertine* (1675) or in the anti-libertine tracts that her life precedes, such as Edward Ward's *The Libertine's Choice; Or, The Mistaken Happiness of the Fool in Fashion* (1709) and Mary Davys's *The Accomplish'd Rake; Or, Modern Fine Gentlemen* (1727)—or, for that matter, the play recently attributed to Behn, *The Debauchee: Or, The Credulous Cuckold* (1677).[19] In a general way, some Hobbesian philosophical tenets tend to inform the frenzied and seemingly purposeless movements of Behn's characters that she synthesizes into a forced march to the end of a piece, as if she were the Lawgiver or great Dame Nature: "The Desires, and other Passions of man, are in themselves no Sin. No more are the Actions, that proceed from those Passions, till they know a Law that forbids them: which till Lawes be made they cannot know" (*Leviathan* 1.13); "Felicity is a continuall progresse of the desire, from one object to another; the attaining of the former, being still but the way to the later" (1.11).[20] One might infer that the artificiality of the forms that Behn practices is a response to such grave sentences, each pastoral or comedy serving as a parody of the genre itself.[21] Her Bellmours and Silvias tend to pursue their desires in spite of forbidding laws in the vain hopes of attaining boundless felicity in a way that Behn seems to endorse in some of her poetry, scornful of those "Who by a fond mistake Created that a Sin / Which freeborn we, by right of Nature claim our own" ("The Golden Age," 113–14).

However, Behn's rakes enjoy no felicity. They seem objects of derision precisely because they misappropriate Hobbes in the aforementioned Rochesterian way, fulfilling La Rochefoucauld's maxim concerning self-deception in spectacular fashion: "Nous sommes si accoutumés à nous déguiser aux autres, qu'enfin nous nous déguisons à nous-mêmes" (*Maximes*, no. 119),[22] which Behn translates: "We are so accustomed to dissemble, that we often jilt our selves" (*Seneca Unmasqued*, no. 80 [W 3:212]). Jilting oneself may include misapplying a concept such as "Life it selfe is but Motion, and can never be without Desire, nor without Feare, no more than without Sense" (*Leviathan* 1.7)[23] to justify debauchery. Men who operate as if it did are lampooned:

> Customs of Countries change even Nature her self, and long Habit takes her place: The Women are taught, by the Lives of the Men, to live up to all their Vices, and are become almost as inconstant; and 'tis but Modesty that makes the difference, and, hardly, inclination; so deprav'd the nicest Appetites grow in time, by bad Examples. ("The History of the Nun; Or, the Fair Vow Breaker" [W 3:212], 1689)

Behn anticipates the usual charge against women's inconstancy by explaining that men teach by their actions, an idea to which she returns frequently in her work. Her Ovidian heroine tells her faithless lover on behalf of all women, "'Tis false and broken Vows make Love a Sin, / Hadst thou been true, We innocent had been" ("*Oenone* to *Paris*," 281–82). Aphra ruefully pillories her supposed lover John Hoyle for his serial inconstancy: "for New Victories he prepares, / And leaves the Old to its Despairs" ("Our Cabal," 175–76). Rakishness can only enable women to harm themselves: "my poor Heart alone is harm'd, / Whilst thine the Victor is, and free" ("Love Arm'd," 15–16). The anger Behn demonstrates in the above passage from "The History of the Nun" helps explain, to some extent, the caprices of her "jilt" heroine Isabella, a Restoration Joan Crawford. A novice who conceives a passion for one man, Henault, and marries him, Isabella weds his best friend Villenoys when Henault is believed lost in war. When her first husband returns eight years later, Isabella smothers him, confesses her murder to Villenoys, and cajoles him into helping her dispose of the body by sewing it into a sack. She resolves her bigamous predicament by surreptitiously stitching Villenoys's collar to the sack so that when he hurls the body of his best friend from a bridge into a river, the laws of physics dictate that he follow and perish into the deep as a matter of course. Behn makes no effort to explain Isabella's psychology or to provide any real motivation for killing either man, the actions themselves suggesting that the life of (wo)man is poor, solitary, nasty, brutish, and short, her inclinations to libertinism irresistible. One might say that such behavior is chosen for her by decadent male aristocrats who decree that life itself is but motion to justify depraving nicer appetites by their bad example.

II

> Men that distrust their own subtilty, are in tumult, and sedition, better disposed for victory, than they that suppose themselves wise, or crafty.
>
> —*Leviathan* 1.11[24]

> Every body thinks himself capable of understanding Love, and that he is a Master in the Art of it; when there is nothing so nice, or difficult, as to be rightly comprehended.
>
> —*La Montre: Or, The Lover's Watch* (W 4: 310)

The Lover's Watch (1686), Behn's translation of Balthazar de Bonnecorse's *La Montre* (1666), a Restoration example of the ancient form of *prosimetron* (mixed prose and verse) practiced by Boethius and Dante, resembles an anti–*Ars amatoria*, a rebuttal to rakehellism.[25] With no cynicism whatever, her garrulous heroine Iris seeks to train her eager swain Damon in the proper and honest way to love for every hour of the day, and her torrent of words proves more effective than Hellena's fencing with Willmore or Sylvia's passionate letters to Philander. The humility of Damon's replies, appropriately enclosed in a subsection entitled "The Case for the Watch," indicates his conversion by this *domina Amoris*, aided in part by the logic of the preceding epigraph. Behn-Iris argues that the lover humble enough not to suppose himself crafty knows honesty and constancy can and should conquer deceit and inconstancy. This warning oddly echoes Hobbes's Machiavellian sentence. Just as the prince who knows his political limitations can thereby conquer those vain men who fail to comprehend their own shortcomings, the wise lover who knows he is no master of love will succeed because he realizes that he has much to learn. These similar sentiments interpenetrate at the site of Behn's libertines, they who think themselves experts on love. In several comedies, *The Dutch Lover* (1673), *The Town-Fopp* (1676), *Sir Patient Fancy* (1678), *The Feign'd Curtizans* (1679), and *The City Heiress* (1682), these characters predictably decline into foppery, indisposed for victory and incapable of understanding love, not nearly distrustful enough of their own subtlety.

This predictability may be occasioned less by the stock forms of Behn's theater than by a pessimistic belief that a lack of subtlety dictates certain results. Her amusing poem, "A Letter to a Brother of the Pen in *Tribulation*," suggests her attitude concerning her male friends who debauch themselves: "who thought thy Wit / An Interlude of Whoring would admit?" (23–24). Behn shows how little wit her rakes possess as they blunder through such interludes, equipped as they are with multiple partners. In *The Dutch Lover*, Alonzo finds himself nonplussed at the prospect of three invitations to love from three different women, one of whom turns out to be his sister, Clarinda. Similarly, Tom Wilding is harassed and overburdened with Lady Galliard, Charlot, and Diana in *The City Heiress*. The dreadful Sir Timothy Tawdrey and the weak and puling Bellmour squabble over the virtuous Celinda and others such as Betty Flauntit in *The Town-Fopp*. Tawdrey, a knave and coward, ducks his duel with Bellmour and then attacks him from behind in public. And Wittmore blunders constantly in his attempts to seduce the extremely willing Lady Fancy in *Sir Patient Fancy*. Behn shows that one should not equate their rakish multiplicity with virility, but with simple incompetence regarding their relations with women: "the most unmanagable Beasts in Nature" (1.1.44–45). She implies that the felicity with which Etherege's Dorimant extricates himself from his several engagements is a perfidious male fantasy, a fairy tale for boys.

Boys who prove somewhat immune to the type of training Iris gives Damon tend to mouth rakish clichés, an almost certain indicator of the aforesaid masculine incompetence in courtship. When Alonzo's less-than-virtuous Dorminda throws a key down to him from her window as an invitation to love, he justifies himself in the expected way: "Now if 'twere to save my life cannot I forbear, I must go in: Should *Euphemia* know this, she would call it levity and incon-

stancey; but I plead necessity, and will be judg'd by the amorous men, and not the jealous women: For certain this
Lady, whoe'er she be, designs me a more speedy Favour
than I can hope from *Euphemia*, and on easier terms, too"
(*The Dutch Lover* 2.3.54–58). Alonzo's expression of regret, to
"all on the sudden to leave delicious whoring, drinking and
fighting" (3.1.122–23) to woo the unfortunate and virtuous
Euphemia, borders on lampoon: "treating all women-kind
alike we seldom err; for where we find one as you profess to
be [i.e., virtuous], we happily light on a hundred of the socia-
ble and reasonable sort" (1.3.48–50). In *The Feign'd Curtizans*, Galliard exclaims: "Constancy! and wou'dst thou have
me one of those dull lovers who believe it their Duty to Love
a Woman till her Hair and Eyes change Colour for fear of
the Scandalous Name of an inconstant?" (1.1.27–29). And Sir
Anthony Meriwill, an aged rake, explains to his nephew Sir
Charles, "women love importunity" (*The City Heiress* 1.1.441).

Yet Behn's plays argue that women love nothing of the
type, and do not mistake levity and inconstancy for necessity. They refuse to be silent when men erect such defenses,
echoing the women's voices in Behn's fiction and poetry, a
corrective to libertinism. Silvia in *Poems upon Several Occasions* complains "'twas as easie to Prevail, / As after to Betray" ("The Reflection," 27–28). Behn herself contributes a
sarcastic aside concerning a word essential to libertinism:
"Inconstancy's the good supream / The rest is airy Notion,
empty Dream!" ("To *Alexis* in Answer to His Poem against
Fruition," 32–33 [W 1:273], 1688). Obviously, persuasion and
constancy are preferable to brutality and inconstancy. The
social-financial "prize" of *The City Heiress*, Charlot, summarizes the rake's behavior: "I've heard enough of *Wilding's*
Vices, to know I am undone" (2.1.1–2). She criticizes his propensity to keep rambling, which hurts her: "You wou'd, perfidious as you are, though all your Fortune, all your future
Health, depended on that Credit" (76–77). Behn even allows
the adulterous Lady Galliard a salvo. She labels Wilding "a
Rakeshame, who have not Esteem enough for the Sex to believe your Mother honest—without Money or Credit, without Land either in present or prospect; and half a dozen
hungry Vices, like so many bauling Brats at your Back, perpetually craving, and more chargeable to keep than twice

the number of Children" (4.1.134–39). Euphemia rebuffs Alonzo as if she shared this opinion. To his crude "come, come, do not lose my little new-gotten good Opinion of thee, by being coy and peevish," she retorts, "You're strangely impatient, Sir" (*The Dutch Lover* 1.3.24), uncomfortable with his conception of easy terms. And Betty Flauntit's riposte to Timothy Tawdrey speaks for all women in the plays: "You see, Sir, how miserable we Women are that love you Men" (*The Town-Fopp* 4.3.385).

As if Behn were revenging these miserable women, she shames her rakes, making them appear foolish to the point of humiliating them. For all of Alonzo's bluster, Euphemia controls him in a vain attempt to school him, forcing him to disguise himself in front of her father; when she veils herself, he is unable to recognize her, which suggests an obtuseness on his part that transcends the conventional efficacy of disguise in comedy. Bellmour, a truly incompetent libertine, accompanies Sir Timothy Tawdrey to a brothel in an attempt to debauch his sorrows away and fails even at this, wailing: "Gods! What an odious thing meer Coupling is!" (*The Town-Fopp* 4.3.394). In *The Fair Curtizans*, Galliard ends up in bed with the odious parson Tickletext by mistake. In *Sir Patient Fancy*, the witless Wittmore is forced to hide under Lady Fancy's bed when her husband comes home unexpectedly because the rake has failed to plan his liaison with the requisite élan. When Wittmore compounds his blunder by inadvertently revealing his hiding place, Lady Fancy is forced to conceal him with her voluminous skirts by using him for a chair; only a boot to his rear manages to keep him quiet. Behn's rendering of La Rochefoucauld is apposite here: " 'Tis certain that those who are caught by our cunning and deceit, do not appear so ridiculous as we do to our selves, when the subtilty of others has intrapped us" (*Seneca Unmasqued*, no. 307 [W 4:55]). Again, in such patterning, Behn implies that certain behaviors are malignant and cannot be unlearned, no matter how many swift kicks are administered to rakish backsides.[26] The perpetrators misappropriate Hobbes, fail to understand the moral imperative that underlies true Epicureanism, and are incapable of mutuality in love.

III

what the Devil, shou'd I do with a virtuous Woman?—a
sort of ill-natur'd Creatures, that take a Pride to torment
a Lover, Virtue is but an infirmity in Woman.
                                        —1 Rover 4.2.257–59

However, at first examination, Behn seems to endorse libertine sentiment in both parts of The Rover (1677, 1681), which
James, Duke of York, known for gallantry and rakishness,
admired.[27] Even virgin ingenue Hellena, on the verge of entering a nunnery, urges her modest sister Florinda, "let's
Ramble" (1 Rover 1.1.168) as she effects three role, costume,
and gender changes (gypsy, female reveller, boy). The term
she uses (like "rover" itself) has unmistakably erotic over-
tones in the Restoration, its primary meaning "to hunt for
sex," just as Rochester intends in his verse satire A Ramble
in St. James Parke. Of course Hellena, in order to properly
distinguish herself from the courtesan Angellica Bianca
with whom she competes for Willmore's affections, remains
chaste throughout the play, yet given his opinion that virtue
is an infirmity, one might wonder why she wants him. Like
Silvia in Love-Letters, Hellena indulges in the aforementioned protean-Ovidian shape-shifting just like a libertine,
and her roving and machinations are perhaps more intricate than those of her quarry. Just as Silvia seems to understand the rakehell's inheritance of the Ovidian notion of
amor as beguiling ars, "Hast thou forgot thy wondrous Art of
loving? Thy pretty cunings, and thy soft deceivings?" (Love-
Letters [W 2: 144]), Hellena reminds Florinda, "if you are not
a Lover, 'tis an Art soon learnt" (1 Rover 3.1.47–48). Florinda,
no more anxious to marry the aged Vincentio whom her
father has chosen than Hellena is to become a nun, prefers
Willmore's companion and mascot Belvile, certainly, one
whom she hopes to reform by marriage. In the guise of car-
nival-masquer, Hellena flirts openly and shamelessly with
her beloved, discovering in the process that he is more in-
terested in variety (a liaison with a reveller) than in constancy (to her original incarnation as a gypsy): "I know you
Captains are such strict Men, and such severe Observers of
your Vows to Chastity, that 'twill be hard to prevail with

your tender Conscience to Marry a young willing Maid"
(3.1.160–63). Her part of this parley is droll indeed, since
there are no recorded testimonials to the chastity of such
men or to the tenderness of their consciences when the pos-
sessor of a maidenhead is in view. She then plays female
libertine (mirroring D'Urfey's *Madame Fickle* [1676] and
foretelling Southerne's *Sir Anthony Love* [1690]) in her sentiment to bring him to the point: "should I in these days of
my Youth, catch a fit of foolish Constancy, I were undone"
(3.1.169–70). Willmore, true to his type, will say virtually the
same thing in the sequel, reflecting, as it happens, on his
marriage to the departed Hellena: "such a fool I was in my
dull days of Constancy, but I am now for change, . . . for
Change, my dear, of Place, Cloathes, Wine, and Women. Variety is the soul of pleasure" (*2 Rover* 1.1.145–48). However,
Hellena is no libertine. She seeks marriage and the satisfaction of reforming her rake, just as Harriet does with Dorimant in *The Man of Mode*. Early in their play together,
Willmore's overture to his "gypsy" Hellena, "I long to come
first to the Banquet of Love! and such as swinging Appetite
I bring," is tactfully and firmly rebuffed with the simple
logic of her question in response: "is there no difference between leave to love me, and leave to lie with me?" (*1 Rover*
1.2.183–84; 188–89).

In such ways, gourmand Willmore's actions and their consequences undercut the benign nature of his libertinism.
His approach to the rose-selling woman in his first scene is
direct, grossly physical, barely veiled with metaphor: "Fair
one, Wou'd you wou'd give me leave to gather at your Bush
this idle Moneth, I wou'd go near to make some Body smell
of it all the year after" (*1 Rover* 1.2.87–89). His remark to his
companions, "there's but one way for a Woman to oblige
me" (1.2.243–44), borders on gross self-definition. In the
play's epicenter, Behn would seem to discredit her hero
somewhat heavily when he drunkenly attempts the virtuous
Florinda, the love of his best friend Mr. Belvile. He meets
her spluttering "what a filthy Beast is this?" with "I am so,
and thou oughtst the sooner to lye with me for that reason"
(3.5.139–41). That Willmore is too inebriated to recognize
his victim hardly excuses his behavior, as Belvile charges:
"Damn your debaucht Opinion" (3.6.217). The episode is

merely a microcosm of his friend Blunt's angry assault on the same woman later in the play, feeling justified as he does by having lost his breeches, his money, and his dignity to two cutpurse-whores: "Cruel, yes, I will kiss and beat thee all over; kiss, and see thee all over; thou shalt lye with me too, not that I care for the injoyment, but to let you see I have taien deliberate Malice to thee, and will be reveng'd on one Whore for the Sins of another" (4.5.611–15). These attempted rapes expose the poisonous nature of the gentle and mocking cavalier lyric that precedes them: "And with kind force he taught the Virgin how / To yield what all his Sighs cou'd never do" (2.1.172–73). Force is unkind, unappreciated by women.[28] Willmore is only slightly more housebroken than the rustic companion who is the butt of his jokes. Even allowing for the convention of disguise and misrecognition, Hellena's change of identity easily fools Willmore. He does not understand the usefulness of going masked himself in the middle of carnival season so that the exasperated Belvile must explain it to him: "whatever Extravagances we commit in these Faces, our own may not be oblig'd to answer 'em" (2.1.2–3). This symbolizes his failure as a rake, an identity that depends absolutely on secrecy and guile—Willmore, as it happens, is made to answer for everything. Belvile confronts him with his notorious lack of savoir-faire: "do'st know the danger of entring the house of an incens'd *Courtizan?*" (252–53), as if he were a Mr. Horner not in on his own joke. In her guise as a boy, Hellena helps torpedo the Willmore-Angellica Bianca relationship by pretending (in the manner of Viola-Cesario and Olivia in *Twelfth Night*) that she is a page helping Willmore woo another woman, right in front of the incensed courtesan with whom he has just spent a gaudy night, who exclaims: "there's no Faith in any thing he says" (4.2.455).

Thus exposed by playwright and characters, it is as if Willmore must be schooled in rakehellism by the women in the play. Angellica Bianca suggests that he lacks a bit in the art of words: "if thou canst not flatter me a little, 'twill please me from thy Mouth"; Willmore's reply confirms her opinion: "Curse on thy charming Tongue! dost thou return / My feign'd contempt with so much subtilty?" (2.2.375–76). But subtlety is beyond him. Annoyed that Blunt has reminded him of Hellena after having spent the night with Angellica Bianca, he confesses, "I had quite forgot her else, and this Night's debauch had drunk her quite down" (3.1.124–25). As the first play ends, Willmore gives himself over to marriage with Hellena, proclaiming in the play's last words: "Lead on, no other Dangers they can dread, / Who Venture in the Storms o'th' Marriage-Bed" (5.1.544–45). As the second play begins, we discover from Willmore that his bride has perished in a real, not metaphorical, storm, perhaps a joke on Behn's part for those who remembered the first part: "poor soul—she would go to Sea with me, and in a Storm—far from Land, she gave up the Ghost" (2 Rover 1.1.126–27). But this proves to be no obstacle to further amorous adventures. The hero cries to his new friend Beaumond, "I am now for softer Joys, for Woman, for Woman in abundance," who replies delightedly, "The same Man still, wild and wanton!" (117–18; 120). Behn's depiction of such behavior elsewhere is so scathing that it is difficult to take this seriously or as something that she endorses, in spite of her fancy preface to the Duke of York thanking him for his patronage.

IV

she is so abominably vile a woman, and rallies not only all Religion but all Virtue in so odious and obscene a manner, that I am heartily sorry she has writ any thing in your commendation.
—Gilbert Burnet to Mrs. Anne Wharton, 1688[29]

Given Behn's negative portrayals of her rakes, it may seem difficult to understand how her various Restoration audiences could possibly accuse her of libertinism. Her published appreciation of Creech's Lucretius demonstrates that she understands the philosophy at its legitimate, classical, and non-hedonistic source. Some modern scholarship argues the impossibility of women's ability to exhibit such libertine behavior at all, given its patriarchal structure and phallocentric essence.[30] Yet the admonishments of Burnet concerning Mrs. Wharton's acknowledgment of "To Mrs. W. On her Excellent Verses" from Poems upon Several Occasions hint at a negative public reception of precisely this kind, one that necessitated the spirited poetical defenses of her character by her sympathetic male colleagues, as we saw in her escort of commenders for her collection. Two years after this publication, Nahum Tate proclaims, in his prefatory verses for Behn's *La Montre* (1686), "The Pride of *Greece* we now out-rival'd see: / *Greece* boasts one *Sappho*; two *Orinda's*, we" ("To the Divine *Astrea*, on her *Môntre*" [S 6:9]), which suggests that she was admired when she was indeed understood. Yet her usurpation of masculine writerly privilege and her boldness in forming her art from rakish matter naturally adhered to and defined her, which always infuriated her, as the preface to *Sir Patient Fancy* reveals: "The play had no other Misfortune but that of coming out for a Womans: had it been owned by a Man, though the most Dull Unthinking Rascally Scribler in Town, it had been a most admirable Play" (W 6:5).[31]

But Behn was not naïve. She knew well that for a woman in Carolean culture to write *The Rover* or "The Disappointment" was the act of a libertine, in spite of attempts to reclaim and cleanse the territory of love poetry on women's terms, or to legitimize herself with Lucretius. Her male speakers in *Poems upon Several Occasions* tend to say rakish things: "Give me but Love and Wine, I'll ne'er / Complain my Destiny's severe" ("A Paraphrase on the Eleventh *Ode* out of the First Book of *Horace*," 13–14); "Kiss me softer than the Dove, / Till my Ravisht Soul does lie / Panting in an Ecstasie" ("A Translation," 14–16). One could argue justifiably that these renderings of Horace and Pseudo-Gallus are indeed translations, without much room to maneuver. These are the things that men have said since antiquity, who insist for their own purposes that "The End to which the Fair are born, / Is not to keep their Charms in store: / But lavishly dispose in haste / Of Joys which none but Youth improve" ("The Counsel," 3–6). Behn simply reproduced her milieu and understood that what she wrote would be used against her because she was a woman. Isabella's disclaimer notwithstanding, that love "teaches feeble Woman how to write" (*The Lover's Watch* [W 4:285]), Behn, hardly feeble, possessed an anguished understanding of this basic injustice, which led to equally elaborate phalanxes of self-defense.

Behn adopts the tactic of disassociation when she portrays female libertinism as a hypocritical characteristic of those who exhibit the behavior for which they criticize her. The aptly-named Lady Galliard, anxious to be seduced by the rake Wilding, insidiously dissembles her desires by claiming that she does not wish to be "A loath'd Extinguisher of filthy flames, / Made use of, and thrown by" (*The City Heiress* 4.1.232–33), in an echo of Behn's rejection of Lysander's offer of sex: "Take in no Partners to your Fire" ("To Lysander . . . Loves Fire," 33). The lustful Puritan Lady Lambert speaks similar language in *The Roundheads*. Ironically, in that play, Behn uses the repulsive Presbyterian divine Ananias to comment on such hypocrisy: "Verily, the Sin lyeth in the Scandal; therefore most of the discreet pious Ladies of the Age, chuse us, upright Men, who make a Conscience of a secret, the Laiety being more regardless of their Fame" (3.2.332–34). "Honour" is simply the supercilious worry about one's reputation to these people, a tool of oppression against women, as Behn intimates elsewhere with the first-person plural: "Thou base Debaucher of the generous heart, / That teachest all our Looks and Actions Art" ("The Golden Age," 140–41). "Honour" is an impediment to the realization of honest desire, the mask for Lambert and Galliard (and for Wycherley's Lady Fidget before them) as they debauch themselves.[32]

Yet Behn knew that the effectiveness of caricature is necessarily limited, open to misinterpretation. *Poems upon Several Occasions* demonstrates her interest in depicting the corrosive effects of libertinism on women, as the abandoned shepherdesses, Oenone most prominently, testify. Likewise, in her most ambitious work of fiction, *Love-Letters between a Nobleman and His Sister*, the same principles apply. The protagonist, Silvia, gradually becomes debased by its malignant essence.[33] The semi-epistolary novel is a deeper investigation of the rambling heroine first proposed in *The Fair Jilt*, Silvia's progress through a number of men to die peacefully in her bed somewhat more troubled than the journey of the motiveless and malign Miranda in the same direction.[34] A person no more "immoral" or "indecent" than the average sort adopts the very behavior she abhors.

However, Behn, neither clumsy nor sentimental, refuses to present a fairy princess led into shame and degradation by a ridiculously evil man. Men's libertinism requires some enabling and consent to take root in women, as the speakers in her poetry so often reveal as they recall "each Recess and Shade where thou and I, / Loves Secrets did Unfold; / And did the dull Unloving World defy" ("On Mr. *J. H.* In a Fit of Sickness," 61–63). In *Love-Letters*, the appropriately named Philander, no worse than he should be, simply stimulates impulses hitherto dormant in Silvia, whom Behn later describes as "too apt to charge others with those Crimes to which she was her self addicted, or had been guilty of: Amorously inclin'd and indiscreet in the Management of her Amours, and constant rather from Pride and Shame than Inclination" (W 2:257). At first, her resistance seems stronger than the power of her brother-in-law's entreaties. She does not seem willing to betray her sister Mertilla, but Philander's magnetism awakens her amorous drives and her own propensity for deceit. Her breathless "I have no Arts Heav'n knows, no guile or double meaning in my soul" (24) guilefully becomes an invitation to Philander—"I may one day in some unlucky hour in some soft bewitching moment, in some spightful critical ravishing minute, yield all" (39)—to consummate their passion, her ambition all along: "I confess I did dissemble a coldness which I was not Mistress of: there lyes a Womans Art, there all her boasted Vertue, it is but well dissembling, and no more" (67).

The pessimistic nature of authentic libertinism suggests that true consummation can never be accomplished, uncertain as we are of the arrival of the happy minute. Hence Philander and Silvia do not easily accomplish the realization of their joys. In the manner of "The Disappointment," Philander is impotent the first time, and laments this imperfect enjoyment with Rochesterian gusto: "Oh *Silvia!* what Demon, malicious at my Glory, seiz'd my vigor?" (56–57). This impotence serves as an omen of the future for the libertinish lovers. Philander's initial failure to perform is a physical emblem of his true nature, to which he alludes in an anguished, pre-coital missive to Silvia: "'tis not enough that we tell those we Love all they love to hear, but one ought to tell 'em too, every secret that we know; and conceal no part of that Heart one has made at present to the person one Loves, 'tis a Treason in Love not to be Pardon'd" (44). Most treasonable in love, Philander specializes in telling Silvia what she wants to hear while always concealing his heart from her, involving Brilljard in his schemes and corrupting him, as well. He learns from his master that "to be the greater Enemy you ought to seem to be the greatest Friend" (152).

Now a stranger to herself, her heart dead and cold at the root, Silvia can only practice what she has learned. Discovering at last the depths of Philander's emotional treason, she decides to encourage his lovesick best friend, Octavio, "in a moment furnisht with all the Art and subtilty that was necessary on this occasion" (200), concluding with that libertine from antiquity, Ovid, *the least I can do is to deceive the deceiver*" (207–8).[35] Octavio is also infected, his definition of love reduced to "*an unthinking Motion of the Soul, that comes and goes as unaccountably as changing Moons, or Ebbs and Flows of Rivers, only with far less certainty*" (370). Behn underscores this lack of certainty in the supremely ironic moment when Octavio is horrified to discover Silvia, having just pledged herself to him, abed with Philander, whom he had aided in infidelity against her. Yet Silvia had already been debased, reasoning with the libertinism she has already imbibed from Philander, too numb to be brokenhearted any longer at his perfidy: "she scorn'd by any vain indeavour to recal him from his passion, she had wit enough to have made those eternal observations, that love once gone is never to be retriev'd, and that it was impossible to cease loving, and then again to love the same person, one may believe for sometime ones love is abated, but when it comes to love a new Object, it can never return with more than pity, compassion, or civility for the first" (220). Silvia finds herself unable to arouse any passion in herself at all, having discovered, along with the Miranda of whom she seems to be a revision, that love "rages beyond the Inspirations of *a God all soft and gentle*, and reigns more like *a Fury from Hell*" (*The Fair Jilt* [W 3:9]).

With fury from hell, Behn exposes the machinations of "that false Creature, Man" (*Sir Patient Fancy* 3.1.12) and, with unusual frankness, portrays women's natural wishes for love, "the most noble and divine Passion of the Soul," without which they are doomed to be "unfinish'd, and unhappy" (*The Fair Jilt* [W 3: 7]). Such passages in her fiction and poetry doubtless appeared rakish to her manifold audience, few of whom understood her portraits of female passion as corrective. Women, Behn seems to say, desperately need the aforesaid love, embraces, and happiness. What they get instead is none of the foregoing, just grasping hands and insensitive fingers. To be groped is to be disappointed, left with "all my Rifled Joy" ("To *Lysander*, on Some Verses He Writ," 24), knowing "'Tis the Glory you seek when you rifle the Spoil" ("The Return," 6), and that "The Rifled Joys no more can Please, / That once oblig'd your Stay" ("The Reflection," 47–48). For that matter, Behn's most eloquent statement of the disjunction between male desire and female response is "The Disappointment," its droll description of male-to-female genital touching dramatizing the very concept of "rifling." Lysander, having pinned the unwillingly willing Cloris, crudely explores her:

> His daring Hand that Altar seiz'd,
> Where Gods of Love do sacrifice:
> That Awful Throne, that Paradice
> Where Rage is calm'd, and Anger pleas'd;
> That Fountain where Delight still flows,
> And gives the Universal World Repose.
>
> (45–50)

With mock-heroic phrasing such as "Altar," "Awful Throne," and "That Fountain where Delight still flows," Behn does not so much praise the essence of biological femaleness as satirize the importance that patriarchal culture attributes to it. For young men such as Lysander, as well as his elders and betters, nothing is more important— this "hinder Place" (116) calms their rage and pleases their anger, (too) easily pacifying them. Yet in her verb "seiz'd," Behn suggests that the experience is decidedly more pleasing for Lysander than for Cloris, the virgin cruelly thwarted in her wish to be rid of her maidenhead, her enjoyment quite imperfect.[36] No word could better epitomize masculine insensitivity and the quest for power, just as the poem's last word, "Impotence" (140), epitomizes the fate of men who refuse to prioritize mutuality.

Poems such as "Song: On Her Loving Two Equally" from *Poems upon Several Occasions* and the later "To the Fair *Clarinda*, Who Made Love to Me, Imagined more than Woman" (1688) attempt to distinguish between honest desire and libertinism, defiant in their unconventionality, championing the quest for "Glorious and Luxurious Ease" ("A Farewel to *Celladon*," 46–47) that marks her pastoral world, informed by Creech's Rapin, Theocritus, and Horace. The monologue featuring an arboreal narrator, "On a *Juniper-Tree*," describes mutual (and multiple) orgasm. "To *Alexis* in Answer to His Poem against Fruition" (1688) constitutes a veritable essay on the dichotomy between men's perfidy and women's desire. Since "Man with that inconstancy was born, / To love the absent, and the present scorn" (15–16), woman cannot depend on him in the way that she can, or should, rely on herself, as the following rhetorical question implies: "Why do we deck, why do we dress / For such a short-liv'd happiness?" (17–18). After all, "With one surrender to the eager will / We're short-liv'd nothing, or a real ill" (13–14 [W 1: 272]). Behn's Ovidian heroine explains how most men follow the pattern of Congreve's double-dealer, Mr. Maskwell: "Till Swains had learn'd the Vice of Perjury, / No yielding Maids were charg'd with Infamy" ("*Oenone* to *Paris*," 279–80). Men compound their falseness not only by charging women with their own crimes but by demonizing female desire, as well. When Lucretia Knowell muses, "to be read in the Arts . . . is the peculiar Province of the other Sex" (*Sir Patient Fancy* 1.1 [4: 13]), this is, in part, what she means. Furthermore, Oenone's Ovidian antiquity is hardly accidental. Behn marshals the *magister artium et Amoris*, the archetypal male libertine from the ancient world, to argue the timelessness and veracity of her case.[37] If the ultimate libertine was unafraid to ventriloquize as a scorned woman critical of male behavior which he himself had seemed to endorse, she in turn gives herself leave to speak bluntly as a true member of the sex who explains how wonderful things could be: "Now uncontroll'd we meet, uncheck'd improve / Each happier Minute in new Joys of

Love!" ("*Oenone* to *Paris*," 66–67), in an age when "it was glory to pursue delight, / And that was lawful all, that Pleasure did invite" ("The Golden Age," 80–81), it being no sin to possess "all that cou'd adorn a Face, / All that cou'd either Sex subdue" ("On the *Death* of Mr. *Grinhil*," 44–45).

In a poem to the physician Thomas Tryon, Behn argues that libertinism spoiled the Golden Age, introducing "wild Debauchery . . . / And Vice, and Luxury" to an unsuspecting people: "By swift degrees we took that Poison in, / Regarding not the danger, nor the sin" (1685) (24–25 [W 1:179).[38] Therefore, a certain dynamic between the sexes is timeless: "The fair young Bigot, full of Love and Prayer, / Doats on the lewd and careless Libertine" (A *Voyage*, 220–21).[39] Lines of this type suggest that her elegy on Rochester not only comments on her prudish detractors and identifies her with a famous and usefully dead poet, but is also literary camouflage. Her public praise of the earl masks a private contempt for bad behavior that she criticizes elsewhere in her fictions, and corrects in "On a *Juniper-Tree*," her most fully realized vision of a healthy alternative to libertinism. This constitutes revenge for Mrs. Barry, if you will, an indication that a woman is not a part or a hole, but a whole.

5

The Juniper-Tree in Behn's
Pastoral World

The blessed Minute he pursu'd
—"On a *Juniper-Tree*, cut down to make *Busks*," 52

The third entry in *POEMS UPON SEVERAL OCCASIONS*, the superb "On A *Juniper-Tree*, cut down to make *Busks*," was first
published four years earlier in Rochester's volume of approximately the same name (1680) under the title "On a *Giniper Tree* now cut down to make Busks," thus by implication
credited to him.[1] The two versions differ in some acciden-
tals (or "minor" substantives, depending on how one views
this issue in textual criticism), to which Behn seems to have
attended in reclaiming her verses from the opus of her dead
hero, all of which suggests what the rest of the collection
implies. She took great care in this act of self-presentation,
this important writerly activity that would make her reputation, implicitly understanding Dryden's contrast between
the ephemerality of stage language and the permanence of
poetry in print.[2] She even seems to have excised a couplet
included in the falsely attributed *"Giniper Tree."* An examination of the excision shows it to be judicious, not simply
the work (or lapse) of a typesetter.[3]

Given Behn's care with her book and with "On a *Juniper-
Tree*" in particular, it is curious indeed that the line that
serves as epigraph to this chapter was allowed to stand with
no corresponding rhyming unit of iambic tetrameter in
some 1684 printings. The following line completed the couplet in 1680: "Whilst *Love*, her fear, and shame subdu'd."
The poem's most recent editor adds it without much fan-
fare; her predecessor does not include it, with no explana-

tion whatsoever, in what might be described as the fashion of his day. Surely the early-twentieth-century editor nods, and his successor improves the poem with her diligence.[4] No seventeenth-century book is free of errors, and such lacunae as *"Juniper-Tree"* features occurred under the auspices of the Tonson brothers on Chancery Lane. Some versions of page 22 (or signature C3 verso) of *Poems upon Several Occasions* complete the couplet with: "While Love and Shame her Soul Subdu'd." So, in 1680, love subdues Cloris's fear and shame as her swain pursues his goal; four years later, love *and* shame subdue her very soul. Fearless and shameless or shamed and somewhat unwilling? Both readings seem out of keeping with the aesthetic of the poem, especially Behn's vision of Cloris at this point. Her (fleeting) postcoital regret occurs later, when she "chid the Swain, for having prest, / What she alas cou'd ["wou'd," in some versions] not resist" (70–71), but then joins him in paying homage to the tree by caressing its bark and kissing its roots (79–82). She is a happy young woman.

Restoration poets generally did not intend to present fractured couplets to their readers.[5] It is unlikely, but at least possible that Behn's minute attention to her text extended to omitting any corresponding rhyme, because it would be completely appropriate to the idea encoded in line 52, the poem, and her poetry itself for her to do so. She fashions "The blessed Minute he pursu'd" in the center of this finely constructed piece of late baroque art, an unabashed celebration of heterosexual love that presents her alternative to cynical masculine libertinism. It is not the poem's climax (this occurs later, literally and figuratively, three times), but the prelude to it, calling attention to itself. Behn, perhaps, wants us to pause and to examine her improvisation on a commonplace of libertine poetry, what her male contemporaries refer to as the "lucky" or "happy minute"—a pseudo-scientific belief derived from the materialism of Lucretius and Hobbes that successful seduction, copulation, and satisfaction depends on the fortunate confluence of random matter. Or, as she herself describes this Cupid-induced phenomenon in the translation that ends *Poems on Several Occasions*, "Agreeing *Attoms* by his pow'r were hurl'd" (*A Voyage to the Isle of Love*, 1676). Her adjective, "blessed," suggests that luck does not, or should not, have anything to do with it, as it surely does in her comedy on the subject, *The Luckey Chance* (1686), or in the words of her hypocritical puritan Lady Lambert, who barely masks her disappointment at the interruption of her assignation: "thou art come in the most lucky Minute—I was just on the point of falling" (*The Roundheads* 2.1.287). If the line were intended to stand by itself, it argues strongly for the singularity of this "blessed" event. Nothing else can compare, an example of what Dorothy Mermin describes as "a background for female sexual freedom" in Behn's pastoral world.[6]

The singularity of this sentiment, be it textual, lexical, or poetical, epitomizes the golden world that most commentators find Behn evoking in her poetry as she hopes to be admired and understood by all. Although "On a *Juniper-Tree*" has received relatively little critical attention, two scholars have written lucidly, if briefly, on the poem, Judith Kegan Gardiner and Elizabeth V. Young.[7] As I analyze Behn's piece and relate it to the rest of *Poems upon Several Occasions*, I will build on Young's optimistic assertion that the poem "opens and expands the possibilities of love and its connections with the natural world, moving it beyond a relationship of opposition to one of community,"[8] and dispute some of Gardiner's more acerbic contentions, that the immortality alluded to in the poem "alludes not to divine truth but simply to the renewed desire for sex" and that it is simply "soft porn."[9] I will also speculate how it may, in some respects, answer the poetry of Katherine Philips. The juniper tree's story constitutes Behn's heterosexual ideal— more so, perhaps, than the bravura translation that opens her collection "The Golden Age," for which some of my predecessors claim similar status.[10] After all, that pindaric laments the effect of the "Ill-natur'd Bus'ey Great" ("The Golden Age," 75) on Arcadia. The carpe diem convention that closes that poem would hardly be necessary if Honour and Nonsense were banished, as they are from "The kind supporting yielding Grass" under the juniper tree ("On a *Juniper-Tree*," 30).

I

> Nor thou *Arceuthis*, art an Enemy
> To the soft Notes of charming Harmony.
> Falsly the chief of Poets would persuade
> That Evil's lodged in thy Eternal shade,
> Thy Aromatick shade, whose verdant Arms
> Even thy own useful fruits secures from harms;
> Many false Crimes to thee they attribute,
> Wou'd no false Virtues too, they wou'd to thee impute.
>
> —*Sylva*, 520–27[11]

Several influences probably coalesced in Behn's mind as she wrote "On a *Juniper-Tree*" besides Creech's translation of Theocritus's *Idyllium* 24, discussed in chapter 3. First, she was compelled to confront an uncomfortable physical fact. Busks, the strips of wood that served as stiffening agents for corsets, were a part of her everyday existence, rubbing under her breasts and against her hips, abdomen, and the small of her back. They were one curse (among others) of womanhood for queens and waiting-gentlewomen alike. Her poem creates its own droll myth to explain and justify this inconvenience. Second, her work on the translation of the sixth book of her beloved Cowley's Latin *Plantarum libri sex* (1668), *Sylva*, surely affected the composition of "On a *Juniper-Tree*," or vice versa. Appended to the edition of Cowley's works published in Behn's last year (1689), *Sylva* features the five couplets above on the juniper (answering Virgil's criticism of this tree in the *Eclogues*),[12] as well as a long speech that foretells the Civil War and the coming of Charles II by the nymph Dryas, concealed in the trunk of an oak (see *Sylva*, 865–1725). Earlier, as a marginal note states, the "translatress speaks in her own person" on behalf of the laurel:

> I by a double right thy Bounties claim,
> Both from my Sex, and in *Apollo's* Name:
> Let me with *Sappho* and *Orinda* be
> Oh ever sacred Nymph, adorn'd by thee;
> And give my Verses immortality.
>
> (*Sylva*, 590–94)

As Mirella Agorni argues, Behn lost no opportunity to improve her literary status by the act of translation.[13] And it should be observed that it was particularly prestigious to associate oneself with the poet from the previous age whom Behn's literary culture respected most, Cowley, as well as with her female predecessors from antiquity and modernity, Sappho and Katherine Philips. Furthermore, *Sylva* provided Behn with several precedents for talking trees in a "Prophetick Mood." The laurel, the oak, and the juniper all possess several interlocking symbolic properties such as heterosexual courtship, poetic immortality, patriotic royalism (the Boscobel Oak, after all, hid Charles as his Parliamentarian captors pursued him), and male fertility. Even a cursory reading of George Sandys's scholarly rendering of the *Metamorphoses* would have provided Behn with the importance of trees concerning the latter issue, this symbolism somewhat obvious regarding the potent Charles, as well.[14] Behn imbues the juniper with all of these qualities as part of her sensual paradisal mythology. Its shade, "Aromatick" (a favorite word of hers, attuned as she was to smell) and "Eternal," cannot be evil if it nurtures lovers such as Cloris and Philocles and is "Grateful" to do so.

A third influence, more remote than corsets and Cowley, may have been Horace's *Satires* 2.8, a suggestion made by Montague Summers in the previous century.[15] Given Behn's ignorance of Latin, the most likely avenue of transmission would have been her friend Creech, whose translation of the poem appears in *The Odes, Satyrs, and Epistles of Horace, Done into English*, printed by her publisher Jacob Tonson in the year that *Poems upon Several Occasions* appeared (1684). As I argue elsewhere, Creech's influence on Behn as a purveyor of antiquity cannot be overstated, even by Behn herself: "So thou by this Translation dost advance / Our Knowledg from the State of Ignorance, / And equals us to Man!" ("To Mr. *Creech*," 41–43). As chapter 3 demonstrates, this rendering of Lucretius provided her with classical precedent for her feminized version of libertinism; his translation of Theocritus helped her landscape her English Arcadia; his Horace, accurate, elegant, and urbane, was her model for poetic *aurea mediocritas*. The sexual dynamic between them (worldly older woman, diffident younger man) seems rather obvious from their poems to each other, as well. Creech states that a reading of Behn's work could fire the blood of the most recalcitrant virgins: "Thy Raptures are transfus'd through every vein, / And thy blest hour in all their heads does reign" ("To the Authour, on her Voyage to the Island of Love," 43–44). Behn is somewhat more frank: "that which Admiration does inspire / In other Souls, kindles in mine a Fire" ("To Mr. *Creech*," 15–16). Indeed.

Horace makes the very well equipped yet ignored and bird-befouled Priapus the narrator of this brief and highly amusing poem. We learn that someone carved him from the stump of an old oak in a wasteland that his patron Maecenas intends to transform into a garden. He recounts a strange middle-of-the-night encounter with two hags, Canidia and Sagana, who have arrived to practice magic, as is customary in this location. Frightened by their spells and appearance, Priapus "reveng'd my self at last" for the years of necromantic and scatological abuse and "stoutly farted from my Arse of Oak," chasing off the unfortunate ladies, attuned as they are to such portents and prodigies.[16] If Behn was influenced by this poem, she brilliantly transfigures its details and incorporates them into "On a *Juniper-Tree*." Her tree, definitely alive in some form (if transfigured into busks) and possibly female as well as male, presides over an amazingly productive sexual encounter between two young lovers, providing a different and effective magic in contrast with Horace's two asexual witches. The wasteland over which the neglected fertility god presides becomes lush and green and supportive under the living juniper, whose lovers' sexual act enacts and evokes the very fertility that Priapus was invented to inculcate in humankind. The reanimated oak, like the transformed juniper, also has feelings that can be hurt or appeased. Priapus feels neglected and inferior: "Let me be spit, let me be piss'd upon / By all the Rogues and Rascals of the Town." The juniper, in contrast, thinks itself quite superior to all other trees: "I hold Supremacy, / (In all the Wood) o'er every Tree" (18–19). Finally, the juniper recounts its transformation just as the oak had previously, happy that Cloris chose to "translate / My being to a happier state" (98–99), in this case always near to her by bodily proximity (busks in her corset), supporting and protecting her so that her sexual activity is, in effect, her choice, securing her useful fruits from harm.[17] Behn's poem is, like that of Horace-Creech, most droll. Horace's god makes an ironic guest appearance in name only as a euphemism for Lysander's tragically flaccid member in "The Disappointment" (105). In these ways, "On a *Juniper-Tree*," like virtually all poems in her collection, reflects her wish to translate her literary being to a happier state.

II

A Conversation at once free
From Passion, and from Subtlety;
A Face that's modest, yet serene,
A sober, and yet lively Meen;
The virtue which does her adorn
By honour guarded, not by scorn.
—Katherine Philips, "The Virgin" (9–14), 1678[18]

Behn's poem is assuredly not "a bit of pastoral pornography" narrated by "a perversely enthusiastic voyeur," nor does it recall religious poetry on the True Cross.[19] In her wistful evocation of her pastoral state in a corrupt world, she transfigures gender and makes love free so that the pernicious untruths of her culture need not repress her young couple (especially her young woman), if only for a blessed minute. One could argue that Behn's poem implicitly attacks concepts such as Philips's paean to virginity, which cannot be reconciled with passion. The ensuing rigid navigation of the mean between extremes results in mediocrity instead as virtue guards her dear, dear honour. Cloris, a virgin such as Philips would instruct, finds her nervous happiness in the moderate acceptance of her natural impulses, while also concerned for honour, albeit as something forgotten and then remembered, like virtue. The rules of civilization do not obtain in Arcadia. One could say that her behavior more closely resembles that of an actual young woman than anything in Philips's poetry, especially the paragon cited above. (That this is indeed a paragon implies that the young women Philips may have known were more like Cloris than she was willing to say. One composes explicit rules because people are not following them in their implicit, unspoken form.) It could be noted in turn that Phil-

ips, since she came first, could not enjoy the poetical freedom that Behn possessed even if she had wished to do so.
And this could be countered with yet another assertion. Reception of Behn's poetry even well into the last century suggests that she did not receive (or expect) approval for her
forays into the erotic. The daughter defies and overcomes
the mother, but then discovers that the same patriarchy vic-
timizes them, conflating punk and poetess.

Philips, given to sententiae as her culture dictated that a
poetess must be, distrusts intensity: "He's his own happiness and his own Law, / Whereby he keeps Passion and Fate
in awe" ("*Mr. Francis Finch*, the Excellent *Palaemon*," 33–34).
Friendship and its moderation are much to be preferred,
simply "Love refin'd and purg'd from all its dross," and "As
strong as Passion is, though not so gross" ("A Friend," 8, 10).
One measures its worth in absence, not community: "when
our Sense is dispossest, / Our labouring Souls will heave
and pant, / And gasp for one anothers breast" ("Parting with
Lucasia," 5–7). Such professions of female friendship suggest the creation of a safe space for passion, out of the grasp
of the patriarchy that tries to grasp it, surreptitiously, for
itself. Some might claim that Behn's androgynous statements of affection, such as "To the Fair *Clarinda*, Who Made
Love to Me, Imagined More Than Woman," explodes notions
such as Philips's, or may gloss the eroticism beneath. Yet in
spite of Philips's confessions of woman-to-woman ardor,
one might even suspect (wrongly) that she fears passion:

> 'Tis true, it looks at distance fair;
>   But if we do approach,
> The fruit of *Sodom* will impair,
>   And perish at a touch:
> In Being than in Fancy less,
> And we expect more than possess.
>   ("Against Pleasure," 7–12)[20]

Can the fruit of Sodom not feed female friendship, also?
Compared to Behn's, Philips's poetry in this vein may be
misunderstood as priggish and simplistic, although one
might better label it as moderate common sense, the cultivation of the *aurea mediocritas* informed by the same tradi-

tion that produced some of the most esteemed poetry in our language.[21] This stanza recalls Shakespeare's Sonnet 129 on lust, Raphael's warnings to Adam about physical love in *Paradise Lost* (8.561–94), and Spenser's allegories on the delusive nature of passion in *The Faerie Queene*, especially Sir Guyon's eye-opening tour of the Bowre of Blis (2.12). It also anticipates some of Behn's own poetry on the subject, which explains how men dispose of women after rifling their sacred stores. "With one surrender to the eager will / We're short-liv'd nothing, or a real ill" ("To *Alexis* in Answer to his Poem against Fruition," 13–14, 1688). Yet Behn's regret seems to be hard-earned, after compliance or aggressive pursuit of her own, with a tinge of embarrassment at her former enthusiasm or gullibility. Philips, although possessed of a devilish and much-underrated sense of humor, rarely gives the impression of venturing anything, much less the impairing fruits of Sodom, so that embarrassment or regret is not necessary or even conceivable. It would have violated her poetical character for her to do so.

Perhaps conscious of her role as Poetess, an exemplar to women usurping masculine writerly privilege, Philips's pose should not surprise, just as Behn's reaction to and modification of it should not be a shock, either. Even a glance at the styles of women's dress between the date of Philips's death (1664) and the publication of *Poems upon Several Occasions* (1684) reveals the differences in concepts of freedom for women in their everyday lives. They are bundled and beribboned at the Restoration from their little lace cuffs to their high-necked collars. By its end, clothing becomes less ornamental, frilly, constraining, choking. The abundance of décolletage by the end of Charles's reign says no less. Some painters abjure even this camouflage and depict their female subjects posing topless. But such "freedoms" are suspect. The sexual self-display so often noted in Behn's poetry (and whose lack has been equally often noted in Philips and her circle) parallels its equivalent in dress style, with similarly mixed results for Aphra's reputation that a plunging neckline or even toplessness could well have produced, fashionable or no. This should also not surprise. It is the rare woman writer who champions Aphra above all others: "The femal Writers thou hast all excell'd, /

Since the first mother of mankind rebell'd" ("A Pindarick to Mrs. *Behn* on her Poem on the Coronation: Written by a Lady, " 96–97, 1688).[22] One might note that all of these ladies are still corseted, and that even the appearance of freedom in dress is illusory, male-dictated.

Some, especially men, prefer poetical décolletage, as we see in the prefatory poems to Behn's main collection. In his dedicatory poem to her *Lycidus* (1688), Dr. Daniel Kendrick compares Behn to Philips and finds the latter wanting: "If we *Orinda* to your works compare, / They uncouth, like her countrys soyle, appear, / Mean as its Pesants, as its Mountains bare" ("To *Mrs. B* on Her Poems" [S 6: 297]). Behn, albeit flattered, would probably not have agreed. The differences between herself and Philips are more subtle. She may have thought of Orinda as a professor of "False Virtues," as some would say of the juniper in her translation of Cowley. Not only does Philips inveigh against passion, but she also champions Behn's bête noire, honor, for the very reason that Behn despises it: its restraining power on women. To Philips, self-restraint, neither repressive nor hypocritical, teaches self-control and leads to modest liberation. She lectures her bosom friend, "Honour's to th' mind as Beauty to the Sence, / The fair result of mixed Excellence" ("To the Truly Competent Judge of Honour, *Lucasia*," 23–28). If another acquaintance would only submit to the (lawful, decent) entreaties of a suitor for whom she has no special esteem, it would be for her own benefit: "Give him his happiness, and know your own. / Thus shall you be as Honour's self esteem'd, / Who have one Sex oblig'd, your own redeem'd" ("To *Mrs. Mary Carne*, When *Philaster* Courted Her," 31–36).[23] So, if Mistress Carne would only repress her natural feelings and oblige the deserving swain by marrying him, she would know true happiness, be viewed as honor itself, and free womankind from the sin of Eve. One is reminded of Etherege's Mr. Medley: "Like a woman I find you must be struggled with before one brings you to what you desire" (*The Man of Mode; Or, Sir Fopling Flutter* 4.1.323–24, 1676).[24] Behn may have recognized Philips's passive-aggressive sense of humor, but this is exactly the thinking that she criticizes as cynical hyperbole elsewhere. The rules of honor teach women to entice and jilt so that they "to themselves prescribe a Cruel Law" ("The Golden Age," 125). That is, they simply replicate and promulgate the means of their own repression, uncouth, mean, and bare. Behn does not subject her Cloris to this cruel law. She might have thought that Philips's vision of a passionless existence guided by honor speaks for itself: "He feels no raptures which are joies diseas'd / And is not much transported, but still pleas'd" ("Against Love," 11–15).[25] Yet in this very statement one can almost hear Philips's molars grinding together. This is the safe thing to say, the good example. Twenty years on, Behn would prefer to be transported to a happier state, if Cloris may be cited as evidence.

Philips's fine "Upon the Graving of Her Name upon a Tree in *Barn-Elms* Walks" might also have served as a spur or goad to Behn in her composition of "*Juniper-Tree.*" Orinda's intriguing and typically moderate set of tetrameter couplets seems to be discussing the condition of women as well as the fruits of nature:

> Alas, how barbarous are we,
> Thus to reward the courteous Tree,
> Who its broad shade affording us,
> Deserves not to be wounded thus!
> See how the Yielding Bark complies
> With our ungrateful injuries!
> And seeing this, say how much then
> Trees are more generous than men,
> Who by a Nobleness so pure
> Can first oblige, and then endure.

$(1-10)^{26}$

The epigram, like Behn's narrative, anthropomorphizes the tree, its "grateful shade" also "kindly lent," yet set in contrast to our "ungrateful injuries," transfigured in some way, ostensibly for the benefit of the female speaker. She does not reveal whether she or an admirer perpetrated this conventional bit of vandalism, or whether the intent was somehow romantic. Then, in an unexpected analogy, the tree, "courteous," "wounded," "Yielding," "generous," noble, and "pure," transforms itself. Oddly, it is not a tree, but womankind, who, after obliging penetration, stoically endures, if we can assume that the referent of

"Who" is "Trees" and not "men." If Behn had this poem in mind (along with Creech, Horace, Cowley, Priapus, and corsets) as she cultivated her own tree, one might speculate that she answers Philips in this fashion. Trees are indeed more generous than men, but if they were allowed to speak (as Behn's is), they would happily preside over a different kind of penetration, a manifestation of great creating Nature. And, paradoxically, the greater "injury," the juniper's dismemberment, results in its greater participation in the human community that Behn envisions. Behn might agree that it is bad to be carved into and abandoned. Yet she might also add that it is worse to be ignored altogether, or spoken for, imagined as a symbol of long-suffering and sterile female sexual response.

III

why an obscene Action may not be describ'd, or an obscene Imagination express'd, *truly* and *lively*, or why either of 'em is not capable of the Graces of correct Versification as well as any other thing, is for ever unintelligible.

—Robert Wolseley, Preface to Rochester's
Valentinian, 1685 (CE 3:23)

the treatment her name has experienced cannot in candour be said to be undeserved. That one of the very grossest offenders against decency, by a license which seems directly designed both to inflame and to shock, should have been a woman, may have been her misfortune; but this plain fact goes far towards justifying the obloquy which has been the grave of her literary reputation.

—Adolphus William Ward, *A History of
English Dramatic Literature*, 1899[27]

Wolsey and Ward, two centuries apart, typify their respective eras with their approach to the erotic dimension in literature, just as our opinion of their views typifies our own. The seventeenth-century commentator's defense of Rochester's oeuvre may seem almost unnecessary to us, given the relative freedom of expression we now enjoy. Even this author's poetical excursions into the lower bodily stratum find their descendants in contemporary television programs for young people: a Bakhtinian carnival of impotence, defecation, menstruation, ejaculation, and smelly linen. And, of course, Ward's justification of his exclusion of Behn from his long-winded history of English drama is reprehensible to most twenty-first-century readers, most of whom would find nothing whatever objectionable in her works, and who must strain to find the aforementioned five entities of her hero anywhere in them. However, as we have seen in the ravings of Robert Gould and even in the measured statements of Dryden, Ward's judgment is simply the culmination of most previous commentary on Behn. Accordingly, Wolseley's observation, as sensible as it may appear to those of us who have championed the freedoms of expression granted to artists such as Robert Mapplethorpe, is quite atypical, even now. One could also say that the majority of readers in both eras found Behn much more troubling than Rochester for the simple act of writing itself. This is why her poems with subtle sexual content make her one of the grossest offenders against decency, more so even than the man who wrote about the bowels of Sue Willis, the six sexual aids procured for Cary Frazer by her parents, and the penile obsessions of the Duchess of Cleveland.

Did Behn herself consider poems such as "On a *Juniper-Tree*" obscene? Probably not. But she surely understood her culture's apprehension of this concept, because she navigates its parameters with great care as she composes her couplets. In this way, she describes "an obscene Action" and expresses "an obscene Imagination ... *truly* and *lively*." Her first step is to distance herself from her subject by personification, more subtly than in the allegorical method she learned from Cowley. A tree serves as narrator. This androgynous speaker at first seems female, and very much like the model of a young woman prescribed by Philips:

> to the touch I must confess, [I]
> Bore an Ungrateful Sullenness.
> My Wealth, like bashful Virgins, I
> Yielded with some Reluctancy;
> For which my vallue should be more,
> Not giving easily my store.
>
> ("On a *Juniper-Tree*," 7–12)

This inanimate creature, like most people, does not like to be touched without its consent. It also thinks of itself in conventional female transactional terms: patriarchy manages the troublesome sexualized body by treating it as a commodity that its owners control for profit. So to pluck its berries (as in *Lycidas*) signals an uncomfortable liberty, just as being fondled might make any bashful young woman sullen, reluctant, ungrateful, conscious of "vallue," not easy. Behn can discuss this conundrum in safe and satisfactory terms because, although seemingly female and resembling the virgin who will be deflowered, this is a tree, not a young woman.[28] Its gradual acceptance of touch foretells Cloris's willing participation in heterosexual womanhood.

Behn's pastoral ideal envisions mutual and productive human sexuality, which Cloris and Philocles's seizing of the blessed minute exemplifies. How was Behn to express this "obscene action" in a true and lively fashion without obscenity? Rochester habitually adopts the pose of the pitiless and objective third-person narrator-poet, generally indistinguishable from the persona he creates. Behn distances herself by allowing the tree to narrate and subtly participate as it can, relating what it has seen in a positive, even joyous manner. Nature, as well as the juniper, "naturally" approves:

> Their trembling Limbs did gently press,
> The kind supporting yielding Grass:
> Ne'er half so blest as now, to bear
> A Swain so Young, a Nimph so fair
>
> (29–32)

Not only is the couple young and fair, but also hesitant, nervous. Therefore, since this is a blessed minute for nature also, its representatives must aid the human pair, kind (natural as well as thoughtful), accommodating, and supportive. And, as is conventional in pastoral from Theocritus to Ambrose Phillips, Ruskin's pathetic fallacy obtains: nature, anthropomorphized, benefits from human contact. The juniper also thinks itself blessed:

> My Grateful Shade I kindly lent,
> And every aiding Bough I bent.

> So low, as sometimes had the blisse
> To rob the Shepherd of a kiss,
> Whilst he in Pleasures far above
> The Sence of that degree of Love
> Permitted every stealth I made,
> Unjealous of his Rival Shade.
>
> (33–41)

Again, the tree itself participates, humanized like the yielding grass, shading and protecting this ultimate symbol of nature as elsewhere in Behn's poetry, where "the Winds that gently rise, / Doe Kiss the yeilding Boughs" ("The Willing Mistriss," 7–8). It is appropriately unclear whether "every aiding Bough" is attached to a male or a female juniper as it appears to kiss Cloris, but Philocles thinks it no robbery. Although circumstances necessitate some "stealth," neither jealousy nor rivalry evince themselves. Here, "Trembling and blushing are not marks of shame, / But the Effect of kindling Flame" ("The Golden Age," 100–101). And the physical aspects of love manifest the spiritual, which the tree defines as "Pleasures far above / The Sence of that degree of Love."

With this neoplatonic foundation, only those of ill will could attribute true obscenity to Behn. Accordingly, her narrator can use more detail and go further in celebrating a love that partakes of and transcends the senses. One could even posit that the purpose of climax is to be translated to that extra-physical state, and that the body simply provides the means, as in Donne's "The Extasie" and Carew's "A Rapture." Behn's vision is, in every way, mutual. Cloris takes her "kindling flame" from "the sighing burning Swain" so that they can meet "all uncontroul'd" ("The Golden Age," 102, 105). One aggressive partner does not overpower the reluctant other:

> Kind was the force on every side,
> Her new desire she could not hide:
> Nor wou'd the Shepherd be deny'd.
> Impatient he waits no consent
> But what she gave by Languishment,
> The blessed Minute he pursu'd
>
> ("On a *Juniper-Tree*," 47–52)

Here, force, which women generally do not appreciate, is natural as well as gentle ("Kind"), and, significantly, the province of both partners in all directions ("on every side"). At this point, given the fluidity of the poem's editorial history, one can add 1680's "Whilst *Love*, her fear, and shame subdu'd," the 1684 variant "While Love and Shame her Soul Subdu'd," or simply leave the blessed minute unrhymed as the epitome of great creating or translating nature. Therefore, the immortality of the "Minute" cannot be "happy" or "lucky" as in libertine tradition, exemplified by Dorimant's suggestion to Harriet: "Let us make use of the lucky minute" (*The Man of Mode; Or, Sir Fopling Flutter* 5.2.103), but must be "blessed," almost mystically religious, and like the eternal beauty of the tree, immortalized in the poem. Hence, the line may best be left unrhymed. Nowhere else does the juniper speculate about the interiority or hidden motivations of the couple coupling. It generally describes only what it can see, in the manner of most animated trees that one finds in the *Metamorphoses* or *The Faerie Queene*. Far from indulging in mere voyeurism, the tree actively participates in what it describes.[29] As Cloris and Philocles "feast on Raptures unconfin'd" (57), their blessed minute is the tree's, also:

> For who but a Divinitie,
> Could mingle Souls to that Degree?
> Now like the *Phenix*, both Expire,
> While from the ashes of their fire,
> Sprung up a new, and soft desire.
> Like Charmers, thrice they did invoke,
> The God! and thrice new vigor took.

(60–66)

Now Behn transcends the metaphysical allusiveness of Donne in "The Extasie" or the innocent theorizing of Adam to Raphael in Milton's epic. To "mingle Souls to that Degree" is orgasm.[30] That "both Expire" like the phoenix implies that it is mutual. That "a new, and soft desire" springs up like the mythical bird denotes that it is multiple, not only for the physically capable Cloris but for the impressive (if youthful) Philocles, who needs no time for reanimation so that the couple can take "new vigor" at least "thrice."

The identity of "The God!" remains mysterious: verbal ejaculation, the Lord's name in vain, the Horace-Creech Priapus which the juniper approximates in its cylindrical and
relatively gigantic shape. This is Behn's pastoral ideal, a
truly blessed minute.

Death does not provide Behn's *et in Arcadia ego*, not even
in the transfiguration of the tree into busks. It is, instead,
honor. Cloris's temporary postcoital regret and the somewhat typical behavior of the swain provides the author's acknowledgment of it:

> Cloris reassum'd her fear,
> And chid the Swain, for having prest,
> What she alas cou'd not resist:
> Whilst he in whom Loves sacred flame,
> Before and after was the same,
> Fondly implor'd she wou'd forget
> A fault, which he wou'd yet repeat.
>
> (68–74)

Behn's juniper does not imply hypocrisy in Cloris because
she upbraids Philocles for doing what she wanted him to
do. Nor does it criticize the swain for his relative lack of
sensitivity to the great change or secret willingness to continue or to schedule a return engagement. Instead, it hu-
morously documents responses quite typical of human
beings at such a moment, especially young people. The prelapsarian nature of their Arcadia dictates precisely why the
couple cannot remain in it, but must take their solitary way
out of it. And the culture that produced Cloris and Philocles
surely shapes their responses, something that they import
to their pastoral interlude and must carry with them always. Behn's focus at this point is, ingeniously, the tree,
whose real sense of abandonment and longing mirrors and
intensifies the brief allusion to the lovers' postcoital psychology:

> if before my Joyes were such,
> In having heard, and seen too much,
> My Grief must be as great and high,
> When all abandon'd I shall be,
> Doom'd to a silent Destinie.
>
> (85–89)

Cloris will not be abandoned; she too will be the same before and after, with one small exception. Like Philips's tree
in Barn-Elms Walks, it is the juniper that will suffer—in this
case, from the lack rather than the presence of human contact. No voyeur, the tree explains its vicarious participation
without regret in what it has seen. It will simply miss, very
much, the couple that it has sheltered, protected, and nur-
tured. And, in its transfiguration as guardian of Cloris's sacred store, it clearly appreciates the lovers' gratitude to it
for making their initiation into adulthood possible. Appropriately, Behn leaves the reason for abandonment mysterious, as Keats will in describing a panel of the amphora in
his famous ode. We can only know what the tree (and the
Grecian Urn) shows us. In this way she remains true to the
aesthetic of the poem. The ideas of assignation, foreplay, female desire, premarital sexual congress, mutual multiple
orgasm, fleeting postcoital regret, happy mutuality, tree
worship, and the construction of feminine unmentionables
are all described in a timely and lively fashion, with great
subtlety, tact, and good humor, with enormous empathy for
inexperienced young people who do not know they are
being watched by a large literary audience as well as a desperately lonely tree. Unlike her hero Rochester, she refuses to humiliate her lovers. Unlike some of her other
predecessors, she does not censor their activities.

IV

Buc, a buske, plated bodie, or other quilted thing, worne
to make, or keepe, the bodie straight.
> —Randle Cotgrave, *A Dictionarie of the
> French and English Tongues*, 1611

A Busk . . . is a strong peece of Wood, or Whalebone
thrust down the middle of the Stomacker.
> —Randle Holme, *The Academy of Armoury: Or,
> a Storehouse of Armoury and Blazon*, 1688[31]

These two historical examples of the definitions of Behn's
chief term from the *Oxford English Dictionary*, although from
opposite ends of her century, nonetheless evoke the mascu-

line rigidity of the device, especially in the verbs "make," "keepe," and "thrust" and in the adjectives "straight" and "strong." Men designed the busk and its successors for women, an entity that wearer's patriarchal culture compelled her to force on herself to embody its conception of the feminine, just as spike heels or short, short skirts exemplify today. One could even note that the term itself narrows (like the thing itself) from a whole to a part. Such linguistic constriction seems ironic since Behn's speaking tree is, except for the tetrameter couplets that make up its speech, the very opposite of rigidity. Between this poetical freedom and the practical bondage of the busk lies, in some respects, Behn's answer to all cavalier poems on the girdle (admittedly a sash rather than a corset), in which the male poet rapturously imagines himself as the article of clothing fortunate enough to encompass the soft warm skin and to caress the curves of the female torso. Waller rhapsodizes, "That which her slender waste confin'd, / Shall now my Joyful Temples bind" ("On a Girdle," 1–2), which surely would have provided a strange sight. As with all fetishes, joyous possession of the article that can be possessed substitutes for the body that it covers that cannot be possessed: "Give me but what this Riban bound, / Take all the rest the Sun goes round" (11–12).[32]

In such imaginings, Waller probably could not have known how uncomfortable the actual device must have been, which, for example, compelled a woman to perch at the end of a seat in a sitting position to prevent the bottom section of the busk(s) from pressing into the lower abdomen and the tops of the thighs, reducing or even eliminating circulation. That Behn makes this thing, created by men to mold women into suitable shapes, celebrate the natural bodily freedom that it was designed to proscribe must have been highly amusing to her. That this thing that makes women suffer suffers itself provides another slyly humorous (or at least ironic) idea. As Cloris makes her retreat, the tree laments, "With grief I bow'd my murmering Head, / And all my Christal Dew I shed" ("On a *Juniper-Tree*," 94–95). From this couplet, a reader can discern the physical business of Philocles' detumesence and ejaculation, as well as his partner's bodily responses toward arousal. She or he can also sense the complementary anthropomorphic workings of nature. The juniper's tendency toward drooping branches and rendering its sap obviously suggests sadness and tears, which moves Cloris, ever the sensitive one "whose Soul is made of Love," to pity (96–97). And what could be misread as symbolic castration, the felling of this phallic-shaped tree, is nothing of the kind. In doing so, Cloris "did translate, / My being to a happier state" (98–99), a martyr for the religion of love (101). She, at least, does not want the juniper to suffer by her absence, as Orinda does for Lucasia. It will, unlike Philocles, always be near her, and "still guard the Sacred Store" of her body, a stern yet flexible gatekeeper of her biological femaleness: "of Loves Temple keep the Door" (106–7). Even Philips could not have imagined a truer example of female friendship. Again, in this way, the juniper does not just protect women's sexual space for male use or exchange. Rather, it ensures that Cloris's sexuality will always be her choice—birth control, if you will.

Finally, speaking of such female autonomy, "On a *Juniper-Tree*" exorcises the dysfunctional sexuality depicted in "The Disappointment" and in other examples of the "imperfect enjoyment" genre.[33] Its theme answers Behn's wry aside in that better-known poem, "The *Nymph's* Resentments none but I / Can well Imagine or Condole" ("The Disappointment," 131–32). She redresses the "Resentments" of one poem in its doppelgänger. It is probably not accidental that the young women in "*Juniper-Tree*" and "Disappointment" are both named Cloris.[34] It is as if they are the same virginal young woman who, frustrated with one unsuitable swain, reaches blessed fulfillment with the other. Or perhaps Lysander and Philocles are interchangeable and thus indistinguishable for Cloris's purpose.[35] Her experience, not their fulfillment, matters most. In the resentful poem, Cloris is surprised and Lysander impatient. Therefore she cannot communicate her own desire before he rashly attempts to sate his own. His inexperience and fear kindles the like in her. She becomes passive, expectant; he is beside himself and unable to appreciate the moment. In fact, he does not understand the value of pacing himself, and tries to make what is desirable more so, "The blessed minutes to improve" (33). Surely this is a mistake, as Marlene Dietrich cautions in her rendition of a famous song from the 1930s.[36] This echo of the "unrhymed" line in "*Juniper-Tree*" suggests the connection between the two poems as well as predicting Lysander's dysfunction. Blessings are just that. They cannot be improved, only appreciated and enjoyed for what they are when they arrive. That Philocles recognizes this gift of his shepherdess and her sponsoring genius of the wood foretells that he will, unlike Lysander, stand to it, and that there will be no disappointments for Cloris, at least for this blessed minute. It is this motif that informs the whole of the concluding poem in the collection, *A Voyage to the Isle of Love,* that features another young man named Lysander as well as Cloris's surrogate, Aminta.

6

"Swoln to Luxurious Heights":
A Voyage to the Isle of Love

You that do seek with Amorous desires,
  To tast the Pleasures of the Life below,
Land on this Island, and renew your Fires,
  For without Love, there is no joy, you know.
                    —*A Voyage to the Isle of Love,* 299–302

Methinks ye Voyage sho'd come last, as being ye largest
volume. You know Mr Cowley's David is last, because a
large poem, and Mrs. Philips her plays for ye same
reason.
                    —Letter to Jacob Tonson, 1684

BEHN ENDS HER COLLECTION WITH A 2196-LINE EPISTOLARY PAS-
toral verse romance, an extensive missive from one Lysander to a Lysidas concerning a fantastical love affair.
This translation of the Abbé Paul Tallemant's *Le Voyage de
l'Isle d'Amour* (1663) demonstrates her considerable dexterity with French, which she also shows in her later renderings of La Rochefoucauld's *Maximes,* Bonnecorse's *La
Montre*, and Fontenelle's *Entretiens sur La Pluralité des Mondes.* The inclusion of *A Voyage* fulfills the subtitle of *Poems
upon Several Occasions*, and demonstrates its importance to
her, if she was indeed responsible for her volume's title.[1]
Like the important shorter poems in the collection, this
lengthy composition profitably repeats and expands on motifs that she treats elsewhere. In some ways, she provides
the ultimate statement of her poetics, the centrality of "Amorous desires," the erotic in love, where "*all is taken, all is
given*" (2069), and mutually. To express this, she challenges
herself by assuming a personality quite different from her

164

own in order to experiment with writing both genders: a young man, both naïve and ardent. To facilitate this exploration, she develops some of the concepts she discovered in Creech's Lucretius, Cowley, and Rochester. She also proves her facility in a longer work, a more difficult form in some respects than a prose comedy with the freedom that its conventions of repartee allow. Though her need to render Tallemant accurately in English verse without losing her identity as she writes must have proved formidable, she succeeds admirably on both counts in her quest to be admired and understood, as Gerard Langbaine argues only two years after her death.[2] A Voyage, very much an Aphra Behn production, anglicizes this product of baroque French culture. Pleasures are tasted, fires are renewed; love and joy are found. One can redeem men without shaming them, even when they are young and slaves to testosterone.

I

Cure then, thou mighty winged God,
This restless Feaver in my Blood
          —"Song: On her Loving Two Equally," 14–15

Tallemant (1642–1713), a wit at the court of Louis XIV, eventually became a member of the French Academy. He wrote Le Voyage de l'Isle d'Amour when he was eighteen and published it three years later (1663). Its subtitles in subsequent editions, le Passe-Partout and La Clef des Cours,[3] [the passkey, the key of hearts] allude to a medieval literary tradition most fully realized in the anonymous Ovidian love-treatise from the thirteenth century, La Clef d'Amors. The much greater poem of that epoch, La Roman de la Rose, also seems present in the erotic allegorical framework of Tallemant's text. The differences between Le Voyage and Behn's rendering of it are significant. One concerns form. Tallemant's brief work could be classified as prosimetron (mixed prose and verse), which Boethius and Dante use in The Consolation of Philosophy and La vita nuova. A Voyage contains no prose. Behn's expansion and rendition of Le

Voyage into poetry represents a notable undertaking and achievement, since it is in effect a one-sided epistolary novella in verse. Although she would later complain, *"The French . . . is of all the hardest to translate into* English" (W 4: 74), her fluent knowledge of this language caused no barrier to her as Latin had.[4] Elizabeth Spearing argues that another difference concerns style: "Behn adds sensational detail to her original, but does so with the conscious, and consciously indecorous, ingenuity that belongs to the baroque or mannerist mode." Part of this ingenuity marks another difference for Spearing, concerning gender: "She takes on a literary equivalent of the adaptability expected of any woman in seventeenth-century society; the politics of translation intersect with the sexual politics to produce a masquerade in which the translatress's power may be at its greatest when it is most completely dissembled."[5]

Some of Behn's subtler variations on Tallemant seem informed by the differences of age and gender, perhaps even of nationality. A hardworking and indigent forty-three-year-old Englishwoman rewrites the "dainty fantasy" of an aristocratic French roué of eighteen, admirable indeed.[6] Yet her "masquerade" cannot conceal the enormous divergence in perspective between them, one that life and writerly skill create. The age-gender gulf resembles that between the worldly Behn and the bookish Creech and repeats that pattern of appropriation and dialectical imitation in which the writer, fortified by her experience, overmasters her younger male mentor by reprocessing the matter and form she inherits from him. The "consciously indecorous" consummation of the lovers reveals the most significant change, to which virtually all of Behn's translation points, even drives, provide a kind of moral for her fable. One could even say that the entire purpose of the poem is for Lysander to have sex with Aminta under the careful supervision of various abstractions.

As we have seen, Behn's letter to Tonson states that she thought of her translation as the keystone of her collection, in the manner of Cowley's *Davideis* and Philips's rendering of Corneille's *La Mort de Pompée*. The tone, even the structure of *A Voyage* suggests such an intention. It possesses the aura of the conclusion to an oratorio. And, like the collection to which it serves as climax, it makes a final, deliberate circle, a spiraling journey that leads to the vortex of the Bower of Bliss, Behn's pseudo-Spenserian re-imagining of Tallemant's Palais du Vray-Plaisir. It may also represent a feminocentric answer to Rochester's somewhat repulsive and misogynistic invocation of the same literary place name as metonym.[7] Here the lovers enjoy the blessed minute that Occasion literally presents. Like Lysander's appropriately thematic "drive," this cyclical pattern appears physiologically and complementarily mimetic, Behn's signature of her biological femaleness. It is the womb of the poem and the collection, as in Spenser's Garden of Adonis rather than his Bower of Bliss (cf. *The Faerie Queene* 3.6 and 2.12) and in Milton's Eden (*Paradise Lost* 4.210–355). In this place, "*Recesses Dark, and Grotto's all conspire*" (*A Voyage*, 2051). In this place, "The Temple Gates are open Night and Day" (1700).

One may label Behn's version of Tallemant a "fantasy," but could hardly apply the adjective "dainty" to it. A poet who disguises her gender recounts the emotional agony of love and its humiliations from a man's point of view. At first reading, this "transvestite ventriloquism" seems to create a parable of nascent feminist wish-fulfillment, as some have argued about the plays of Thomas Southerne in the decade following Behn's death—if women of her time were so empowered, this is what they would do or be.[8] Yet Behn extends herself even further, because her surrogate in the poem is not Aminta, but Lysander.[9] In the guise of a man, Behn figures woman as Other in *A Voyage*, although she, unlike Tallemant, allows Aminta to speak and gives her the outline of a psychology (e.g., 415–20; 1313–18; 2141–50). Lysander finds himself befuddled by (and then must accept) the stereotypical capriciousness of Aminta's behavior: her first flight with Honour and unexplained escape from him to the company of Rivals (1315–18; 1476–90); her mysterious final yielding after he repents for no discernible offense (see the Pindaric "The Penitent," 1613–38). Naturally, Behn possesses an authorial advantage that a man cannot. As a woman, she certainly understands Aminta very well, as her two portraits of the hotly pursued and youthfully inarticulate Cloris in "On a *Juniper-Tree*" and "The Disappointment" attest. Yet she does not overtly betray this understanding of Aminta for polemical purposes and thus violate her "masquerade." We sit on Lysander's shoulder, but Behn appropriately occludes our perception of his beloved. We cannot see her any more clearly than he can; Behn does not satirize him for this lack of perception. Women, she implies, can make themselves difficult to read for reasons of their own, as her heroine Ismena explains in her early comedy *The Amorous Prince* (1671): "This unlucky restraint upon our Sex, / Makes us all cunning" (2.2.182–83).

Yet Behn intends our vision of Lysander to be transparent. Her portrayal of him in some ways answers her own earlier depictions of men in love, such as the rakes in *The Dutch Lover* and the play's fundamental critique of "the blind indiscriminateness of male desire."[10] This protagonist, the opposite of both shallow foppery and cynical libertinage—ardent, sensitive, articulate, faithful—represents her paradigm of what men ought to be. Although the realization of his physical desires provides the main theme of *A Voyage*, his clumsy courtliness suggests his attempts to socialize these drives. Nor are his speeches to attain this goal merely clichés meant to manipulate Aminta into bringing his love to fruition. Moreover, Behn encodes Lysander's ideal nature in his emotional pliability, his willingness to be taught as well as his ability to learn. And the conspiracy of personifications in the translation, with Behn as puppetmaster, provides plenty of pedagogy: Respect, Little Cares, Confidence, Occasion, Love himself and his *putti*. Behn simplifies this pattern when she repeats it in her translation of Bonnecorse's *La Montre* (1686) with the ardent Damon and the garrulous Iris, as we saw in chapter 4. Her verses addressed to a Lysander in the rest of *Poems upon Several Occasions* also feature Behn as educator and this young man as a pupil: "To *Lysander* who made some Verses on a Discourse of Loves Fire" (discussed in chapter 2); "To *Lysander* at the *Musick-Meeting*"; "To *Lysander* on some Verses he writ, and asking more for his Heart than 'twas worth." One might note that the protagonist of *A Voyage* is also a poet, so to speak, in his act of narrating the poem that Behn writes, of a similar degree of sensitivity and sentiment as his creator. Through this speaker, Behn demonstrates her mastery of various forms as she does in the rest of her collection, especially the heroic couplet, the ballad-hymn stanza, and the irregular odes of which she was so fond. And in this writerly act, one man, through a woman, in effect educates another man about love. Finally, it may not be accidental that the dysfunctional shepherd of "The Disappointment" and the speaker of *A Voyage* share the same name, given the similar (but temporary) amorous difficulties of the latter (2081–94). This "final" Lysander exorcises all the others: he does not ask more for his heart than it is worth; he understands music; he writes good poetry; he does not betray the woman he loves; he can satisfy her.

II

the soft tale of Love She breathes
—"A Farewel to *Celladon*," 91

A summary of this neglected work is in order. The opening consists of a miniature verse epistle from Lysander to Lysidas, a paean to friendship and a warning that the story will "renew" his grief and "rowse [it] into a storm" (1–42). A Pindaric, "The Truce," describes the fanciful compromise between Lysander and his weeping eyes (43–65). He then explains that it has been a year since his experience on the Isle and the voyage thence, which he proceeds to describe (66–201). En route, a Man sings a ballad about the dangers of the place, its "pleasing Pain" (129–60), and then breaks into Pindarics on the same subject, "Love's Power" (202–36). Immediately on landing, Lysander sees the unnamed Aminta and falls in love with her (237–51). He describes her charms in "The Character" (252–65). His senses "Ravisht," he encounters Cupids who sing to him and encourage him to achieve the object of his sudden passion. He finds her asleep in a bank of flowers *en déshabillé* (266–387).

It is at this point that the somewhat opaque erotic allegory begins. A man with mysterious powers who "aw'd" Lysander "with th'Majesty of his Eyes" (377) appears, whom one of the Cupids identifies as Respect. The putto describes him approvingly in a Pindaric (387–408). As Lysander approaches him for instruction, Aminta awakes, is naturally surprised and frightened, but then, with the help of Respect, is assured by her amorous swain that his intentions are honorable, and she departs (409–45). Now envenomed with love, Lysander pursues her to the palace of Inquietude, kept by a "Woman of a strange deform'd Aspect" of the same name (446–68). Taking to his bed, he muses on his situation in "The Reflection," another Pindaric (469–96), and then on "Little Cares, or Little Arts to please" the next morning (497–552). Another day passes, with the predictable amplification of desire (553–88) and ensuing dream (including a Pindaric, "The Dream") at nightfall, from which he wakes at the fantasized moment of fruition (589–600). Love pleasantly torments Lysander more. He revisits Little Cares and suffers Rivals, but Aminta happily goes to Good Reception (601–62), which impels him to visit the City of Hope, on the bank of the dangerous River of Pretension (663–710). He describes the princess Hope as treacherous, the goddess of her river. She entices two men who love the same woman, one pretentious, one humble, certainly abstractions that serve as surrogates for Lysander's psyche (711–826). He decides that humility is the best course for the present time.

Hope encourages Lysander. Love then guides him to Declaration, and Respect cautions him to avoid expressing himself with ridiculous boldness to Aminta, whereby the god protests in "Love's Resentment" (827–49). Respect wins out, however, and Lysander complies with his wishes, which causes the three of them to visit the City of Discretion (850–921). Discretion, as it happens, is Respect's sister, and plays hostess to Aminta, so that the anxious Lysander can refine his courtship skills there. Although he attempts to channel his feelings in "The silent Confession," Aminta guesses his feelings, calls Pride to her defense, and retreats into the Den of Cruelty, an abstraction that is naturally female and, like Inquietude, intimidating (922–89). Near the Den is, as one might expect, the River of Despair, whose waters naturally depress Lysander. Yet he chooses not to drink from them and then decides to take action in "The Resolve" (990–1035). First, however, he resolves to rehearse "as if *Aminta present were*" in "The Question" (1036–55). This does not seem to help. An interlude follows, which consists of a colloquy between Lysander and Love, who chastens him and encourages him not to give up. Love himself even attempts to reason with Aminta, but to no purpose (1056–128).

At this point, events take a welcome turn for Lysander. Pity, in her own way as treacherous as Hope, vows to combat her enemy Cruelty and to soften Aminta's heart. She suggests that the time has come for Lysander to declare his feelings, even those bordering on irrationality. Aminta then (in modified ballad stanza) accepts his entreaties and promises *"in time your Passion may receive / All you dare take, and all a Maid may give"* (1129–201). Lysander (as well as, presumably, Lysidas) has been waiting a long time for this, which his Pindaric "The Transport" emphasizes. Pity has been most helpful, and continues to be so in obliging Aminta to visit Confidence in her villa, from which Jealousy and Rivals are duly banished. Lysander follows and tells Aminta the secrets of his soul and pauses for "The Reflection" so that we can learn what these secrets are. Aminta then encourages him, but he mistakes her confidence for love and compliance, not yet attained (1202–304).

Then the bogeyman from the rest of Behn's collection appears, Honour, who snatches Aminta. Inconsolable, Lysander reencounters Respect, who, like Love before, encourages him to maintain his equilibrium. On a downward course, he wanders and finds the castle of Absence, a queen like Cruelty, although not as well attended. She is in fact burdened with only one soft, silent maid, Melancholy. Lysander then parleys with her and they find common cause. He abandons them both for solitude and finds it in the woods near the castle, where he reproaches his sponsor in "To Love" (1305–461). Love conveys some encouraging letters from Aminta. Lysander then seeks her, but finds her in the village of Rivals, where Aminta, now freed from Honour (and, it appears, Duty), entertains the competition and plays the jilt (1462–510). Love, seeing that Lysander is beside himself, takes him to lodgings at the palace of Jealousy, which naturally has no salutary effect upon him, as his "The Complaint" implies (1511–612). Although the narrative does not explain Aminta's capriciousness or any action of Lysander's that may have caused it, he then apologizes to her in "The Penitent." Its triple refrain "my [faithful, tender, fond]

Heart adores you still" provides the charm that banishes his rivals as well as his jealousy (1613–44).

Now the real business can begin in earnest. Lysander and Aminta take their first journey together, to the City of Love and its Temple. Therein, the couple proceed to exchange hearts before entering the Bower of Bliss. Tyrant Honour, however, blocks the gate. Naturally, he is worshipped at this entrance, to the chagrin of all Lysanders. Aminta heeds his counsel and flees; Lysander mourns his loss. Love, undaunted, rescues her and returns her to Lysander's arms, and the procession to the Bower continues. Respect makes a brief appearance, but yields to Occasion, the allegorical representation of the blessed (not lucky) minute (1645–969). Lysander describes the Bower in intimate detail, replete with flora, fountains, paths, and various recesses suggestive of the *mons Veneris* (1970–2072) in the manner of Spenser and Milton.

The bout commences, something not found in Tallemant. However, Behn provides a further surprise. In a merging of the trysts recounted in "The Disappointment" and "On a *Juniper-Tree*," Behn's Lysander at first finds himself unable to perform, but then (thankfully) experiences "vast Seas" that come "rowling on" and discovers himself, unlike the Lysander of "The Disappointment," happily "Swoln to Luxurious heights." The sex, it would appear, is tantric, unending, mutual (2073–112). Alas, however, these days of joy must end, because Aminta dies just as mysteriously as she jilts and obliges. Lysander seeks the Desert of Remembrance, from which he has been addressing the patient Lysidas, and then makes his circle complete as he finishes his tale (2113–96).

Again, several things seem remarkable about Behn's bending of Tallemant's allegory. She does not appear to write from the feminine point of view but almost uncritically from the masculine. Nor does her narrator seem unreliable so that his long story becomes an implicit and ironic attack on men and their erotic misbehavior. Concurrently, and without contradiction, *A Voyage* prescribes proper masculine behavior in love. All men, even the nice ones, need to be trained, and without humiliation. They should respect women; observe discretion of some sort; be willing to apologize, even to grovel when the beloved deems it necessary. Honour may appear at times demonic, especially if recalled in context with Behn's diatribe against it in "The Golden Age," but Behn symbolizes women's reliance on it as social fact. This is to say that, regardless of the patina of the semi-pastoral setting, the pliable Lysander, and the Baroque putti flittering about, *A Voyage* does not romanticize love, but rightly analyzes it as process, fraught with Little Cares, Despair, Rivals, Inquietude, and the sometimes incomprehensible behavior of the beloved. And, finally, climactically, Behn envisions the entire drive of Lysander's passion as physical, nothing shameful, only natural: the vaginal recesses of the Bower of Bliss; Lysander's arousal at the charms of the sleeping Aminta; not the slightest mention of proper marriage; the shared climaxes. Even Aminta's mysterious death, operatic and tragic, appears sexual somehow, perhaps a glance at *le petit mort*, as one may infer from Behn's "In Imitation of *Horace*": "To taste these Sweets lets in a Certain Death" (11). To Behn, this must have seemed the perfect ending to the soft tale of love that she breathed. Throughout, Behn's sexual morality appears to be mutuality, as she phrases it succinctly elsewhere in her book: "A Heart requires a Heart Unfeign'd and True" ("To *Lysander*, on some Verses he writ," 9).

III

Where e're she be, I still am there;
What-ere she do, I that prefer

—*A Voyage*, 933–34

Behn constantly revises and reprocesses her mentors and her own writing, which demonstrates "her habit of intermeshing works to form a single coded fictional world."[11] This intertextuality (and even "intratextuality") informs her attempts to remain faithful to Lysander's point of view and to preserve her masquerade of gender in *A Voyage*, just as she does in various pieces in the rest of *Poems upon Several Occasions,* in which she assumes a number of personae, male and female. Lysander's lines above, simultaneously selfless and sensitive, recall the devoted and self-effacing Cowley that inspired Behn in her appropriations from *The Mistress:* "Let me but *love*, what ere she be, / Shee cannot seem *deform'd* to *me*" ("The Request," 10–11).[12] One who reads carefully through *A Voyage* will note many "intratextual" echoes of other lines from the rest of the collection. The larger poem and its precedents comment on one another. Just as Honour serves as Behn's enemy in "The Golden Age," an entity "that hindred mankind first" (120), so it fulfills the same function for Lysander, *"His pow'r, is robbing Lovers of delight"* (*A Voyage*, 1794), abducting Aminta at the very gates of the temple of the Bower. In an equally simple example, Lysander's collapse before the River of Despair (990–1016) expands on "The Complaint" and "Song: To *Pesibles* Tune" in which Amyntas, prostrate before a stream, bewails Silvia's perfidy, and serves as tragic-operatic answer to the Monmouth parody in "Silvio's Complaint," where "A Noble Youth but all Forlorn, / Lig'd Sighing by a Spring" (5–6). Amyntas and Silvio-Monmouth, of course, do not achieve the object of their desires, and deserve to despair, unlike Lysander. That the River's *"doleful Murmurs have such Eloquence / That even the neighbouring Trees and flow'rs have pitying sense"* (*A Voyage*, 994–95) may recall the reanimated juniper tree that shades the entire collection, eloquent and empathetic.

Naturally, there are more complex instances of this authorial phenomenon. Two dream episodes from *A Voyage* and *Poems upon Several Occasions* strangely complement each other. The frustrated Lysander engages in a somewhat typical male fantasy in which he dreams of Aminta *"All Trembling in my Arms . . . / Defending of the Bliss I strove to take / . . . Her force so charming was and weak"* (589–90, 592) and then awakens at the point of consummation, in a lather over the possibilities of overcoming his beloved's pitiful resistance. However, in "On a Copy of Verses made in a Dream, and sent to me in a Morning before I was Awake," the female speaker in a position similar to Aminta's (i.e., dreamed of, fantasized about) recounts her own more complicated scenario. A man sends her poetry written during a dream similar to Lysander's, but which possesses much more seductive power than the protagonist of *A Voyage* can muster. She too is asleep when his poetic epistle awakens her and arouses her. In effect, Behn's persona recounts what it is like to be the recipient of the product of a man's dream, which is not sex, but poetry that has the same effect with its "welcome Mischiefs" (8) to ensure that "Fancy ev'ry where does gently play" (37). So, in "On a Copy of Verses," Behn imagines what it would have been like for Aminta to have received a poetical record of Lysander's phantasm. Or, in a similarly complicated echo, when Respect admonishes Cupid and Lysander, "Amintas *Cruelty you need not dread, / Your Passion by your Eyes will soon be known*" (845–46), the distich recalls and refracts the manifold references to the effect of the male gaze, particularly the "Lovely Eies" of Hoyle ("On Mr. *J. H.* In a Fit of Sickness," 25) and their terrible powers: "no Softness in 'em move. / They kill with Fierceness, not with Love" ("Our Cabal," 161–62). Behn exorcises her lover's devastating projective sensory effect on her by neutralizing it in Lysander. She cannot know what it is like for Hoyle to view her; she only knows what it means to her to be viewed, and, in some senses, ravished without even Hoyle's lips grazing her skin. Yet in contrast, Aminta does not serve as victim in this way, but as receptive arbiter, master of herself and her swain. She will determine how she is to be viewed.[13] When the chaperoning abstractions (and she, most importantly) deem it appropriate, they will be a reclining bucolic couple like their predecessors in the Bower. Near its spring, *"The verdant Banks no other Prints retain, / But where young Lovers, and young Loves have lain"* (*A Voyage*, 1993–94). Behn recycles this delicate and sensual image from *"Oenone to Paris,"* when that forlorn shepherdess wistfully remembers "Where the dear Grass, still sacred, does retain / The print, where thee and I so oft have lain" (185–86). Oenone can only long for what Aminta has yet to experience. As we will see, Aminta may not be so anxious to partake of this activity.

The image appropriately emblematizes other imprintings in the landscape of Behn's Isle. Two words at the beginning of the translation, "Doubt" and "Uncertainty," enunciate a theme that Behn frequently utilizes elsewhere, a pairing obviously characteristic of her century and her understanding of its thinkers, as her readings of Descartes and La

Rochefoucauld attest.[14] The purpose of the following passage—Lysander's assurance to his friendly reader that he will tell his story—appears disingenuously simple:

> At last, dear *Lysidas*, I'l set thee Free,
> From the disorders of Uncertainty;
> Doubt's the worst Torment of a generous Mind,
> Who ever searching what it cannot find,
> Is roving still from wearied thought to thought,
> And to no settled Calmness can be brought
>
> (1–6)

Doubt and uncertainty necessarily trouble Lysander the lover once he embarks on his journey to the Isle—the evanescence of Aminta, the mysteries of her behavior and her reactions to his own, the advice given by various abstractions, especially when Honour, Love, and Respect contradict one another. Behn frequently uses doubt as a motif in the rest of the collection—the fate of the consciousness of the juniper tree after its transformation, the advice to Amoret about Hoyle's enigmatic behavior ("A Ballad on Mr. *J. H.* to *Amoret*, asking why I was so sad"), the arbitrary nature of tyrant Cupid in "Love Arm'd" and the paradox that the speaker's "poor Heart alone is harm'd" while the beloved's is "free" (15–16), the mysterious impotence of Lysander and Cloris's befuddlement at it in "The Disappointment," and Oenone's aggrieved incomprehension of Paris's preference for Helen. The adjective applied to "Mind," "generous," is multiplex in meaning, also—not just magnanimous, but copious, free, and endlessly reproductive, as the three following lines imply. Much like Behn's own, there is no rest, only motion, for it, anticipatory of Locke's twin categories of knowledge, observation and reflection.[15] One cannot be free from the disorders of uncertainty, but must accept them and not allow oneself to be overmastered by them, as Lysander's aforementioned *"I still am there"* suggests. There are many benefits to staying the course in this way. Although Honour may sometimes trump Love, Respect may still yield to Occasion.

Behn's authorial cunning sometimes resembles that of one of her heroines, such as Hellena in *1 Rover*. This restlessness ensures that she reworks the medieval poetic conventions that Tallemant uses, such as the erotic allegory of *Le Roman de la Rose*. She appears to invoke another, the Ship of Fools, during the actual voyage to the Isle, as if an artistic ancestor of Hogarth had extended Bosch's famous painting on this subject into a progressive cartoon:

> All pray, and promise fair, protest and weep,
> And make those Vows they want the pow'r to keep,
> And sure with some the angry Gods were pleas'd;
> For by degrees their Rage and Thunder ceas'd
>
> (100–104)

Here, to ensure their safe passage in rough weather, the future lovers utter their specious vows—as false, presumably, as the promises they will enunciate to the ones they love to complete an entirely different type of progression. Lysander later remarks on just this phenomenon in his Pindaric, "The Reflection," on *"all the stealths forgetful Lovers make, / When they their* Little Covenants *break"* (1274–75). That he does not participate in this shallow activity suggests that he will not "want the pow'r to keep" any vows he makes.

Another related passage occurs when Lysander describes the Fools more precisely. The social comedy or city satire may remind some readers of Rochester's Artemiza, writing of the strange town ways to her country cousin Chloe, or of the clownish behavior of the holiday crowd in "Tunbridge Wells." It may also owe something to the conception of the *charivari*, the street-carnival motif in some forms of Augustan poetry.[16] At the same time, the women therein seem to be surrogates for Behn and some of her characters from the plays and stories:

> I laught to see a Lady out of date,
> A worn out Beauty, once of the first rate;
> With youthful Dress, and more fantastick Prate,
> Setting her wither'd Face in thousand forms,
> And thinks the while she Dresses it in charms;
> Disturbing with her Court: the busier throng
> Ever Addressing to the Gay and Young;
> There an old Batter'd Fop, you might behold,

Lavish his Love, Discretion, and his Gold
On a fair she, that has a Trick in Art,
To cheat him of his Politicks and Heart

(186–96)

The "Lady out of date" may represent Behn's amusement at her present condition, just as her portrait of Onahal, the cast-off mistress of the king in *Oroonoko*, may fulfill the same function: "certainly, nothing is more afflicting to a decay'd Beauty, than to behold in it self declining Charms, that were once ador'd; and to find those Caresses paid to new Beauties, to which onece she laid a Claim; to hear 'em whisper as she passes by, *That once was a delicate Woman*" (W 3:71). The "fair she" who cheats the old battered fop is reminiscent of the heroine of *The Fair Jilt*, and perhaps the author in her youth. If this is tacit self-representation, it may provide an ironic commentary on the way that some of her more urbane detractors, such as Wycherley, saw her: "Once, to your Shame, your Parts to all were shown" ("To the *Sappho* of the Age, suppos'd to Ly-In of a *Love-Distemper*, or a *Play*").[17] Although he may be alluding to the consequences of an unfortunate fall on the ice in an age before undergarments, these two portraits can be seen as "Parts" of her, shown without shame.

Again, Behn fashions her narrator as male, a challenging divergence from the many female-androgynous speakers in *Poems upon Several Occasions*. One might even apply Patrocinio P. Schweickart's theory of "immasculation" to Behn's technique. The "androcentricity" of the text compels all readers to adopt the perspective of heterosexual men.[18] Although this authorial shift can be difficult for her to maintain, she usually acquits herself happily in this subterfuge. Her years of playwrighting surely accustomed her to this kind of projection and transference. Characters such as Willmore in the *Rover* plays indicate that she understood not only how men think, but how men think about themselves: "I have a heart with a hole quite through it too, no Prison mine to keep a Mistress in" (*1 Rover* 3.1.175–76). He is simultaneously heartbroken, shallow, and unpossessive— and knows it. Sometimes, as if to overcompensate for the gender difference in *A Voyage*, her Lysander's perspective appears snortingly masculine, without the subtlety of the observer of "Our Cabal," for example. The anonymous Man imagines love in phallocratic, even sadomasochistic terms for voyagers of both sexes, appropriately brought to the Isle by a storm (presumably of passion): *"They Kiss the Shaft, and Bless the Foe, / That gives the pleasing Pain"* (*A Voyage*, 159–60). Love proves as disorderly, dangerous, and difficult for the humble Lysander as it is for the presumptuous Fools on deck to whom Respect and Occasion pay scant attention. Perhaps this authorial-emotional turbulence accounts for this odd simile:

> In the rude War no more the Winds engage,
> And the destructive Waves were tir'd with their own Rage;
> Like a young Ravisher, that has won the day,
> O're-toil'd and Panting, Calm and Breathless lay,
> While so much Vigour in the Incounter's lost,
> They want the pow'r a second Rape to Boast.
>
> (105–9)

Curiously, and perhaps jarringly, Behn describes the miraculously spent deep as if it were a successful rapist. Does Lysander mean to demonize the storm, or does he unconsciously project his own desires? Though the comparison has no precise correlative elsewhere in *A Voyage* or in the rest of the collection, Lysander uses language with a tinge of sexual violence in his initial pitiful remembrance of *"the lovely yielding Maid,"* the departed Aminta: *"Just in the Ravishing hour, when all her Charms / A willing Victim to thy Love was laid"* (60–63). At worst, perhaps, he may be mouthing conventional "cavalier" terms that our age, so different from the Restoration in this way, would read as referring to rape.[19] When Lysander observes the sleeping, unclothed, and therefore completely vulnerable Aminta, he limits his perusal to the visual rather than the tactlessly tactile until she attempts to flee his words: "grasping fast her Robe, oblig'd her stay" (420) only so that he can be heard. He is in the process of learning to obey Respect, who *"even requires that you shou'd silent be, / And understand no language but from Eyes"* (397–98). One might also note that Lysander's actions never approach such violence, and that *"yielding,"*

"*Ravishing*," and "*Victim*" recall the atmosphere and circumstances of "The Disappointment" and "On a *Juniper-Tree*," benign poems that feature the young woman as equal participant and even provocative agent in erotic congress. Perhaps Behn attempts to portray women's lives as she knew them, the authentic behavior of Philips's virgins (and her own). Perhaps she wishes to appeal to certain desires in her male readership, whose ultimate fantasy includes a willing and aggressive female partner.

At the same time, Behn tacitly criticizes Lysander on some occasions and invites us to scrutinize some of his utterances. Sometimes men (even the nice ones) wish for foolish things. One section of the anonymous Man's Pindaric, "Love's Power," describes the aforementioned male fantasy:

> The tender Maid to the Rough Warrior yields;
>   Unfrighted at his Wounds and Scars,
>   Pursues him through the Camps and Fields,
> And Courts the story of his dangerous Wars,
> With Pleasure hears his Scapes, and does not fail
> To pay him with a Joy for every Tale.
>
> (214–19)

One can see why the male passengers anxiously make their voyage to the Isle. The reversal of courtship roles suggests that not all on the Ship are Fools. "*There no Reproaches dwell; that Vice / Is banisht with the Coy and Nice*" (520–21). Women may pursue men, in spite of the appearance of Honour and his minions. Nausikaa tackles Odysseus on the beach rather than leading him back to her father's home. Desdemona seduces Othello, not reverting to the device of proffering a hint on which he might speak. One might also say that Lysander alludes to the sorts of freedoms for which Behn's recognizably female speakers long, a type of wish fulfillment that transcends traditional gender roles. Still, at times, *A Voyage* even contains an obstreporously male-oriented disapproval of women and their "wiles." In apparent answer to the passage where Love merely prods the "Shepherd uninspir'd" in "The Golden Age" (96), the same deity punishes the shepherdess whose coyness prevents her from yielding:

Sometimes to be reveng'd on those,
    Whose Beauty makes 'em proudly nice,
He does a Flame on them impose
    To some unworthy choice.

(A Voyage, 231–34)

Oberon humiliates Titania with Bottom—and, one suspects
Lysander would add, rightly so. The gender aggression es-
calates. When Aminta flees with Honour, Cupid "Re-
proach'd" Lysander's "Courage, and condemn'd my Wit, /
That meanly cou'd t'a Womans scorn submit" (1081–82).
Behn also depicts another female personification to whom
Aminta flees (970), whom Cupid criticizes as well: "Shall
Cruelty a peevish Woman prove, / Too strong to be overcome
by Youth and Love?" (1094–95). As one would expect, Ly-
sander criticizes Honour, but in antifeminist terms:

> *Some Woman sure, ill-natur'd, old, and proud,*
> *Too ugly ever to have been deceiv'd;*
> *Unskill'd in Love; in Virtue, or in Truth,*
> *Preach'd thy false Notions first, and so debaucht our Youth*

(1805–8)

However, it would be unwise to confuse Behn herself with
Lysander, even though she deploys him as surrogate.[20] First,
she fashions him as young and inexperienced and prone to
the outbursts that some men make when, agitated by lust,
they approach their desired objects and find themselves rebuffed. We observe his progressive education. He will transcend his natural and expected fallibility in his adolescent
ranting that only ugly, old, and unlovable women love Honour. Second, we should also note that not all female abstractions meddle disconcertingly or work against him. The lady
Absence commiserates with him: "To all her Humours, I
conform my own, / Together Sigh, together Weep, and Moan"
(1391–92). Occasion, the blessed minute personified, is not
only female, but obligingly naked, and even Respect yields
to her (1939). Pity, Lysander's strongest ally, is also figured
as a woman, and "knows all the subtillest Arts to move, /
And teach the timorous Virgin how to love" (1150–51). Lysander, in fact, manipulates Pity into pitying him, who then
approaches Aminta, "And oft repeats th'insinuating Tale, /

And does insensibly the Maid betray" (1168–69). Third, although Aminta unexpectedly plays the jilt in her flight with Honour and her allegiance with Rivals, Behn explains, through Lysander's consciousness, that in such an agitated state, his perceptions lend themselves to error:

> I listen to each low breath'd Word she says,
> And the returns the happy Answerer pays:
> When catching half the Sense, the rest Invent,
> And turn it still to what will most Torment.
>
> (1550–53)

This excellent passage reproduces the anguished psychology of sexual jealousy, especially its irrationality, roving from thought to thought, unable to be brought to a "settled Calmness," one that we have seen Behn treat extensively in *Poems upon Several Occasions*. The lover falsely completes the sense of what he has already misapprehended, which foments his tendency to self-flagellation at repeated intervals ("still"). One may compare this with similar conceptions in the collection as a whole: the subtlety of the advice to Amoret regarding Hoyle and his perfidy, especially the telling adjective in the second line that follows: "With all these Charms he did Address / Himself to every Shepherdess" ("A Ballad on Mr. *J. H.* to *Amoret*," 55–56); Oenone's scorn for Helen: "I had rather this way wretched prove, / Than be a Queen and faithless in my Love" ("*Oenone* to *Paris*," 246–47). Jealousy, the nausea of the soul, is universal. A certain gender irony then applies in Behn's pastoral universe. When men feel jealousy, it is usually unjustified, but they denigrate all women in response. When women suffer from it, it is not without reason, and they blame one man, not all. Lysander represents an ideal, but he is not perfect. Behn invites us to question him, but refuses to humiliate him or satirize men through him.

Again, Behn proves almost dogged in her attempts to force the reader to view events through Lysander's perspective, failure as well as success, the consequences of "*Loves insatiate Luxury*" (1279). Mimetically, she fashions images of sight to facilitate our own view of the proceedings. Behn evokes Lysander's desire by underscoring the visual perusal of love's physicality in the poetry that she invents and translates. For creator and created, desire, gallantry, and literary creativity beget progeny on one another:

> At my approach new Fires my Bosom warm;
> New vigor I receive from every Charm:
> I found invention with my Love increase;
> And both instruct me with new Arts to please
>
> (553–56)

Poetic ability, arts to please, and new fires increase with specific visualization. Whether one can equate Behn's constant revision of her writing with authorial narcissism may be too difficult to fathom, but her intratextuality creates unity rather than uniformity. Just as the Lysander of "The Disappointment" sees Cloris's "rising Bosom bare" (62), his namesake in *A Voyage* discerns Aminta's "*half discover'd rising Bosome bare*" (267). This prologue to desire has a physiological source in the observer. Lysander's "*all my Blood as in a Feaver burns*" (472) recalls "This restless Feaver in my Blood" of the female speaker of "On Her Loving Two Equally" (14). For better viewing, Behn positions her heroine in a Rubenesque odalisque. This "lovely Maid extended lay" (*A Voyage*, 353), to be apprehended by the male gaze:

> With what transported Joy my Soul was fill'd,
> When I, the Object of my wish beheld!
> My greedy View each lovely part survey'd
>
> (356–58)

Although Lysander euphemistically describes his ardor for Aminta as "transported Joy," his blazon of Aminta's parts as he surveys them is indeed "greedy." Immasculation appears to be fully in operation:

> On her white Hand, her Blushing Cheek was laid
> Half hid in Roses; yet did so appear
> As if with those, the Lillys mingled were;
> Her thin loose Robe did all her shape betray,
> (Her wondrous shape that negligently lay)
>
> (359–63)

In spite of this conventional floral picture to depict Aminta's complexion, Lysander naturally and appropriately
fixes his interest on the figure beneath the peignoir, just as
his namesake does in another poem as he views the languishing Cloris: "Her loose thin Robes, through which
appear / A Shape design'd for Love and Play" ("The Disappointment," 63–64). For that matter, the reader might also
detect an echo of Behn's appraisal of Lysander elsewhere.
Women may also demonstrate their erotic appreciation of a
sleeping male form: "Your Body easey and all tempting lay, /
Inspiring wishes which the Eyes betray" ("To *Lysander* at
the *Musick-Meeting*," 21–22). Behn then recreates a figure
from antiquity, *Venus pudica*, with a hand or thigh concealing the ultimate object of visual desire. Aminta

> every Tempting Beauty did reveal,
> But what young bashful Maids wou'd still conceal;
> Impatient I, more apt to hope than fear,
> Approacht the Heav'nly sleeping Maid more near;
> The place, my flame, and all her Charms invite
> To tast the sacred Joys of stoln delight.
>
> (364–69)

Lysander may be a voyeur, but he is no rapist. The many
small symbolic references to "*Love's* Altar" (534), which take
their inspiration from the "Altar" of "The Disappointment,"
the "Awful Throne, that Paradice / Where Rage is calm'd"
(45, 47–48), suggest the comical reverence in which Behn
knows that men hold this body part, later figured as the temple gates in the Bower: " *'Tis only* Love, *fond* Love *finds entrance here*" (*A Voyage*, 2032). And, fittingly, she does not
allow us to see this "entrance." The delights that Aminta's
charms promise, especially from that august location
("*here*"), must be willingly bestowed, as the appearance of
Respect implies, "*the eldest Son of* Love; / Esteem *his Mother
is*" (389–90). This is only his first appearance in the poem, as
telling, perhaps, as his last, before the prospect of the
Bower, when he happily yields to Occasion, assured, then
as now, that Lysander has been properly schooled. Not only
does he learn to value his own pleasure, but willingly contributes to Aminta's: "*perfect the desires, / That fill two Hearts*

that burn with equal Fires" (1927–28). Visualization merely represents the first step.

Behn's restlessness takes other forms in the poem, especially where gender is concerned. Commentators have noted that she does not anticipate the dicta of twentieth-century French feminists such as Hélène Cixous that command women to "write themselves" and put themselves into their texts. At the same time, Behn surely understood the foregoing theorist's idea of "transgression" for women to speak at all, particularly in her own time. She also appears to have been aware of the considerable number of women in the audience for her comedies.[21] In her first play, *The Forc'd Marriage* (1671), "an Actress" interrupts the presumably male Prologue and, *"pointing to the Ladies,"* challenges them to say, at the conclusion of the comedy, *"A Woman shall not Victor prove to day"* (W 5: 8). The first speaker in her next play, *The Amorous Prince* (1671), Cloris, is female. Both *1 Rover* (1677) and *Sir Patient Fancy* (1678) open with two young women (Florinda and Hellena, Isabella and Lucretia, respectively) who cheerfully analyze their fathers's oppression of them, expressing their exasperation with the role of "Obedient Daughter" (*Sir Patient Fancy* 1.1.17). So, Behn frequently and happily transgresses in her very utterance as a woman author, and seems to inscribe herself and her gender's perspective into her texts. However, she does not appear to "write herself" in *A Voyage*, given her fidelity to maintaining Lysander's perspective. Yet her "masculine part," her pen, insists that the feminine assert itself. One of the few instances in which one can detect slippage in her assumed masculine point of view occurs when Lysander describes his feelings for Lysidas to him:

> That friendship which our Infant hearts inspir'd,
> E're them Ambition or false Love had fir'd:
> Friendship! Man's noblest bus'ness! without whom
> The out-cast Life finds nothing it can own,
> But Dully dyes unknowing and unknown.
> (*A Voyage*, 12–17)

Although she imagines one man speaking to another, her diction describes the relationship in feminine terms of the conventional type that Philips uses in her tributes to members of her circle ("Infant hearts"). This appears doubly unusual because Behn's poetry generally does not concern non-erotic friendship, much less the distinctively feminine. Even the poem to Anne Wharton concerns her uncle Rochester, not any relationship between her and Behn. At the same time, the passage contains echoes from her other work. The criticism of ambition resembles the contempt for civilization's tendency to despoil ideal bonds that we find elsewhere, such as "The Golden Age." The rhetoric of the third line foretells "Man! our great business and our aim" in a pessimistic poem that discounts the possibility of lasting bonds between men and women ("To *Alexis* in Answer to his Poem against Fruition," 27), one to read in opposition against the larger, optimistic work. Concerning other types of bonds, Behn uses a familiar rhyme a few lines later to explain how the friendship preserved itself in spite of the intercession of Aminta: "This tye, which equal to my new desires / Preserv'd it self amidst Loves softer Fires" (*A Voyage*, 31–32). Since Behn usually pairs "desires" / "fires" to describe erotic heterosexual love (cf. "On a *Juniper-Tree*," 41–42; "Love Arm'd," 5, 7; "Song to *Ceres*," 7–8; "The Disappointment," 111–12), Lysander's equation of his friendship with Lysidas to his physical passion for Aminta seems curious, also, although there appears to be no further hint of any alternative sexualities. In fact, as if to dissipate this idea, Behn deploys the same rhyme at Lysander's first mention of Aminta, from whose eyes the *putti* shoot their darts: "Some from her Smiles they point with soft desires, / Whilst others from her Motion take their Fires" (*A Voyage*, 243–44). We hear the same chime in the strange ballad by the unnamed Man (125) who tends to enunciate what Behn's speakers state elsewhere as belief:

> All thither come, early or late,
> Directed by Desire,
> Not Glory can divert their fate,
> Nor quench the Amorous fire.

(145–48)

One may detect a hint of materialism, even libertinism, in the quatrain, as if all people were bundles of matter irresistibly drawn to each other, always in motion, never at rest, in quest for the suggestively physical *"Enterances on every side"* (149) of the Isle, Temple, and Bower. In Behn's narrative contortions, a woman writes as a man to another man as if both men were women, but those who arrive to quench their fires, including Lysander, are definitely heterosexual.

Behn's masculine part asserts the woman's perspective in other ways. She has been accused of "exaggerating the femaleness of her characters and narrators" to challenge literary convention, but it may be difficult to apply this argument to *A Voyage*—or, frankly, to the rest of the poems in the volume.[22] Although Aminta does appear capricious and vacillating, we must remember that Behn filters everything through Lysander's perspective. The protagonist, infected by desire, would naturally misread his beloved's hesitancy as fickleness. One might also notice that, in contrast with Tallemant's Aminta, Behn's actually speaks, in the manner of her personified sisters in the poem, Hope, Occasion, and Confidence. (Perhaps Behn thought this transgressive enough and wished to maintain her aesthetic.) Moreover, she ensures that Lysander commend Aminta for her intellectual abilities, "the entertainment of her Wit," that "Beyond her Beauty did my Soul surprize" (434–35). Perhaps we should examine the few passages in which Aminta demonstrates this entertaining wit, what Behn deems important enough for her to say to break Lysander's torrent of words—or, better yet, what he remembers of her speech to report to Lysidas.

It is appropriate that Aminta's first words are in self-defense. Her hesitancy seems unremarkable. She does not know Lysander or even his name, conventional prerequisites for friendship, love, and consummation. Half-naked and drowsy, surprised by an amorous and ardent young man,

> Where are my LOVES, she crys! all fled away?
> And left me in this gloomy shade alone?
> And with a Man! Alas, I am undone.
>
> (416–18)

Although a modern reader may wish for more profundity from Aminta at this juncture, she or he might observe that she does not faint or collapse into spasms of weeping, but asserts herself by speaking, and in a way that, again, Lysander remembers well enough to relate to his male addressee. This self-possession carries over into the rest of the poem. Lysander rarely functions independently of her. She acts, and he reacts to her. At the conclusion of his ardent pindaric "The Transport" (1210–25), Aminta visits Confidence, another one of Behn's additions to Tallemant's narrative.[23] This personification, as we later learn, allegorizes her psyche, not Lysander's. Strictly speaking, it represents Aminta's *self*-confidence, which he mistakes for "her Complysance" to his desires (1291) before she finds herself ready to acquiesce to them. Lysander must learn that women should be confident in themselves before bonding with others.

Behn enacts Aminta's subjectivity in other statements, even those that appear to suggest the opposite of empowerment or free will. She asserts herself again when she refuses Lysander, in the allegorical guise of Honour snatching her from her pursuer's grasp. In paradoxically deterministic language, the heroine expresses her right to make her own choices:

> *Forgive*, Lysander, *what by force I do,*
> *Since nothing else can ravish me from you;*
> *Make no resistance, I obey* Devoir,
> *Who values not thy Tears, thy Force or Prayer,*
> *Retain thy Faith and Love* Aminta *still,*
> *Since she abandons thee against her Will.*

(1313–18)

In spite of her protest at the absence of free will, that Honour forcefully compels her away from Lysander, her instinct for virtue represents her own choice. Behn does not seem to castigate her for it, in spite of Lysander's bewildered incomprehension. The obedience to Honour is a powerful cultural force, as Behn acknowledges not only in "The Golden Age," in which she excoriates it, but in the previously discussed "To *Lysander*, who made some Verses on a Discourse of Loves Fire," in which she invokes it herself by refusing to become part of a ménage à trois: "Take in no

Partners to your Fire" (33). Perhaps a ghostly intratextual echo also reverberates from "To *Alexis* in Answer to his Poem against Fruition" (1685): "With one surrender to the eager will / We're short-liv'd nothing, or a real ill" (13–14 [W 1:272]). The fire of experience seems seared into those lines, as if their speaker knew what she was talking about. Aminta, far from helpless, chooses to obey Devoir as if she had read this poem, and commands Lysander to love in spite of her reluctance. She will not surrender to the eager will for nothing.

Even in Aminta's yielding, she asserts herself by speech. Just as she allows Honour to steal her away, she commands Love to bring her back. She must enunciate and explain the choice she makes:

> Lead on, young Charming Boy, I follow thee;
> Lead to Lysander, quickly let's be gone,
> I am resolv'd to Love, and be undone;
> I must not, cannot, Love at cheaper rate,
> Love is the word, Lysander and my fate.
>
> (A Voyage, 1903–7)

Again, the contemporary reader may wish for something more memorably phrased, not so much in the service of enforced immasculation to heighten our vicarious enjoyment of Lysander's precoital desire but to represent Aminta with more depth or verve. To resolve to *"be undone"* and not *"at cheaper rate"* sounds not only unromantic but mercenary, a cliché that a clever maid might suggest to her kept mistress on the verge of marrying a rich old fool for his money, as Betty does to Diana in *The City-Heiress* (1682): "He'll quickly die and leave you rich, and then do what you please" (5.1.242). Yet this missed opportunity for profundity may be part of Behn's point. At this juncture, things must be phrased simply, without sparkling wit. Perhaps this is all that Lysander can remember, or how her words sounded to him. Or, to distill the matter to its essence, it would not be out of order to suggest that Aminta's sense of self-worth is bound up with her decision to dispense with her chastity or not (prefiguring Richardson's Clarissa and Pamela). All of Charles's mistresses confronted a similar dilemma, chose the former course, and suffered the consequences, not all of them good. So did Monmouth's mother, Lucy Walters. Therefore, at the moment of seduction, the target of Lysander's drive and thematic center of Behn's circular narration, what will she allow Aminta to say?

> *Take, charming Victor—what you must—subdue—*
> *'Tis* Love—*and not* Aminta *gives it you,*
> Love *that o're all, and every part does reign,*
> *And I shou'd plead—and struggle—but in vain;*
> *Take what a yielding Virgin—can bestow,*
> *I am—dis-arm'd—of all resistance now.—*
>
> (1910–15)

She must say that she acts against her will, although the verbs that govern her rhetoric are in the imperative mood: *"Take," "subdue," "Take."* In choosing to "submit" and thereby exercising her will, she behaves as if she has no choice. This verbal schizophrenia represents the consequences for women whose culture inflicts androcentric conceptions of Honour on them, as Behn argues in "The Golden Age": "cursed Honour! thou who first didst damn / A Woman to the Sin of shame" (117–18). Carol Barash's statement on the politics of gender applies very well to Behn and Aminta. The author "calls attention to both the female speaker and the female translator as linguistic and political actors, or subjects. She thus suggests implicitly that women's professions of desire are not natural, but culturally constructed (and culturally contested) forms of poetic address."[24] Simply put, Aminta's words are indeed culturally constructed, just as Cloris's similar verbal resistance to her Lysander in "The Disappointment" are, even as she pulls him atop her into position: *"My Dearer Honour ev'n to You / I cannot, must not give"* (27–28). She cannot act as though she wants what she wants. Yet there are exceptions to this conundrum for the author. Her Aminta seems more informed than Cloris, who flees at the touch of a flaccid penis. At Lysander's temporary impotence, he notes: "I saw the trembling dis-appointed Maid, / With charming angry Eyes my fault upbraid" (*A Voyage*, 2085–86). Her culture dictates that she keep such knowledge to herself—Behn subtly violates the norms of the same culture, her own, by expressing the knowledge for her. Perhaps she felt she could not transgress any more explicitly than this, having already usurped the masculine prerogative by writing in the first place. As her adversary Robert Gould put it so succinctly concerning women readers and writers, "Farces and Songs obscene, remote from Wit, / (Such as our *Sappho* to *Lisander* writ)" ("To a Gentlewoman who had written many fine Things, and not seen Mrs. *Phillips's* Poems").[25] Of course, "our *Sappho*" is Behn, her addressee with a name too familiar to require glossing.

IV

New Charms each minute did appear in view,
And each appointment Ravishing and New.

—*A Voyage*, 2109–10

Lysander's ecstatic appreciation of his newly consummated relationship with Aminta represents the apotheosis of the mutuality that Behn, or indeed any lover, desires: "our Joyes of equal Love" ("The Invitation," 2). Such rapture almost demands scrutiny, particularly from a poet not prone to such pronouncements. To conclude my discussion of *A Voyage*, I compare this ideal to its antithesis in a poem from the collection "To My Lady *Morland* at *Tunbridge*."[26] Though *A Voyage* and "Lady *Morland*" appear to have little in common, they share a similar genre and form, the love-oriented verse epistle consisting largely of pentameter couplets.[27] This fact alone invites comparison and investigation, as do similar formal and prosodic twinnings in *Poems upon Several Occasions*. The longer poem and "Lady *Morland*" also subtly echo each other, if refractorily.

A Voyage and "Lady *Morland*" exhibit Behn's tendency toward auto-intertextuality (or intratextuality), which encourages the reader to investigate her revisions of herself within her opus. *A Voyage*, serious and sometimes even operatic in tone, features one man writing to another about a woman in whom they have no common interest, but who mysteriously dies after having been won. Behn complicates this relatively simple story with the device of allegory and by challenging the reader to determine Lysander's narrative reliability. He strains and struggles to attain the love and favors of Aminta, refusing to give up. "Lady *Morland*," lighter in tone and equipped with a subtly satiric bite, presents one woman writing to another concerning a man in whom they share an extremely pointed interest. Such "life stories," generally quite complicated already, are often even more complex after poets attempt to immortalize them in verse, with the added twist that their many lacunae require filling in from the available evidence that the speaker deigns to provide for us. The speaker in "Lady *Morland*" appears to have worked very hard indeed for the man, Amyntas, she eventually loses to the addressee, Cloris, and appears to have given up quite easily to her social superior. Again, the two poems, discrepant in size, refract each other. They possess approximately the same theme with the same results for the speaker—crushing disappointment, elements of humiliation, the need to recount loss. Also, neither focuses on the objects of affection (Amyntas and Aminta), but rather on the psychology of the speaker.

This parallelism suggests how "Lady *Morland*" and *A Voyage* can be mutually illuminatory. Behn uses the former to question the idealism of its much larger counterpart, as if to say that such arrangements are never simple, but are actually labyrinthine entanglements, instead. Rather than joys of equal love with its appointments ever ravishing and new, one must conclude, *"rarely equal Hearts in Love you'l find"* (*A Voyage*, 235). Yet we can also posit that she fashions *A Voyage* to counter the mild cynicism of "Lady *Morland*," just as poets paint Golden Ages to express their (childish) disappointment in the present one.

In any case, it may be unsettling to learn that *"every thing begets desire"* (*A Voyage*, 494), or to discover that language itself perpetrates such begettings. Behn uses similar verbiage in both poems for wildly different purposes to suggest the transience of words, their general unreliability. Lysander's overweening ardor for Aminta utilizes the same rhetoric that Behn features in her gentle and not altogether benevolent flattery for Her Ladyship. However, this extravagant praise concerns Morland's physical attributes exclusively. As we have seen, Lysander prizes Aminta's "Wit," which affected him "Beyond her Beauty" (434–35), and *A Voyage* subtly organizes itself around her choices, to which her swain reacts. Both poems problematize the concept of womanly beauty itself by measuring its effects on the flatterer as well as the flattered. In the case of Lady Morland, Behn implies, like Oscar Wilde, that those who go beneath the surface do so at their peril. Aminta's general wariness, as opposed to Morland's apparent lack of this survival skill, suggests that she will not share the fate of the wronged women in *Poems upon Several Occasions*, those who complain that they have been "By such dear Perjuries won" ("The Reflection," 42).

That Morland may find herself entrapped by such perjuries is implied in the poem that precedes it, "On a Copy of Verses made in a Dream" (already discussed in this chapter for its resonance in the translation). Behn's speaker in that poem recounts being awakened by the delivery of a verse epistle, itself composed in a dream by Amyntas, whose erotic poetical skills promise their complementary physical reward. This happy consummation, however, is subverted, because it is precisely this Amyntas whom Behn's speaker loses to Lady Morland in the following poem. Two verbal prompts provide further linkages. The same simile appears twice, Amyntas "Like an unwearied Conqueror" ("On a Copy of Verses," 39), and Morland "As when a Conqu'ror does in Triumph come" (1). The last word of the preceding poem is "Defeat" ("On a Copy of Verses," 44), because it is precisely what Behn's speaker will suffer in losing the much-pursued Amyntas to her aristocratic rival. How will she negotiate this rather difficult situation? She must express her disappointment, even anger, with tact and savoir faire, and with no small amount of passive-aggression. Again, the opening simile of "Lady *Morland*" compares her to "a Conqu'ror," intriguingly male, explaining how he would have been described by those not fortunate enough to witness his triumphant entry:

> How brave the Prince, how gay the Chariot was,
> How beautiful he look'd, with what a Grace;
> Whether upon his Head he Plumes did wear;

Or if a Wreath of Bays adorn'd his Hair:
They hear 'tis wondrous fine, and long much more
To see the *Hero* then they did before.

(5–11)

Behn's speaker gives the language of compliment full force, perfectly legitimate—or bland, which may be the point. Stock adjectives such as "brave," "gay," "beautiful," "wondrous fine" appear gratuitous, empty. She was certainly capable of more pointed, original language. One may wonder, then, why Lysander uses similarly vacuous terminology when he first meets and then describes Aminta:

Such Charms of Youth, such Ravishment
Through all her Form appear'd,
As if in her Creation Nature meant,
She shou'd a-lone be ador'd and fear'd.

(*A Voyage*, 252–55)

Rather than bland adjectives, Lysander uses somewhat stock nouns: "Charms," "Ravishment," "Form," "Creation." The situational contrast, of course, is that Lysander does not know better; Behn's speaker does. In his naiveté, before his education in courtship and love commences, he stresses in the best way he can that Aminta is supernaturally beautiful and affects him overwhelmingly, as a novice. Behn's speaker, a professional, in words that appear to say just as much as Lysander's, may be implying the opposite.

Behn's speaker, much more sophisticated than Lysander, disguises her real agenda for twenty lines in the verse epistle beneath the veneer of flattery. Amyntas (and by extension, Morland) lacks depth and she (and again, perhaps, Morland) deserves better—but the speaker herself is perhaps more deserving still. One is reminded of Dryden's technique in "To the Memory of Mr. *Oldham*" (1683–84), in which he subtly criticizes the recently deceased young satirist while appearing to praise him. Although the Laureate seems to commend Oldham by comparing him to the victorious runner Euryalus and himself to his fallen friend Nisus, one must remember that Euryalus only wins because Nisus trips Salius, who was outdistancing Euryalus (*Aeneid* 5.315–39), the allusion hardly a strong endorsement of the young man's poetical skill. Furthermore, Dryden suggests that further life would not have improved Oldham's poetry, "What could advancing Age have added more?" (12), because his wit was disfigured by "the harsh cadence of a rugged line" (16), betrayed "by too much force" (18). Behn's speaker perpetrates similar underminings, as if to argue that love is more complicated than Lysander depicts it in A *Voyage*, whom Behn depicts as similarly thunderstruck at the first sight of Aminta, and then also saddled with the indignity of amorous competition for her, allegorized in the corporate abstraction Rivals.

The seemingly innocuous "I came and saw, and blest my Destiny; / I found it Just you should out-Rival me" ("Lady *Morland*," 19–20) signals the commencement of the aforesaid agenda. In some respects, to bless her "destiny" compliments the addressee. She feels privileged to arrive at the place where, along with everyone else, she can be conquered by the sight of so much beauty. At the same time, since another type of destiny altogether operates in the poem, to lose the fickle Amyntas, Behn may imply that this loss represents a different kind of blessing. Her other compliments for Morland sprout fangs in similar ways. In "Ev'n my Devotion, *Cloris*, you betray'd" (31) suggests on the surface that Behn, like the officiating clergyman who "Forgot the Gospel, and began to Pray" (27), was distracted from the ostensible purpose of Sunday worship. Beneath the surface, however, it seems that Cloris has betrayed other kinds of "devotion," namely, her friendship with Behn's speaker, which would have included respect for her relationship with Amyntas, not to mention his purported, yet apparently quite false, "devotion" to the speaker herself. As the poem proceeds, the sarcasm of Behn's speaker becomes simultaneously subtler and bolder:

> I call'd *Amyntas* Faithless *Swain* before,
> But now I find 'tis Just he should Adore.
> Not to love you, a wonder sure would be,
> Greater than all his Perjuries to me.
> And whilst I Blame him, I Excuse him too;
> Who would not venture Heav'n to purchase you?
> ("Lady *Morland*," 35–40)

At the River of Pretension, Lysander discovers that "LOVE / Maliciously wou'd needs my Conduct prove" (*A Voyage*, 691–92). No such river courses through the poem under comparison here. Yet Love tests the conduct of all three principals with just as much malice and finds them all wanting, even the speaker herself. Surely she cannot find it justified for Amyntas to reverse his affections so completely, given his faithlessness. The implication is clearly that he will prove just as faithless to Morland. Given this, the sarcasm of the next couplet seems almost baldfaced. Amyntas, fickle and prone to excessive lying ("all his Perjuries to me"), will desert Lady Morland, also. Although the speaker claims to exculpate him ("Excuse"), the parallel term in the line ("Blame"), as well as the adverb ("too") implies that she blames more than she excuses, although the object of these verbs might secretly better read "you" rather than "him." The hyperbole of the last line at this point seems almost comical. One hears an echo of Aminta's self-assessment by fiscal metaphor discussed earlier, "*I must not, cannot*, Love *at cheaper rate*" (*A Voyage*, 1906), without the accompanying naiveté. Amyntas's "purchase" seems almost coldblooded by comparison, as does the object acquired. They love with money and no heart.

Jealousie is only one of the abstractions that Lysander finds himself with the felicitous leisure to visit, designed to mirror his state of mind and then correct it so that he can love better, along with Pretension, Hope, Absence, Respect, Occasion. It tends to "*render things that are not, to the Eyes*" (1520), the jealous themselves "*Faithless, as Couzen'd Maids, by Men undone*" (1534). Behn's speaker is certainly inflamed by jealousy in "Lady *Morland*." Yet since she cannot openly criticize her addressee or express the possibility that she was an agent in the destruction of her relationship with Amyntas, she must say, behind her hand, that she is too good for him: "you too meanly prize / The more deserving Glories of your Eyes" (41–42). Amyntas, more deserving of blame than excuse and surely faithless now as before, "oft has Fetters worn, and can with ease / Admit 'em or dismiss 'em when he please" (45–46), no slave to Morland's charms as he claims. Her Ladyship may be even more innocent than Lysander, prone to the bad judgment of the uninitiated and naïve, deserving, snarls Behn, of "A Virgin-Heart" (47) to love her rather than the libertine who claims to do so, one possessed of "a *Soul* as Great as you are Fair" (50). Behn's speaker makes explicit that Amyntas possesses no such greatness of soul. In this she may also imply that Morland is afflicted with a similar dearth, lovely to look at, but not much else to recommend her. Again, the world of "Lady *Morland"* comments and is commented on by *A Voyage*. Unequal triangles and the bad feelings that ensue and that cannot be plainly stated become rerouted as sarcasm. Or, rather than sarcasm, Behn expresses disappointment that the ideals of *A Voyage*—the felt can be expressed, enjoyment waits on desire, mutuality, *"The Virgin here shows no disdain, / Nor does the Shepherd Sigh in vain"* (2027–28)—cannot be realized.

A *Voyage* represents more than an apprenticeship for the world of fiction that would occupy Behn for the rest of her writing career, more than a move dictated by market forces (although it was certainly excellent preparation, albeit in verse, not prose). It also summarizes and reconfigures many of the motifs in *Poems upon Several Occasions* and creates the sense of unity she sought in the collection. Honor need not always be demonic, but a friend to women just as it is in the poetry of Philips. The psychology of Lysander in some senses illuminates that of every amorous swain who precedes him, although his intentions are somewhat nobler. Mutuality can be fulfilled in some senses, but in others, problematized as an ideal whose attempted realization results in frustration and loss. Gender can be amorphous in a writer. A woman can assume a man's identity and write to another man about a woman without writing from a conventionally feminine point of view. Such auto-intertextuality indeed suggests that Behn's collection, capped by *A Voyage*, was not conceived or written in haste, but designed with the intention of its author being admired and understood.

Afterword: Welcome Mischiefs

In Maiden Verse, there shou'd no Words be seen
But what reveals the Innocence within.
                    —Gould, "The Poetess: A Satyr,
                    Being a Reply to Silvia's Revenge"

I FINISH MY STUDY WITH A COUPLET FROM THE WORKS OF BEHN'S most notorious detractor. It does not resemble other quotations I have culled from Gould's satires (scathing, frenzied, *ad feminam*), yet is equally revealing. It explains what the same critic of such strong opinions thinks a woman writing poetry should exemplify in her verses and in her character, two entities that for him can never be disentangled. But few women, poets or not, would care to recognize themselves in this distich: surely not Aphra Behn, and probably not Katherine Philips. If Behn was not supposed to be herself, what was expected? Gould's corset-couplet answers this question, and also explains why Behn could never fulfill its narrow scope, even as she strove to be admired and understood. His insistence on demure, virginal verse essentially encapsulates the reception (or, better yet, the lack of it) of Behn's poetry from the end of the seventeenth century until the last decade of the twentieth. She could never be the constructed Orinda. Nor could she have been Emily Dickinson or Adrienne Rich, poets with sharply individual modernist voices.

Again, recent scholarship argues that in spite of the (carefully qualified and controlled) approval of Philips in Carolean literary culture, it considered a woman's act of writing obscene, regardless of the subject matter. As the theory goes, this very standard of obscenity accounts not only for the intense assertion of Behn's "looseness," but also for the maniacal insistence on Philips's chastity and

198

rectitude by the same voices, female as well as male, Finch as well as Gould. I see no reason to discredit this idea or even to question it. My predecessors, especially Dorothy Mermin and Carol Barash, have eloquently explained that women writing poetry after Behn were forced to adopt different strategies than hers if they wished to be read or respected—strategies that would result, ironically, no less in their marginalization in the history of English literature than Behn's.[1] Male literary historians dismissed most of them as insipid just as they ignored Behn because of her alleged indecency. Her subversive discourses of poetical desire could not be models for her successors, however disguised by the objective Augustan voice and its positional style, however intriguing and liberating on the private level for those who looked beneath the surface. I agree with Mermin that these women writing did not wish to be demonized, and that many were content to use words that would reveal only the innocence within. Although one cannot apply this idea to every woman writing poetry in the eighteenth century, it amounts to a normative prescription for them, which most male critics who judged them (well into the middle of the twentieth century) were only too happy to apply. That Behn was an "educated woman" did not matter much to these authoritative voices, either, or that she discussed other matters besides the erotic. It is only recently that her prefaces to her plays have been thought worthy to be labeled literary criticism, as Ros Ballaster and Laurie Finke explain in recent studies.[2] Indeed, Behn's most scholarly piece of prose, her introduction to her translation of Fontenelle, became available in a modern edition only in the last decade. Even a cursory reading of this wide-ranging essay (translation, science, religion)—which includes a demonstration that Copernicanism need not conflict with biblical accounts of the cosmos—reveals Biblical exegesis not unworthy of her enemy, Gilbert Burnet (see W 4:79–86). It is all the more remarkable, then, that the Reverend Summers compiled his edition of Behn's writings during World War I and thus attempted to give her the status accorded to Wycherley and Shadwell, whose plays and poetry he had also edited: *opera*, "Works."[3]

Various historicist discourses assert that a literary culture values and appropriates texts for reasons of its own, independent of a universal standard of value, even if the literary culture champions such a standard and claims it is universal. As the argument goes, the enunciation of such a standard is particularly suspect, itself (almost conspiratorially) a product of the culture that uses it to contain attempts at subverting its dominant ideology. This theory, if it is valid, certainly explains the demonization of Behn and the silencing of her poetical voice after her death. It may also account for the contemporary interest in her, especially in a culture of criticism that generally disdains universal standards as hopelessly essentialist. In an age that values women writers of the early modern period because, among many other reasons, they are women writers in the early modern period, a writer like Behn who is, curiously, not terribly feminist in sympathy or given to poetical intimacy, is irresistible. She is not Jane Barker or Sylvia Plath. In an age that attaches importance to matters of race and class in situating texts historically, it is predictable that most commentary about Behn would focus on a work of hers that appears to concern itself with issues of race and class, *Oroonoko*. And, finally, in an age in which any subject may be discussed without embarrassment, it is not surprising that much criticism of her poetry should value "The Disappointment," a poem subtle but explicit in its rendering of dysfunctional sexuality. It would not be untoward to suggest that Behn's collection of poetry in itself should receive the same attention, even though it is not largely concerned with these matters. It is a remarkable achievement for other reasons.

One of the finest recent studies of Restoration and eighteenth-century poetry, one generally inclusive of marginalized poets male and female and authoritative in its readings of canonical authors of the period—a study I rely on—makes no mention of Behn or her poetry whatsoever. Although I found this book somewhat late in the progress of my own research, the following passage from it creates an interesting counterpoint to *Poems upon Several Occasions*:

Indeed, women poets had a particularly hard time qualifying as "Augustans," not only since the classics were supposedly closed to them, but also because they (legally powerless) were officially supposed ignorant of politics, history, and of the large world that makes a life outside the self. The boldness and appetite which seizes the world and absorbs it into poetry are not "feminine" qualities. Women were supposed to write elegies on the death of pet linnets and so on, weak versions of the sort of lyric verse despised and discarded by the major movements of the period. Significantly, they did not write long poems at a time when the long poem was most valued. They were rarely satirical (satire is critical and aggressive). Nor were women supposed to write poetry derived from the inner self without the strictest self-censorship. Women poets hardly ever attempted the charivari, the daring dispersal of reality in favor of a crazed version of it. They were certainly not encouraged to attempt it; perhaps their contemporaries uneasily felt that if a topic often representing the female powers and sexual unease were seriously invoked by a female, matters would get out of hand.[4]

Behn's collection proves the exception to these negative pronouncements about women writing poetry in the period. Her extensive knowledge of classical literature, which she demonstrates in her odes and in her infusions of Horace, Lucretius, Theocritus, and Ovid, argues that the classics were not closed to her. She does not appear to have been legally powerless or financially dependent. Her collection shows that she was surely not ignorant of politics, history, and "the large world . . . outside the self." Her "boldness and appetite" in fashioning herself and in constructing her collection so intricately may not have seemed "feminine" to some of her reading public, but her methods do not necessarily reproduce masculine conventions of self-promotion and artistic unity. Her one death elegy is not for a pet linnet but for the painter Thomas Greenhill (or Grinhil). "*Oenone to Paris*" and *A Voyage to the Isle of Love* are both long, "major" poems. "A Letter to a Brother of the Pen in Tribulation" and "To my Lady *Morland* at *Tunbridge*" both qualify as satires, albeit neither "critical" nor "aggressive." Indeed, she does not "write poetry derived from the inner self," but then neither do her contemporaries, according to the critic's own overriding thesis about Augustan poetry. (Actually, in the critic's terms, Behn is Augustan indeed.)

Although the *charivari* is not invoked much in her collection, many other methods of "representing the female powers and sexual unease" appear in it: the utopian longings of "The Golden Age"; the feminocentricity of "On a *Juniper-Tree*" and "The Disappointment"; the constants of the poetry to and about Hoyle (sex, sorrow, and men's eyes). Even the prevalence of "languish" and its derivatives, evocative of the poses of the court painter Peter Lely's female subjects, suggests this twinning of women's powers and the unease they can cause in a phallocentric culture. That Behn's poetry overturns the ideas of this culture, admirably summarized in the paragraph above, suggests why it was savaged by Gould, ignored and then forgotten or scorned by Wagenknecht and Sutherland. *Poems upon Several Occasions*, then, suggests that matters got quite out of hand. Its author was, after all, buried in Westminster Abbey, as were Chaucer, Spenser, and Cowley.

Notes

INTRODUCTION

The epigraphs are from, respectively, *The Works of Mr. Robert Gould*, 2 vols. (London: Printed for R. Lewis, 1709), 2:17; *Colophon* 18 (1934): 17–32.

1. Derek Hughes, *The Theatre of Aphra Behn* (London: Palgrave, 2001), 9.

2. Behn understood her age's conception of "female frailty" and utilized it for satiric purposes when necessary: "All I ask, is the Priviledge for my Masculine Part the Poet in me, (if any such you will allow me) to tread in those successful Paths my Predecessors have so long thriv'd in, to take those Measures that both the Ancient and Modern Writers have set me, and by which they have pleas'd the World so well. If I must not, because of my Sex, have this Freedom, but that you will usurp all to your selves; I lay down my Quill, and you shall hear no more of me, no not so much as to make Comparisons, because I will be kinder to my Brothers of the Pen, than they have been to a defenceless Woman" (Preface to *The Luckey Chance*, 1686 [W 7:217]).

3. James R. Sutherland, *English Literature of the Late Seventeenth Century* (Oxford: Clarendon Press, 1969), 134, 132–33.

4. "Aphra Behn and the Ideological Construction of Restoration Literary Theory," in *Rereading Aphra Behn: History, Theory, and Criticism*, ed. Heidi Hutner (Charlottesville: University Press of Virginia, 1993), 25. Other important studies that make similar observations include Catherine Gallagher, "Who Was That Masked Woman? The Prostitute and the Playwright in the Comedies of Aphra Behn," *Women's Studies* 15 (1988): 23–42; Katherine Eisaman Maus, "'Playhouse Flesh and Blood': Sexual Ideology and the Restoration Actress," *English Literary History* 46 (1979): 595–617; Jessica Munns, "'I by a Double Right Thy Bounties Claim': Aphra Behn and Sexual Space," in *Curtain Calls: British and American Women and the Theater, 1660–1820*, ed. Mary Anne Schofield and Cecelia Macheski (Athens: Ohio University Press, 1991), 193–210; and Angeline Goreau, *Reconstructing Aphra: A Social Biography of Aphra Behn* (Oxford: Oxford University Press, 1980), 23–42.

5. "Literature, Culture, and Society in Restoration England," in *Culture and Society in the Stuart Restoration*, ed. Gerald MacLean (Cambridge: Cambridge University Press, 1995), 4, 12.

6. *The Secret Life of Aphra Behn* (New Brunswick, N.J.: Rutgers University Press, 1997), 5.

7. See Goreau, *Reconstructing Aphra*, 268; Ballaster, " 'Prentices of

State': Aphra Behn and the Female Plot," in *Rereading Aphra Behn*, ed. Hutner, 189–90.

8. N. H. Keeble makes these observations about Margaret Cavendish (applicable to Behn) in "Obedient Subjects? The Loyal Self in Some Later Seventeenth-Century Royalist Women's Memoirs," in *Culture and Society in the Stuart Restoration*, ed. MacLean, 213.

9. See note 2 above.

10. Catherine Labio makes the same argument about Behn's fiction—that she knew she wrote for an audience that did not value novelty as much as the observance of convention. See "'What's in Fashion Vent': Behn, LaFayette, and the Market for Novels and Novelty," *Journal of Medieval and Early Modern Studies* 28 (1998): 119–38.

11. *The Letters of John Dryden, with Letters Addressed to Him*, ed. Charles Eugene Ward (Durham, N.C.: Duke University Press, 1942), 127. For an article on Thomas and Dryden, see Anne McWhir, "Elizabeth Thomas and the Two Corinnas: Giving the Woman Writer a Bad Name," *English Literary History* 62 (1995): 105–19. Behn castigates Dryden for his timely conversion to Catholicism at the accession of James II: "resolv'd to stand and constant to the times / fix't to thy lewdness, settl'd in thy crimes" ("A Satyr on Doctor Dryden," 23–24 [W 1:231]).

12. Behn uses "loosely" in this sense. Rochester's spirit "School'd my loose neglect" ("To Mrs. W," 38).

13. Barbara M. Benedict states that Behn's works, especially *Miscellany* (1685), "reveal how carefully her collections were tailored for the contemporary audience." See *Making the Modern Reader: Cultural Mediation in Early Modern Literary Anthologies* (Princeton: Princeton University Press, 1996), 88.

14. I.e., the concept of Spenser self-consciously presenting himself as the New Poet to his literary culture. See *Self-Crowned Laureates: Spenser, Jonson, Milton, and the Literary System* (Berkeley: University of California Press, 1983), 55–100.

15. See Finke, "Aphra Behn and the Ideological Construction of Restoration Literary Theory," 29; Salzman, "Aphra Behn: Poetry and Masquerade," in *Aphra Behn Studies*, ed. Janet Todd (Cambridge: Cambridge University Press, 1996), 111; Spearing, "Aphra Behn: The Politics of Translation," in *Aphra Behn Studies*, ed. Todd, 171.

16. Labio assumes that the Tonson brothers controlled this part of Behn's publication (125–26). Gallagher (56–66) and Goreau (280) argue that Behn's turn to print media from playwrighting was partially motivated by her desire to control her own literary production.

17. They are: the Earls of Orrery and Roscommon; Abraham Cowley (who provides two commendatory poems); "Philo-Philippa"; Thomas Flatman; James Tyrell. See *Minor Poets of the Caroline Period*, 3 vols., ed. George Saintsbury (Oxford: Clarendon Press, 1905–21), 1:493–503.

18. I have provided line numbers for all prefatory material, taken from *Poems upon Several Occasions* (London: Printed for R. Tonson and J. Tonson, 1684), sigs. a5r-b8v.

19. Goreau posits that Dryden wrote this poem (*Reconstructing Aphra*, 14).

20. Keeble, "Obedient Subjects?" 217.

21. In *Aphra Behn's Afterlife* (Oxford: Oxford University Press, 2000), Jane Spencer provides the best single account of the reception of Behn's poetry (43–61) as well as an analysis of the women writing drama and fiction after her (143–86). In some ways, Spencer reaches the same conclusion about the decline of Behn's reputation that Dorothy Mermin does a decade earlier—both her female successors and her male critics thought of her as a woman who had devoted her life to sex (20). See Mermin's "Women Becoming Poets: Katherine Philips, Aphra Behn, Anne Finch," *English Literary History* 57 (1990): 335–55.

22. *Seductive Forms: Women's Amatory Fiction from 1684 to 1740* (Oxford: Clarendon Press, 1992), 69.

23. "Women Becoming Poets," 336, 441.

24. Salzman, "Aphra Behn: Poetry and Masquerade," 127.

25. *English Women's Poetry, 1649–1714: Politics, Community, and Linguistic Authority* (Oxford: Clarendon Press, 1996), 102–3.

26. "'Be Impudent, Be Saucy, Forward, Bold, Touzing, and Leud': The Politics of Masculine Sexuality and Feminine Desire in Behn's Tory Comedies," in *Cultural Readings of Restoration and Eighteenth-Century Theater*, ed. J. Douglas Canfield and Deborah C. Payne (Athens: University of Georgia Press, 1995), 116.

27. "Aphra Behn: The Politics of Translation," 155.

28. "Liberty, Equality, Fraternity: Utopian Longings in Behn's Lyric Poetry," in *Rereading Aphra Behn*, ed. Hutner, 273.

29. I.e., "All women together ought to let flowers fall upon the tomb of Aphra Behn, for it was she who earned them the right to speak their minds." See *A Room of One's Own and Three Guineas* (London: Chatto & Windus, 1984), 61.

30. See Sarah Lewis Carol Clapp, ed., *Jacob Tonson, In Ten Letters by and about Him* (Austin: University of Texas Press, 1948), 324–25.

31. Spencer sees masculine encomiastic praise of Behn for beauty as well as literary talent as the primary reason for the decline of her reputation as a poet. "Female writing" becomes "a natural extension of the female body and is equally to be valued for sexual purposes." See *Aphra Behn's Afterlife*, 47. Jonathan Goldberg takes a slightly different view in *Desiring Women Writing: English Renaissance Examples* (Stanford, Calif.: Stanford University Press, 1997).

32. "Aphra Behn and the Ideological Construction of Restoration Literary Theory," 21.

33. *OED* cites its first usage of "dramatist" from Ralph Cudworth's *The True Intellectual System of the Universe* (London: Printed for Richard Royston, 1678), 879; for "playwright," it cites Martin Clifford, *Notes upon Mr. Dryden's Poems in Four Letters* (London: n.p., 1687), 4. 16.

34. See *Forming the Critical Mind: Dryden to Coleridge* (Cambridge: Harvard University Press, 1989), 19, 29.

35. "Aphra Behn and the Ideological Construction of Restoration Literary Theory."

36. *The Just and the Lively: The Literary Criticism of John Dryden* (Manchester: Manchester University Press, 1999), 124.

37. Sutherland devotes a section to poetry (154–201) and discusses Restoration criticism, but almost exclusively concerning drama (393–416). Margaret Anne Doody's *The Daring Muse: Augustan Poetry Reconsidered* (Cambridge: Cambridge University Press, 1985) and Eric Rothstein's *Restoration and Eighteenth-Century Poetry 1660–1780* (London: Routledge & Kegan Paul, 1981) are both excellent studies of poetical practice but derive their theory from close readings of the poetry under discussion rather than from critical prose of the period. Neither makes mention of Behn's poetry, although both include women in their studies and treat them in the mainstream of Augustan literature rather than segregating and stigmatizing them as "women poets."

38. On these controversies, see Doody (1–3) and Rothstein (x-xii).

39. Gelber's conception of the "just": "The language, which is always correct, is simple, clear, lucid, and direct; and metre . . . however much it may be varied, never violates the rhythm of its basic measure or pattern." His definition of the "lively": "in every aspect of a work a poet, though without ever succumbing to obscenity or treason or blasphemy, may flout or completely ignore the rules of strict decorum." See *The Just and the Lively*, 12, 13. Gelber argues for an overall consistency in Dryden's criticism, disagreeing with virtually all of his predecessors back to Dr. Johnson, and takes issue with Robert D. Hume's observation about the alleged banality of Restoration dramatic theory, which might well be applied to contemporary concepts of poetry as well: "The numerous late seventeenth-century pronouncements on comedy have never proved notably helpful in reading the plays of the time. Critic after critic tells us that comedy must instruct and please by 'holding the glass' to a society in need of satiric correction—and faced with such platitudes, modern readers have tended to look elsewhere for help." See *The Development of English Drama in the Late Seventeenth Century* (Oxford: Clarendon Press, 1976), 32.

40. See Rothstein (x-xi) and Doody (1) for a critique of nineteenth and twentieth-century misreadings of Augustan poetry.

41. *Restoration and Eighteenth-Century Poetry*, 51. Rothstein bases his concept on Roman Jakobson's conception of metonymy: "poems interact with previous poems, and speakers with audiences who appraise and vicariously engage in the speakers' roles" (51).

42. For the text of this poem, see *The Works of John Dryden*, 18 vols., ed. Alan Roper et al., (Berkeley: University of California Press, 1956-), 2:54–62.

43. Behn's "On the Death of *E. Waller*, Esq." (1685), in praise of this poet, makes the same point that Dryden does in dispraising Shadwell: "Long did the untun'd World in Ign'rance stray, / . . . / Till taught, by thee, the true Poetick way" (33, 35). For the text of this poem, see W 1:289–90.

44. Gelber's discussion of wit is brief yet comprehensive (107–13). The age's anxiety in defining it had larger implications: "The concern was widespread: it preoccupied not only men of letters but also members of the Royal Society, churchmen and scientists alike. For all of them a mistaken sense of the intellectual virtues did more than produce bad poems.

Love of false eloquence made men vulnerable to forms of unreason of every kind: the deceits of orators, the blandishments of Rome, the ravings of the sects" (108).

45. Much of the ensuing historical material (with exceptions noted) is taken from Ronald Hutton, *Charles II: King of England, Scotland, and Ireland* (Oxford: Clarendon Press, 1989) and François Bluche, *Louis XIV*, trans. Mark Greengrass (New York: Watt, 1990).

46. See *The Complete Works of William Wycherley*, 4 vols., ed. Montague Summers, (London, 1924; reprint, New York: Russell and Russell, 1964), 3:156.

47. See James Anderson Winn, *John Dryden and His World* (New Haven: Yale University Press, 1987), 390–95. His biography is essential to understanding the period, albeit from Dryden's point of view.

48. Robert King, *Henry Purcell* (London: Thames and Hudson, 1994), 108–10.

49. See Todd, *Secret Life*, 289.

50. For lucid and readable accounts of these politicized modes of writing, see Thomas Corns, *Uncloister'd Virtue: English Political Literature, 1640–1660* (Oxford: Clarendon Press, 1992), 294–308; the work of Christopher Hill, especially *The World Turned Upside Down: Radical Ideas During the English Revolution* (New York: Penguin, 1991), 218–43; and MacLean, "Literature, Culture, and Society," 10.

51. Hondius's *A Frost Fair on the Thames at Temple Stairs* (1684) hangs in the Museum of London.

52. All quotations from Evelyn: *The Diary of John Evelyn*, 6 vols., ed. E. S. De Beer (Oxford: Clarendon Press, 1955), 4:360–83.

CHAPTER 1: "A FANCY STRONG MAY DO THE FEAT"

1. Gould, *Works*, 1:67

2. *Selected Poems of Anne Finch, Countess of Winchelsea*, ed. Katharine M. Rogers (New York: Ungar, 1979), 72.

3. Rothstein, *Restoration and Eighteenth-Century Poetry*, 21.

4. *The Idea of Christian Love, Being a Translation at the Instance of Mr. Waller of a Latin Sermon upon John XIII. 34, 35* (London: Jonathan Robinson, 1688), vii.

5. The epithet belongs to Pierre Bordieu, who uses it to describe the value of writing flattering prefaces to patrons who could then help poets with public access and funds. See *Outline of a Theory of a Practice*, trans. Richard Nice (Cambridge: Cambridge University Press, 1977), 178. Deborah C. Payne discusses this practice specifically in "The Restoration Dramatic Dedication as Symbolic Capital," *Studies in Eighteenth-Century Culture* 20 (1990): 27–42.

6. *Poems upon Several Occasions*, sigs. A2 and A3, respectively.

7. *Shakespearean Negotiations: The Circulation of Social Energy in Renaissance England* (Berkeley: University of California Press, 1988).

8. In the *Inferno* (4.73–105), Dante puts himself in company with Homer, Virgil, Ovid, Horace, and Lucan.

9. The letter was first published in *The Gentleman's Magazine*, n.s. 5 (1836): 482. Kathleen Lynch reprints it in *Jacob Tonson: Kit-Cat Publisher* (Knoxville: University of Tennessee Press, 1971), 99–100.

10. See Hughes, *The Theatre of Aphra Behn*, 158–59.

11. So argues John Barnard in "Dryden, Tonson, and the Subscriptions for the 1697 *Virgil*," *Papers of the Bibliographical Society of America* 57 (1963): 129–51. Winn does not mention a figure of this magnitude, but discusses some financial arrangements between Tonson and Dryden, including payments in four installments of £50. See *John Dryden and His World*, 477.

12. Todd notes that the code name of Behn's possible lover during her period of espionage, William Scot, was "Celadon" (*Secret Life*, 86).

13. See W 1:xxiii–xxiv.

14. Behn's poem is a great compliment to Edward Howard, a poor poet, whose *The Women's Conquest* brings up the ghost of Ben Jonson to speak a prologue. See Winn, *John Dryden and His World*, 222.

15. Rothstein's essay on the Pindaric ode is infinitely valuable (*Restoration and Eighteenth-Century Poetry*, 4–10). "With it, unlike narrative, poets could choose whether or not to build on any historical event. Fashion and practicality declared for it. So did the ode's ability to absorb the methods of the heroic narrative: emblems (symbolic images with commentary), persuasive analogy, some degree of narrative sequence, running motifs, and division into sections of discourse" (4).

16. "Literature, Culture, and Society," 6.

17. See *Restoration and Eighteenth-Century Poetry*, 6. Furthermore, as Doody explains, the Pindaric, "so firmly associated with greatness and freedom, answered to the Augustan wish for unconstricted versing, formless form" (*The Daring Muse*, 250).

18. See *The Daring Muse*, 240. "The tetrameter verses ostensibly deny themselves room for large serious tagements, or for prosodic experiments. Though they really achieve these things, all is brought off with an appearance of casualness, of hurry mixed with ease. We no sooner finish one quick couplet than we are thrust into the next, pelted with quick rhythms and snapping rhymes. The presence of the iambic tetrameter verse in this era acts as an implicit critique of the central iambic pentameter verse pattern. An ill-done or padded-out iambic pentameter couplet may unwittingly display its tendency to slip back into lighter verses" (241).

19. Todd relates Lovelace's poem to Behn, W 1:385.

20. See, for example, "A Pindarick on The Death of Our Late Sovereign"; "A Poem . . . To . . . Catherine Queen Dowager"; "A Pindarick Poem on the Happy Coronation Of His most Sacred Majesty James II" (W 1:190–221).

CHAPTER 2: NOTIONS OF THE LYRIC AND PINDARIC

1. See Gelber, *The Just and the Lively*, 68.

2. See Gardner, ed., *The Metaphysical Poets*, revised ed. (London: Pen-

guin, 1966), 308. Similarly, Sutherland writes that the Pindaric ode is "fatally easy to write, almost impossible to write well" (*English Literature of the Late Seventeenth Century*, 154).

3. See Rothstein, *Restoration and Eighteenth-Century Poetry*, 6.

4. Finke views Behn's reading of ancient writers as subversive (35). For more discussion of the issue, see Stella P. Revard, "Katherine Philips, Aphra Behn, and the Female Pindaric," in *Representing Women in Renaissance England*, ed. Claude J. Summers and Ted-Larry Pebworth (Columbia: University of Missouri Press, 1997), 227–41.

5. See *The Writings of Jonathan Swift*, ed. Robert A. Greenberg and William B. Piper (New York: Norton, 1973), 391. One might also note that Behn benefits enormously in receiving mention, worthy of battle with Pindar and dignified enough to follow Cowley in defeat. Swift also mentions Thomas Creech (390) in the battle.

6. "The Politics of Translation," 154–55.

7. *Lives of the English Poets*, 3 vols., ed. George Birkbeck Hill (Oxford: Clarendon Press, 1905), 1:42.

8. All references to poems from *The Mistress* follow *The Collected Works of Abraham Cowley*, 6 vols., ed. Thomas O. Calhoun et al. (Newark: University of Delaware Press, 1989-), vol. 2, pt. 1.

9. *The Seventeenth Century: The Intellectual and Cultural Context of English Literature, 1603–1700* (New York: Longman, 1989), 87. The best single analysis of *The Mistress* and its reception is Calhoun et al., eds., *Collected Works*, 2.1:219–36.

10. Ibid., 2.1:303–642.

11. *Secret Life*, 218–19.

12. *The Complete Works in Verse and Prose of Abraham Cowley*, 2 vols., ed. Alexander Grosart (Edinburgh: Constable, 1881; reprint, New York: AMS Press, 1967), 2:5.

13. See Raymond Astbury, "The Renewal of the Licensing Act in 1693 and Its Lapse in 1695," *The Library*, 5th ser. 33 (1978): 296–322.

14. See Thomas M. Greene, *The Light in Troy: Imitation and Discovery in Renaissance Poetry* (New Haven: Yale University Press, 1982).

15. Dryden's tripartite distinction: "metaphrase, or turning an author word by word, and line by line, from one language into another . . . paraphrase, or translation with latitude, where the author is kept in view by the translator, so as never to be lost, but his words are not so strictly followed as his sense; and that too is admitted to be amplified, but not altered . . . imitation, where the translator (if now he has not lost that name) assumes the liberty, not only to vary from words and sense, but to forsake them both as he sees occasion; and taking only some general hints from the original, to run division on the groundwork, as he pleases" (Preface to the Translation of *Ovid's Epistles*, 1680 [K 1:237]).

16. Love distinguishes between seven Restoration modes of "translation": strict metaphrase and a slight loosening with the verbal texture of the original, such as long lines or strange syntax; strict and free paraphrase; strict and free imitation; reconstruction. See "The Art of Adaptation: Some Restoration Treatments of Ovid," in *Poetry and Drama*

1570–1700: Essays in Honour of Harold F. Brooks, ed. Antony Coleman and Antony Hammond (New York: Methuen, 1981), 139. Weinbrot's equally painstaking work on the topic can be found in *The Formal Strain: Studies in Augustan Imitation and Satire* (Chicago: University of Chicago Press, 1969), which distinguishes between imitation-as-borrowing and the Imitation (1–58), and "'An Ambition to Excell': The Aesthetics of Emulation in the Seventeenth and Eighteenth Centuries," *Huntington Library Quarterly* 48 (1985): 121–39, which applies contemporary theory regarding Renaissance imitation practice to Augustan poetry (i.e., Greene, *The Light in Troy*). In "Aphra Behn: The Politics of Translation," Elizabeth Spearing argues (wrongly) that Behn was indifferent to Carolean translation theory (156). Behn's own preface to *A Discovery of New Worlds* (1688), itself a translation of Bernard Fontenelle's *Entretiens sur La Pluralité des Mondes* (1686), reflects her knowledge of the subject in almost excruciating detail.

17. *English Women's Poetry*, 108.

18. *The Poetical Works of Sir John Denham,* ed. Theodore Howard Banks (New Haven: Yale University Press, 1928), 159–60.

19. See Greene, 28–53. Langbaine: "whatever she borrows she improves for the better." See *An Account of the English Dramatick Poets* (Oxford: Printed by L. L. for George West and Henry Clements, 1691), 18.

20. The text of this poem is taken from Cowley's *Poems* (London: Printed [by Thomas Newcombe] for Humphrey Moseley, 1656). The line numbers are those of modern editions.

21. Some typical definitions of wit from Behn's time: Davenant, "Wit is the laborious and the lucky resultances of thought, having towards its excellence, as we say of the strokes of Painting, as well a happinesse as care. It is a Webb consisting of the subt'lest threds; and like that of the *Spider* is considerately woven out of our selves. . . . Wit is not only the luck and labour, but also the dexterity of thought, rounding the world, like the Sun, with unimaginable motion, and bringing swiftly home to the memory universal surveys" (Preface to *Gondibert,* 1650 [CE 2:20]). Sir Robert Howard: "Wit should be chaste, and those that have it can only write well" (Preface to *Four New Plays,* 1665 [CE 2:101]). Sprat: "the true perfection of Wit is to be plyable to all occasions, to walk or flye, according to the Nature of every subject" (*An Account,* 1668 [CE 2:138]). Dryden: "Wit . . . is a propriety of thoughts and words; or, in other terms, thoughts and words elegantly adapted to the subject." (*The Author's Apology for Heroic Poetry and Poetic Licence,* 1677 [K 1:190]). Mulgrave: "True Wit is everlasting, like the Sun, / Which though sometimes beneath a cloud retir'd, / Breaks out again, and is by all admir'd" ("An Essay upon Poetry," 1682 [CE 2:286]).

22. See *Is There a Text in This Class? The Authority of Interpretive Communities* (Cambridge: Harvard University Press, 1980).

23. "Liberty, Equality, Fraternity," 275.

24. *Seductive Forms,* 69.

CHAPTER 3: THE DEBT TO DAPHNIS

1. "So thou by this Translation dost advance / Our Knowledg from the State of Ignorance, / And equals us to Man!" ("To Mr. *Creech*," 41–43). She also praises him in the same poem as the poetical successor to Rochester (109–10). Of the debt to translators such as Creech, Barash writes, "Behn and many other women who could not read Latin or Greek were able, in Dryden's terms, more freely to 'paraphrase' or 'imitate' myth" (*English Women's Poetry*, 105).

2. In addition to the works discussed here, Creech edited and annotated a Latin edition of Lucretius, *Titi Lucretii Cari De rerum natura libri sex* (Oxford: Ab. Swall. & Tim. Child., 1695), and translated the following: Marcus Manilius the astronomer, *The Five Books of M. Manilius* (London: J. Tonson, 1697); Plutarch's life of Cleomenes for Dryden's tragedy *Cleomenes, the Spartan Heroe* (London: J. Tonson, 1692); and Juvenal's thirteenth satire for the Dryden-sponsored edition of Juvenal and Persius (1697). His dazzling explanatory notes for his translations, rife with quotations from Greek and Latin, demonstrate his encyclopedic familiarity with the *auctores* of antiquity.

3. I.e., Lady Knowell, in *Sir Patient Fancy* (1678), described in the dramatis personae as "An Affected Learned Woman," played, ironically, by the illiterate Nell Gwyn (W 6:6). At one point, the character exclaims, "Can any thing that's great or moving be exprest in filthy *English*[?]" (1.1.93).

4. In complementary fashion, Behn thinks of Creech's Lucretius as an aphrodisiac as well as a liberating model for nascent writers: "May Timerous Maids learn how to Love from thence / And the Glad Shepherd *Arts of Eloquence*" ("To Mr. *Creech*," 131–32).

5. All references to Rapin and Theocritus are taken from *The Idylliums of Theocritus with Rapin's Discourse of Pastorals Done into English* (Oxford: L. Lichfield for A. Stephens, 1684). It should be noted that the Rapin preface is separately gathered and paginated from the translation of the *Idylliums*, but also with Arabic numerals (i.e., Rapin, 1–68; Theocritus, 1–160). To reduce the number of footnotes, I will include the page number from Creech in square brackets after the number of the Idyllium, e.g., (*Idyllium* 24 [126]).

6. The best general introduction to the subject is still Thomas G. Rosenmeyer, *The Green Cabinet: Theocritus and the European Pastoral Lyric* (Berkeley: University of California Press, 1969), especially 1–44. For a more concise account of both Greek and Latin pastoral traditions, see *The Oxford Classical Dictionary*, 3d ed., ed. Simon Hornblower and Anthony Spawnforth (Oxford: Oxford University Press, 1996), 1118–20. See also Annabel Patterson, *Pastoral and Ideology: Virgil to Valéry* (Berkeley: University of California Press, 1987), and Paul Alpers, *What Is Pastoral?* (Chicago: University of Chicago Press, 1996).

7. *Monsieur Rapin's Reflections on Aristotle's Treatise of Poesie: Containing the Necessary, Rational and Universal Rules for Epick, Dramatick, and*

the Other Sorts of Poetry (London: Printed by T. Warren for H. Herringman, 1694).

8. In the last quarter of the seventeenth century, "pastoral was not simply an exercise in applying convention, but the much more difficult exercise of employing convention in order to break it"; "Behn . . . is able to manipulate and complicate pastoral convention and to write poetry that is daring and heavily ironic." In this pastoral guise, women can garner power normally closed to them in the urban masculine world. See Elizabeth V. Young, "Aphra Behn, Gender, and Pastoral," *Studies in English Literature* 33 (1993): 525, 541.

9. Mermin, "Women Becoming Poets," 336.

10. J. M. Edmonds, trans., *The Greek Bucolic Poets* (Cambridge: Harvard University Press, 1977), 344–45.

11. For an account of Theocritus, see *The Oxford Classical Dictionary*, 1498–99.

12. Todd notes that the king's musician John Banister had public concerts and recitals in Whitefriars where Behn lived, and that she was literally surrounded by music in the theater, as well. See *Secret Life*, 174.

13. Creech's translation holds up well after three centuries. Doody dismisses it as "workmanlike but uninspired" (90). All references to it here follow the 1684 text (London: Printed for Jacob Tonson and Anthony Stephens), including the book and ode number in Arabic numerals, followed in brackets by the traditional device of the Horatian first line as the poem's title, as well as the page number in Creech's edition so that the reader may easily consult it as well as the classical sourcetext for comparative purposes. All references to the Latin Horace: *Q. Horati Flacci Opera*, 2d ed., ed. E. C. Wickham and H. W. Garrod (Oxford: Clarendon Press, 1912). Although not strictly related to the present business, it should be mentioned that Creech's edition contains some irregularities regarding pagination, most notably the omission of page numbers 184–368 between the epodes and the satires, the latter of which begin on page 369, signature Aar. Creech follows one manuscript tradition no longer observed by including his fine version of the *Ars poetica* among the epistles (numbered 2.3 in his edition) rather than separating it as most modern editors do, declaring his indebtedness to the version by the Earl of Roscommon (A8) that preceded his: *Horace's Art of Poetry made English by the Right Honourable Earl of Roscommon* (London: Printed for Henry Herringman, 1680). He does not translate the *Carmen Saeculare*, as well as six of the odes.

14. Concerning this latter point, Elizabeth V. Young, in her article "Aphra Behn's Horace," *Restoration: Studies in English Literary Culture 1660–1700* 23 (1999): 76–90, makes a number of claims about Behn's "translations" of *Carmina* 1.5 and 1.11. "Though Behn's Latin is limited, her understanding of Latin metrics and her ability to imitate the rhythm of the Horatian poem are so strong that the subversion of the content is largely hidden by the formal proficiency Behn displays" (81). Since Behn had no Latin whatsoever, she would have lacked the sophisticated proficiency required for the mere understanding of Latin meter, not to mention the

ability to imitate it. Her alternating iambic trimeter and tetrameter provide only the barest approximation of Horace's prosody—Behn uses these forms in the manner of her male contemporaries who write in the lyrical mode. Young mentions Creech only twice in the text of her article (76, 82), and chides him because he "makes virtually no attempt to imitate Horace's complicated metrical pattern" (89 n. 29) even though it was clearly not his intention to do so. Nor does she mention Behn's flattery of Creech in her poem praising his Lucretius.

15. Again, Young makes large claims for Behn's renditions, which she reads as "socially pragmatic poems" (87). Furthermore, "In the logic of both poems, the indistinctness of the speaker's sexuality serves to de-emphasize the importance of gender, to depoliticize it, and thereby to empower women, who—Behn recognized—were consistently oppressed by the other sex" (87). Young argues that Behn's revision-imitation-paraphrase of these Horatian lyrics is feminist in sympathy, that "women need not be complicit in the commodification of women" (80); that "in Behn's hands the original text is 'stolen' in order to give voice to the traditionally silenced and possessed" (82); and that most of the poetry reflects an attempt "to debunk masculine authority" (84).

16. Cf. Young: "Behn's translations are suspect to her peers: the distinction between the male poet's province of tighter translation of words and sound from one language to another and Behn's looser, more interpretive rendition of classical ideas is value-laden among her contemporaries, with accurate language proficiency the trump card played when critics needed to underscore masculine supremacy" (76).

17. Perhaps some of these six untranslated odes would have been construed as too allusive to contemporary events at the latter part of the reign of Charles II for inclusion in Creech's text. Although *Carmina* 3.21 ("O nota mecum") and 3.25 ("Quo me, Bacche, rapis"), apostrophes to a wine jar and to Bacchus, respectively, seem harmless enough, the other four *carmina* may have seemed dangerously topical in England in 1684, with the succession and the state religion in question. 3.3 ("Iustum et tenacem"), with its references to mistresses and foreign queens, could well have been interpreted as a slap at Charles, his concubines, and Catherine of Braganza. 3.6 ("Delicta maiorum immeritus") concerns atonement for the crimes of one's fathers, potentially offensive to the Stuarts or to their Cromwellian rivals. (One must remember that Marvell's superb *An Horatian Ode on Cromwel's Return from Ireland* was cancelled from all editions of his poetry until 1776 for the same reason.) 4.4 ("Qualem ministrum"), on the military victories of Augustus's stepsons Tiberius and Drusus, the former his successor as emperor, might have seemed praiseworthy of the dangerously ascendant Monmouth. And, most regrettably, Creech did not or could not render 3.27 ("Impios parrae"), a retelling of the myth of Europa and Jove, *post raptum*, in which Venus and Europa's father chide her for being ashamed. The goddess of love remarks at one point, "nisi erile mavis / carpere pensum / regius sanguis, dominaeque tradi / barbarae paelex" (63–66), i.e., "unless you would prefer to card wool as a mistress of royal blood and to be handed over as a concubine

to a barbarian queen." That Louise de Keroualle, Duchess of Portsmouth, fit this description almost precisely in 1684 would not have been
lost on Creech's readers: as explained in the Introduction, she served as
go-between for Charles and Louis XIV, was in essence *maîtresse en titre*,
and had been lady-in-waiting to Catherine.

18. The reader of recent Behn studies might not be allowed to appreciate this phenomenon, given the stress on alternative sexualities in this
criticism. See, especially, Arlene Steibel, "Not Since Sappho: The Erotic
in Poems of Katherine Philips and Aphra Behn," in *Homosexuality in Renaissance and Enlightenment England: Literary Representations in Historical Context*, ed. Claude J. Summers and Ted-Larry Pebworth (New York:
Harrington Park, 1992), 153–71; and "Subversive Sexuality: Masking the
Erotic in Poems by Katherine Philips and Aphra Behn," in *Renaissance
Discourses of Desire*, ed. Claude J. Summers and Ted-Larry Pebworth (Columbia: University of Missouri Press, 1993), 223–36. Bernard Duyfhuizen
states that "To the fair *Clarinda*" (in Lycidus, 1688) "unmistakably celebrates lesbian love." See "'That which I dare not name': Aphra Behn's
'The Willing Mistress,'" *English Literary History* 58 (1991): 78. In Behn's
The False Count (c. 1681), a reference to lesbianism seems slighting, although she portrays the speaker, Francisco, as jealous and stupid: "I
have heard of two Women that Married each other—oh abominable, as if
there were so Prodigious a Scarcity of Christian Man's Flesh" (2.1.54–56).

19. Citation of this text can be difficult for the modern scholar because
of its three gatherings, all separately paginated: the prefatory letter and
Life and dedicatory poems, A-F2v; the poem itself, 1–223; the Notes to the
poem, 1–59. I clarify these separate gatherings by context. References to
the translation itself include the book followed by page number in brackets, all in parentheses. See *T. Lucretius Carus, the Epicurean Philosopher,
His Six Books De Natura Rerum, Done into English Verse, with Notes*, 2d ed.
(Oxford: L. Lichfield for Anthony Stevens, 1683).

20. Anthony Stevens (or Creech himself) may well have been responsi-
ble for the following modification. This passage of "To Mr. *Creech*" in
Poems upon Several Occasions reads: "Beyond poor Feeble Faith's dull
Oracles, / Faith the despairing Souls content / Faith the last Shift of
Routed Argument" (56–58). In *T. Lucretius Carus*, it reads "As strong as
Faiths resistless Oracles, / Faith the Religious Souls content, / Faith the
secure Retreat of Routed Argument" (d4-d4v).

21. For concise accounts of these three *auctores*, see *The Oxford Classical Dictionary*, 888–90, 532–34, and 454–55, respectively.

22. I.e., "Nothing thou Elder Brother ev'n to shade, / Thou hadst a
Being, e'er the World was made" (1–2). See *The Poems of John Wilmot, Second Earl of Rochester*, ed. Keith Walker (Oxford: Blackwell, 1984). All subsequent references to his poetry will be taken from this edition.

23. Dryden's translation can be found in *Works*, 3:57–65, from which the
line numbers are taken. The editors carefully note the many phrases and
rhyme words that Dryden purloins from Creech's translation (*Works*, 3:
271–74; 285–96). See also James Anderson Winn, "Dryden's Epistle before
Creech's Lucretius: A Study in Restoration Ghostwriting," *Philological
Quarterly* 71 (1992): 47–68.

24. Stevens (or Creech) modifies this epithet to "or by Religion" (*T. Lucretius Carus*, d4v).

25. Maureen Duffy posits that this commender is Dryden. See *The Passionate Shepherdess: Aphra Behn 1640–89* (London: Methuen, 1989), 14. In the Introduction, I suggest that the writer could well have been Behn herself.

CHAPTER 4: BEHN'S GODLIKE ROCHESTER AND LIBERTINISM

In addition to the sentiments expressed in the first epigraph, in "To Mr. Creech," Behn says that Rochester ("Strephon") "Writ, and Lov'd, and Lookt like any God" (91).

1. For the controversy over the authorship of "A Session," see *Poems*, ed. Walker, 312. Todd suggests the poem may well have been by Elkanah Settle. She speculates that for this reason, Behn "was perhaps more gratified to be included in a widely read satire" than offended by the "Ace" reference, a term that resists most attempts to gloss it, but which must have some connection to the female genitalia (*Secret Life*, 209–10).

2. On Behn's conception of poetry and gender, consult Bronwen Price, "Playing the 'Masculine Part': Finding a Difference within Behn's Poetry," *Voicing Women: Gender and Sexuality in Early Modern Writing*, ed. Kate Chedgzoy, Melanie Hansen, and Suzanne Trill (Pittsburgh: Duquesne University Press, 1997), 129–51.

3. *The Works of Mr. Robert Gould*, 2:24.

4. See Jessica Munns, "'Good, Sweet, Honey, Sugar-Candied Reader': Aphra Behn's Foreplay in Forewords," *Rereading Aphra Behn*, ed. Hutner, 44–62.

5. To my knowledge, no study devoted solely to the Behn-Barry relationship exists. Some articles that discuss Barry: Robert Hume, "Elizabeth Barry's First Roles and the Cast of *The Man of Mode*," *Theatre History Studies* 5 (1985): 16–19; Helga Drougge, "Love, Death, and Mrs. Barry in Thomas Southerne's Plays," *Comparative Drama* 27 (1993–94): 408–25; Cynthia Lowenthal, "Sticks, Rags, Bodies and Brocade: Essentializing Discourses and the Late Restoration Playhouse," in *Broken Boundaries: Women and Feminism in Restoration Drama*, ed. Katherine Quinsey (Lexington: University Press of Kentucky, 1996), 219–33. See also Elizabeth Howe, *The First English Actresses: Women and Drama, 1660–1700* (Cambridge: Cambridge University Press, 1992), and Simon Hampton, "Rochester, *The Man of Mode*, and Mrs. Barry, in *That Second Bottle: Essays on John Wilmot, Earl of Rochester*, ed. Nicholas Fisher (Manchester: Manchester University Press, 2000), 165–78.

6. *The Letters of John Wilmot, Earl of Rochester*, ed. Jeremy Treglown (Chicago: University of Chicago Press, 1980), 181.

7. Rochester, *A Letter from Artemiza in the Towne to Chloe in the Countrey*, 26–27. This doubling is common in Carolean poetry, e.g., Gould's

"For *Punk* and *Poetess* agree so Pat, / You cannot well be *This*, and not be *That*."

8. Jones DeRitter, "The Gypsy, *The Rover*, and the Wanderer: Aphra Behn's Revision of Thomas Killigrew," *Restoration: Studies in English Literary Culture, 1660–1700* 10 (1986): 82–92.

9. I.e., "Song [Love a *Woman!* y'are an *Ass*]," 15–16. Behn reproduces the situation in *Love-Letters*. Philander, unable to recognize Silvia beneath her disguise as the page Fillmond, agonizes: "he was extreamly charm'd with her pretty gayety, and an unusual Air and life in her address and motion, he felt a secret joy and pleasure play about his Soul he knew not why; and was almost angry that he felt such an emotion for a youth, tho the most lovely that he ever saw" (W 2:123). It should also be noted that Willmore in *2 Rover* sets himself up as a mountebank, a stunt that Rochester was reputed to have performed.

10. Most current studies of Behn do not discuss libertinism in a sustained fashion. None to my knowledge analyze her Lucretian influence. Barash writes that Behn uses "the male libertine position to criticize cultural codes about sexual desire," an idea "consistent with the gender play and sexual repartee of Restoration comedy, where multiple male and well as female sexual subjectivities are enacted" (*English Women's Poetry*, 109).

11. *Complete Prose Works of John Milton*, 8 vols., Don M. Wolfe, general ed. (New Haven: Yale University Press, 1953–82), 1:570. See also 1:541; 2:342.

12. Hill, *The World Turned Upside Down*, 186. See also 210, 254.

13. Turner's work on libertinism includes "The Properties of Libertinism," *Eighteenth-Century Life* 9 (1985): 75–87; *One Flesh: Paradisal Marriage and Sexual Relations in the Age of Milton* (Oxford: Clarendon Press, 1987), 164–73 passim; "The Libertine Sublime: Love and Death in Restoration England," *Studies in Eighteenth-Century Culture* 19 (1989): 99–115; *Libertines and Radicals in Early Modern London: Sexuality, Politics and Literary Culture, 1630–1685* (Cambridge: Cambridge University Press, 2002); *Schooling Sex: Libertine Literature and Erotic Education in Italy, France, and England, 1534–1685* (Oxford: Oxford University Press, 2003). For broader accounts of the phenomenon, especially in the Augustan book trade, see D. M. Foxon, *Libertine Literature in England 1660–1745* (New Hyde Park, N.Y.: University Books, 1965), and Roger Thompson, *Unfit for Modest Ears: A Study of Pornographic, Obscene, and Bawdy Works Written or Published in England in the Second Half of the Seventeenth Century* (London: Macmillan, 1979).

14. "The Properties of Libertinism," 84. To some extent, Alvin Snider answers Turner's call in "Professing a Libertine in *The Way of the World*," *Papers on Language and Literature* 25 (1989): 376–97, arguing that the roots of libertinism can be found in French and English interpretations of Epicureanism.

15. Sade's version differs from that of his predecessors in that it is not directly informed by Hobbes, Voltaire, or other *philosophes*, and the books he lists as important to him differ only slightly from simple pornog-

raphy: *La Rhetorica della putana* (1612), *La Puttana errante* (1650), Milot's *L'Escole des filles* (1655), and Barrin's *Vénus dans las cloître* (1683), all of which were quickly translated into English and whose translators were subsequently prosecuted. See Leona Rostenberg, "Robert Stephens, Messenger of the Press: An Episode in 17th-Century Censorship," *Publications of the Bibliographical Society of America* 49 (1955): 131–52; David Saunders, "Copyright, Obscenity, and Literary History," *English Literary History* 57 (1990): 431–44.

16. For more sustained discussions of these matters, see Jean A. Perkins, "Irony and Candour in Certain Libertine Novels," *Studies on Voltaire and the Eighteenth Century* 60 (1968): 248–59; Barry Ivker, "Towards a Definition of Libertinism in 18th-Century French Fiction," *Studies on Voltaire and the Eighteenth Century* 73 (1970): 221–39; Lloyd R. Free, "Crebillon fils, Laclos, and the Code of the Libertine," *Eighteenth-Century Life* 1 (1974): 36–40; Beatrice C. Fink, "Sade's Libertine: A Pluralistic Approach," *Eighteenth-Century Life* 2 (1975): 34–37; Sylvie Romanowski, "Montesquieu's *Lettres persanes* and the Libertine Traditions," in *Libertinage and the Art of Writing*, ed. David Rubin (New York: AMS Press, 1992), 59–86. Also of use is Francine du Plessix Gray, *At Home with the Marquis de Sade: A Life* (New York: Penguin, 1999).

17. "The Properties of Libertinism," 81, 84. Compare Finke, 28: "For all his rebellious promiscuity, the aristocratic rake believed in the ideology that promoted patriarchy, primogeniture, and legitimate monarchy."

18. See "Pepys and the Private Parts of Monarchy," in *Culture and Society in the Stuart Restoration*, ed. MacLean, 103–5.

19. See W 5:389–443.

20. *Leviathan*, ed. C. B. MacPherson (New York: Pelican, 1968), 187, 160.

21. Barash: "More directly than any other woman writer between the death of Charles I in 1649 and the death of Anne in 1714, Behn calls the reader's attention to the conventions within which her cultural narratives operate" (103). See also Peggy Thompson, "Closure and Subversion in Behn's Comedies," in *Broken Boundaries: Women and Feminism in Restoration Drama*, ed. Katherine Quinsey (Lexington: University Press of Kentucky, 1996), 71–88.

22. *Maximes et Réflexions Diverses*, ed. Jean-Pol Caput (Paris: Larousse, 1975), 42.

23. *Leviathan*, ed. MacPherson, 129–30.

24. Ibid., 163.

25. Behn's flattering dedication to Peter Weston indicates her distaste for libertinism: "Many fine Gentleman I had in view, of Wit and Beauty; but still, though their Education, or a natural Propensity to Debauchery, I found those Vertues wanting, that should compleat that delicate Character, *Iris* gives her Lover; and which, at first Thought of You, I found center'd there to Perfection" (W 4:279).

26. As with so many other Restoration playwrights, Behn's indictment of foppery describes most of her rakes as well: "by a dire Mistake, conducted by vast Opinionatreism, and a greater portion of Self-love, than the rest of the Race of Man, he believes that the Affection in his Mein

and Dress, that Mathematical Movement, that Formality in every Action, that a Face manag'd with Care, and soften'd into Ridicule, the languishing Turn, the Toss, and the Back shake of the Periwig, is the direct Way to the Heart of the fine Person he adores; and instead of curing *Love* in his Soul, serves only to advance his Folly; and the more he is enamour'd, the more industriously he assumes (every Hour) the Coxcomb" (*The Fair Jilt* [W 3:8]).

27. "This more than Human Goodness, with the incouragement Your Royal Highness was pleas'd to give the Rover at his first appearance, and the concern You were pleas'd to have for his second, makes me presume to lay him at Your feet; he is a wanderer too, distrest; belov'd, the unfortunate, and ever constant to Loyalty; were he Legions he should follow and suffer still with so Excellent a Prince and Master" (Preface to *2 Rover* [W 6:228–29]).

28. For a discussion of the issue in the play, see Dagny Boebel, "In the Carnival World of Adam's Garden: Roving and Rape in Behn's *Rover*," in *Broken Boundaries: Women and Feminism in Restoration Drama*, ed. Katherine Quinsey, (Lexington: University Press of Kentucky, 1996), 54–70.

29. Burnet, later Bishop of Salisbury, gained great fame for his alleged bedside conversion of Rochester from libertinism to Anglicanism, which he recounts in *Some Passages of the Life and Death of the Right Honourable John Earl of Rochester, who Died the 26th of July, 1680* (London: Richard Chiswel, 1680). He chastises Rochester's niece Anne Wharton for her literary correspondence with Behn, which included an exchange of poems. The quotation is taken from *Letters between the Rev. J[ames]. G[ranger]., M. A., and Many of the Most Eminent Literary Men of His Time, Composing a Copious History and Illustration of His Biographical History of England*, ed. James P. Malcolm (London: Longman, 1805), 234. Aware of the Bishop's scorn for her, Behn's "A *Pindaric Poem* to the Reverend Doctor *Burnet*, on the Honour He Did Me of Enquiring after Me and My *Muse*" drips with sarcasm: "What must I suffer when I cannot pay / Your Goodness, your own generous way? / And make my stubborn Muse your Just Commands obey[?]" (46–48 [W 1:308–9]).

30. Finke makes this claim based on gender. With the conquest of the female object, the rake loses interest and pursues his interest in variety. "For this reason, a woman could never achieve a sexual conquest, because her only power lay in withholding sex" (27), apparently the "reason for the asymmetry in the libertine pose, for the impossibility of conceiving a truly female libertinism" that Finke states elsewhere (28). In her literary psychobiography of Behn, Todd speculates: "Suspecting but rarely admitting her own obsessive nature, she believed that sexual passion should result in enjoyment in the flesh and not be allowed to develop into a mind-binding construction such as love or romance. Love was the enemy of necessary self-promotion and she saw it as a mistaken result of culture. Sexual desire was implicated in women's social and psychological oppression, and, was an inevitably masochistic and addictive drug. Nowhere was sexual desire free from other desires, for ease, for significance, for mastery, and for degradation" (*Secret Life*, 333).

31. Her particular animus was that women themselves objected to the play, crying it down, offended by the portrayals of female libertinism in Lady Fancy and Lady Knowell. "I Printed this Play with all the impatient haste one ought to do, who would be vindicated from the most unjust and silly aspersion, Woman could invent to cast on Woman; and which only my being a Woman has procured me; *That it was Baudy*, the least and most Excusable fault in the Men writers, to whose Plays they all crowd, as if they came to no other end than to hear what they condemn in this: *but from a Woman it was unnaturall*" (W 6:5). She makes the same complaint about her female spectators later, especially their tendency to "Cry *Faugh*—at Words and Actions Innocent, / And make that naughty that was never meant" ("To *Henry Higden*, Esq; on his Translation of the *Tenth Satyr* of *Juvenal*," 1685, 79–80 [W 1:230]).

32. For example, In Act 4 of *The Country-Wife*, Lady Fidget admonishes Mr. Horner as he persuades her into the china-closet, "you must have a care of my dear Honour." See *The Complete Plays of William Wycherley*, ed. Gerald Weales (New York: Anchor, 1966), 324.

33. This thinly veiled retelling of a scandal involving Ford, Lord Grey, one of the principals in the Monmouth rebellion, depicts a man (Philander) who has an affair with his wife's sister (Silvia) by marrying her to someone else (Brilljard), the union providing the appropriate cover for the lovers' enjoyment, but complicated by the jealousy of the husband and the interest in Silvia by Philander's best friend (Cesario) after the pair flees to exile to avoid the revenge of her family once it discovers the ruse (W 2:vii-xiii and 443–61). Behn uses a mixture of the first- and third-person modes to show us Sylvia's awareness that she exhibits and reproduces the behavior that she abhors. See also Janet Todd, "Who Is Silvia? What Is She? Feminine Identity in Aphra Behn's *Love-Letters between a Nobleman and His Sister*," in *Aphra Behn Studies*, ed. Janet Todd (Cambridge: Cambridge University Press, 1996, 199–218.

34. Miranda, insatiable in her sexual appetites and political ambitions, attempts to seduce one lover even when he is in the confessional, disguised as a priest; she then cries rape when he refuses her and has him put in prison (W 3:13–26). She poisons the sister of a second lover who knows her true nature, "resolv'd to be the *Lucretia* that this young *Tarquin* should ravish" (28). "She was naturally Amorous, but extreamly Inconstant: She lov'd one for his Wit, another for his Face, and a third for his Mein; but above all, she admir'd *Quality*: *Quality* alone had the Power to attach her entirely; yet not to one Man, but that Virtue was still admir'd by her in all: wherever she found that, she lov'd, or at least acted the *Lover* with such Art, that (deceiving well) she fail'd not to compleat her Conquest" (11).

35. Cf. "fallite fallentes" (*Ars amatoria* 1.645).

36. Cloris is aggressive: "Her Hands his Bosom softly meet, / But not to put him back design'd, / Rather to draw 'em on inclin'd" (178); "Her timerous Hand she gently laid / (Or guided by Design or Chance) / Upon that Fabulous *Priapus*" (181). Two useful recent articles on the poem: Jessica Munns, " 'But to the Touch Were Soft': Pleasure, Power, and Impotence in

'The Disappointment' and 'The Golden Age,'" in *Aphra Behn Studies*, ed. Todd, 178–98; Lisa Zeitz and Peter Thoms, "Power, Gender, and Identity in Aphra Behn's 'The Disappointment,'" *Studies in English Literature* 37 (1997): 501–16.

37. Several poets, including Behn, Rochester, and the mysterious "Ephelia" among them, adopted the Ovidian poetic epistle as a means of expression, creating a site for discourse on gender relations in the Restoration that mirrors the business of Drury Lane. Edward Burns gives a brief overview of this late Restoration phenomenon, describing the conduciveness of Ovidian dramatic monologues of women abandoned by the heroic and egotistical men they love to the intrigues of Charles's court. These imitations of the *Heroides* "engage in a discourse of gender [so] that by using explicit and distinct 'male' or 'female' voices as a matter of writerly convention," these voices are "equally available as writing strategies to both men and women." See "Rochester, Lady Betty, and the Post-Boy," in *Reading Rochester*, ed. Edward Burns (New York: St. Martin's, 1995), 76.

38. See "On the Author of that Excellent Book Intituled *The Way to Health, Long Life, and Happiness*" (W 1:179–80). Tryon (1634–1703), committed to women's health issues, recommended vegetarianism as well as abstention from tobacco and alcohol.

39. Behn's use of "Bigot" with "Prayer" is metaphorical, consistent with the primary meaning of the word in her time, "A person obstinately and unreasonably wedded to a particular religious creed, opinion, or ritual" *(OED)*.

Chapter 5: The Juniper-Tree in Behn's Pastoral World

1. See *Poems on Several Occasions by the Right Honourable, the E. of R—*. There is no publisher and the place of publication is falsely listed as Antwerp. This collection ends with a triad of poems by Behn which she later reclaims: "The Disappointment"; "On a *Giniper Tree* now cut down to make *Busks*"; "On the Death of Mr. *Greenhill* The Famous *Painter*" (92–103). All three continued to be attributed to Rochester well into the eighteenth century. David M. Vieth discusses the bibliographic issues concerning these early printings in his landmark study, *Attribution in Restoration Poetry: A Study of Rochester's "Poems" of 1680* (New Haven: Yale University Press, 1963), 448–52. The first three letters of "Giniper" suggest the uses to which juniper berries would later be put as an opiate of the English masses during the Industrial Revolution.

2. See Dryden's prologue to *The Spanish Friar* (1680): "as 'tis my interest to please my audiences, so 'tis my ambition to be read: that I am sure is the more lasting and the nobler design: for the propriety of thoughts and words, which are the hidden beauties of a play, are but confusedly judged in the vehemence of action" (K 1:248). In contrast, Derek Hughes observes of Behn and her attitude to the publication of her plays: "she

did not revere the written page as the ultimate recourse"; "the stage was not a conjuring trick to divert attention from the text; it was a text in itself" (*The Theatre of Aphra Behn*, 192). However, as I argue here and elsewhere, her attitude toward the printing of her poetry was another matter entirely.

3. After line 66 of the copy text for this study, the description of triple mutual orgasm, the 1680 Rochester version includes "And had the *Nymph*, been half so kind, / As was the *Shepherd*, well inclin'd" to precede line 68, "Nor had the Mysterie ended there." If this couplet was Behn's or interpolated into her poem, she was wise to have excised it, since Cloris seems "kind" enough, most of the "Mysterie" having been explored. For a brief critical apparatus, see W 1:464.

4. See Todd (W 1:40; 1:464) and Summers (S 6:149), respectively. Todd adds the 1680 line in brackets and does not account for the alternate line in some 1684 printings. Germaine Greer, Jeslyn Medoff, Melinda Sansone, and Susan Hastings, ed., *Kissing the Rod: An Anthology of Seventeenth-Century Women's Verse* (New York: Farrar Straus Giroux, 1989) provides a handsome annotated edition of the poem (243–48), including an apparatus with variants from 1680. Like Todd's, the copy-text for the *Kissing the Rod* edition was a 1684 printing. It too omits a rhyming line, and like Summers, these editors provide no explanation or even knowledge that such a line exists in 1680 or in some versions of 1684. Nonetheless, Greer and her cohorts provide useful information in the commentary: "*Giniper-Tree*" was circulated in manuscript, of which a fair copy exists; juniper was a source of savin, known as an abortofacient; no other reference to juniper wood as ballast for corsets is known.

5. Rothstein's observations on the craft of the couplet during the period: "one would expect such poetry to be syntactically involved, so that each word, each idea has its proper place in the unit of the sentence. Such poetry should also bind line to line with care, and give each poetic unit an exact relationship to those around it. . . . One can argue . . . that its polish often contrasts ironically with the openness of the subject matter which it makes accessible to us but which it cannot tame" (*Restoration and Eighteenth-Century Poetry*, 59, 61).

6. "Women Becoming Poets," 345.

7. See Gardiner, "Liberty, Equality, Fraternity," 283–86; and Young, "Aphra Behn, Gender, and Pastoral," 526–30. Another recent study of interest is Alvin Snider, "Cartesian Bodies," *Modern Philology* 98 (2000): 299–319. This essay claims that "On a *Juniper-Tree*" partakes of the notion of Cartesian dualism between the mechanized and the human, the tree fulfilling the former category. "Behn's poem reveals an unexpected solidarity between human and non-human beings, . . . imagining an absolute alterity in the 'person' of a metaphorized tree" (302). Snider suggests that Behn learned about Descartes from her translation of Fontenelle's *Entretiens sur La Pluralité des Mondes* (1686), *A Discovery of New Worlds* (1688). He also suggests that Behn's poem promulgates "ethical hedonism and libertinism" (312), an idea with which I strongly disagree.

8. "Aphra Behn, Gender, and Pastoral," 529.

9. "Liberty, Equality, Fraternity," 284–85.

10. See Robert Markley and Molly Rothenberg, "Contestations of Nature: Aphra Behn's 'The Golden Age' and Sexualizing of Politics," in *Rereading Aphra Behn*, ed. Hutner, 301–3; and Jessica Munns, "'But to the Touch Were Soft': Pleasure, Power, and Impotence in 'The Disappointment' and 'The Golden Age,'" in *Aphra Behn Studies*, ed. Todd, 187. See also Germaine Greer, "'Alme in Liberate Avvezze': Aphra Behn's Version of Tasso's Golden Age," in *Aphra Behn: Identity, Alterity, Ambiguity*, ed. Mary Ann O'Donnell, Bernard Dhuic, and Guyonne Leduc (Paris: L'Harmattan, 2000), 225–33.

11. For the text and line numbers for *Sylva*, see W 1:311–53. The heading for Behn's section of the translation reads "*Of Plants*. Book VI. *Sylva*." The purpose of the Latin word is obscure. "Sylva" or "silva" (nominative singular) means "forest," "wood." If the subtitle was intended to offer a Latin equivalent of "trees" or "concerning trees," it should probably read either "arbores" (nominative plural), or, more correctly, "de arboribus" (dative plural).

12. See W 1:443–44. Virgil reads: "iuniperi grauis umbra; nocent et frugibus umbrae" (10.76); "the shade of the juniper [is] heavy; and the shade is harmful to the fruit." He also mentions the tree somewhat earlier in the collection: "stant et iuniperi" (*Eclogues* 7.53); "the junipers are still."

13. See "The Voice of the 'Translatress': From Aphra Behn to Elizabeth Carter," *Yearbook of English Studies* 28 (1998): 181–95.

14. The equation of trees with male potency is well known in anthropological studies from Sir James Frazier to Joseph Campbell. Ovid treats several juniper-like evergreens in *Metamorphoses* 10. Attis becomes a pine for Cybele, Adonis is born from Myrrha. Also, the poet Orpheus tells the story of Cyparissus, beloved of Apollo, the god of poetry, who is transformed into a cypress, another evergreen. In "On the *Death* of *Mr. Grinhil*," Behn instructs the nymphs to fashion wreaths of flowers "Mixt with the dismal *Cypress*" (69–70).

15. See S 6:422.

16. See Creech, trans., *The Odes, Satyrs, and Epistles of Horace*, 410.

17. Gardiner views the tree as simply the guardian of patriarchal values (284).

18. See *Poems by the Most Deservedly Admired Mrs. Katherine Philips, The Matchless Orinda: To Which Is Added Monsieur Corneille's Pompey & Horace, Tragedies, with Several Other Translations Out of French* (London: Printed by T. N. for Henry Herringman, 1678), 136. All citations from Philips are taken from this edition. Since it is without line-numbers, I use those established by George Saintsbury's edition of her poetry in *Minor Poets of the Caroline Period*, 1:485–612.

19. These are Gardiner's points, 285, 283, respectively.

20. For the foregoing four quotations, see *Poems*, 72, 94, 65–66, 67, respectively.

21. Rothstein's comments on Philips typify the dismissive tendency of earlier scholarship: "Her verse has the feeling of sincerity and it floats

on graceful cadences, but the content and expression are banal: these meditative lyrics, retirement poems, and verse of friendship have little to distinguish them apart from their having been written by the first Englishwoman not of noble blood to be celebrated for her writing" (*Restoration and Eighteenth-Century Poetry*, 170). In theory, such opinions differ little from those of James Sutherland and others cited in the Introduction that criticize Behn for immorality—the silencing effect is quite the same.

22. See Greer et al., ed., *Kissing the Rod*, 263.

23. The two foregoing quotations: *Works*, 45, 32.

24. All references to this playwright are taken from *The Plays of Sir George Etherege*, ed. Michael Cordner (Cambridge: Cambridge University Press, 1982).

25. *Works*, 143.

26. Ibid., 137.

27. *A History of English Dramatic Literature*, 2d ed., 3 vols. (Cambridge: Cambridge University Press, 1899; reprint, New York: Frederick Ungar, 1970), 3:453.

28. Young: "The identity of the juniper tree reveals confidence mitigated by subjectivity: strength restricted by external action and evaluation" ("Aphra Behn, Gender, and Pastoral," 526).

29. Compare Gardiner: "only sexual voyeurism provides Behn's tree a semblance of pleasure" (284).

30. Compare Greer et al., ed., *Kissing the Rod*, which argues that the phoenix merely symbolizes tumescence and detumescence (247).

31. Cotgrave (London: A. Islip) and Holme (Chester: Printed for the Author) provide the examples from *OED* s.v. "busk." The noun appears to have derived from the Middle English verb, which means "to prepare oneself, to dress."

32. *The Poems of Edmund Waller*, ed. G. Thorn Drury (London: Lawrence & Bullen, 1893), 95.

33. For a revealing look at the subject, see Valerie Steele, *The Corset: A Cultural History* (New Haven: Yale University Press, 2001).

34. For three somewhat contemporary essays on this subject in Restoration poetry, see Bruce Thomas Boehrer, "Behn's 'Disappointment' and Nashe's 'Choise of Valentines': Pornographic Poetry and the Influence of Anxiety," *Essays in Literature* 16 (1989): 172–87; Jim McGhee, "Obscene Libel and the Language of 'The Imperfect Enjoyment,'" in *Reading Rochester*, ed. Burns, 42–65; Zeitz and Thoms, "Power, Gender, and Identity in Aphra Behn's 'The Disappointment,'" 501–16. Each essay also contains an extensive survey of the seemingly inexhaustible number of studies on this topic. The Zeitz-Thoms study proposes the interesting idea that "The Disappointment" demonstrates the equality of Nature's operations for men and women. It also takes great delight in finding Lysander deficient, misunderstanding or ignoring Behn's empathy for inexperienced young men such as he. For example, it misreads "The Insensible fell weeping in his Hand" ("Disappointment," 90) as an instance of premature ejaculation (Zeitz and Thoms, 503). Actually, Behn's language implies that Ly-

sander manages to achieve only a momentary erection, frightened into impotence by his first sexual experience: "Faintness its slack'ned Nerves invade" ("Disappointment," 84). Therefore, the "weeping" may well be the presence of preejaculate in the penis, a common physical response in the sexually agitated male about which a mature and experienced person such as Behn must have known.

35. Behn probably lifted the name from the anonymous English translation, "The Lost Opportunity Recovered," of the French source-text for "The Disappointment," de Cantenac's "Sur une Impuissance" (1682), whose young man is named Lisandre. See W 1:392–93. The matter is discussed further in the next chapter.

36. I.e., Ralph Rainger's "A Guy What Takes His Time," *The Cosmopolitan Marlene Dietrich* (Columbia/Legacy CK 53209, 1993). Mae West had made this song famous in *I'm No Angel* (1933).

CHAPTER 6: "SWOLN TO LUXURIOUS HEIGHTS"

The second epigraph is quoted in Lynch, *Jacob Tonson*, 100.

1. It should be noted that the title page of *Poems on Several Occasions* names it *A Voyage to the Island of Love*, but this appears to be a nonce usage. The running title in the collection itself shortens the fifth word to *Isle*, hence this usage in the present study.

2. "Those who will take the pains to compare them, will find the English rather Paraphrases, than just Translations: but which sufficiently shew the Fancy and excellent Abilities of our Authress." See *An Account of the English Dramatick Poets*, 23.

3. See S 6:223 for biographical information about Tallemant and the publication history of *Le Voyage*.

4. Behn's preface to her translation of Fontenelle represents her clearest statement of translation theory, especially the many difficulties inherent in rendering French into English. Although she thinks one language more economical than the other, *"it runs a little rough in English, to express one French word, by two or three of ours,"* she prefers her native tongue because the French *"are not satisfied with the Advantages they have, but confound their own Language with needless Repetitions and Tautologies"* (W 4:75–76). Jane Jones points out that the Kent of Behn's childhood was full of Huguenot refugees, which would have facilitated her ability to learn French. See "New Light on the Background and Early Life of Aphra Behn," in *Aphra Behn Studies*, ed. Todd, 315. Also on the subject: Joanna Lipking, "At London and Paris: Pursuing Behn's French Connections," in *Aphra Behn: Identity, Alterity, Ambiguity*, ed. O'Donnell et al., 259–76.

5. See "The Politics of Translation," 165 and 174, respectively. Spearing's account is probably the best commentary on *A Voyage*. Her ultimate point is that in the translation, Behn uses "femini[ni]ty as a masquerade" (171). "The work is distinctively baroque in its layers of artifice: Behn is pretending that she is a man who is pretending to be dying of love. Her

art as a translator becomes at once that of a dramatist and that of an actress in a breeches role" (170). Naturally, this creates a number of paradoxes: "She enters into the text adopting the masculine subject-position of her French original, yet the very completeness of her impersonation turns it into a piece of acting, a masquerade" (166). Ellen Brinks argues that Behn had other influences besides that of her stated source-text. See "Meeting Over the Map: Madeleine de Scudéry's *Carte du Pays de Tendre* and Aphra Behn's *Voyage to the Isle of Love*," *Restoration: Studies in English Literary Culture 1660–1700* 17 (1993): 39–52.

6. The phrase is Summers's (S 6:223).

7. I.e., "Satyr [Say *Heav'n-born Muse*, for only thou canst tell]." Line 20 mentions a "*Bow'r* of Bliss" and then describes it in physiologically topographical terms. See *The Works of John Wilmot, Earl of Rochester*, ed. Harold Love (Oxford: Clarendon Press, 1999), 81–85.

8. Helga Drougge argues that Southerne generally subverts the sexual double-standard, and that women in his comedies "incorporat[e] . . . patterns of Restoration masculinity," particularly the cross-dressing Lucia ("Anthony") in *Sir Anthony Love* (1695). She "is a fantasy for women: the personification of adventurousness and carnival freedom, through imitation of a male pattern, and appropriately displaced in a foreign country." See "Love, Death, and Mrs. Barry in Thomas Southerne's Plays," 410, 415. One could easily say the same of Hellena in *1 Rover*. I have co-opted the phrase "transvestite ventriloquism" from Spearing (170), who applies it to Behn's "To a Brother of the Pen in *Tribulation*."

9. For an essay devoted to the subject of Behn's transgendering, see Susannah Quinsee, "Aphra Behn and the Male Muse," in *Aphra Behn: Identity, Alterity, Ambiguity*, ed. O'Donnell et al., 203–13. Todd claims that Behn often uses the name Aminta "for self-images in her pastoral poetry" (*Secret Life*, 141). If this is true, it may explain why she lifted it from Tallemant unchanged. Her predecessor's hero is named Tirsis. In renaming him Lysander, Behn may well have appropriated the moniker from the Lisandre of "Sur un impuissance," the source-text for "The Disappointment," apparently composed before all other poems in which the name "Lysander" appears, given its inclusion in the 1680 Rochester. In the headnote to *A Voyage*, the spelling of the name is "Lisander," but "Lysander" is the most common form in the text. Similarly, his correspondent's name is variously "Lysidas" and (Miltonically) "Lycidas"; the later version of the translation that features him is entitled *Lycidus* (1688). Tallemant's own poem is posthumously revised and expanded in 1685.

10. Hughes, *The Theatre of Aphra Behn*, 52.

11. Todd, *Secret Life*, 282.

12. See *The Collected Works of Abraham Cowley*, ed. Calhoun et al., vol. 2, pt. 1.

13. Ballaster notes that in the pseudo-Behn work *The Dumb Virgin* (1700), Maria is presented as "an object to be possessed to complete the male gazer's selfhood by perfectly mirroring his desire." It is also worth noting that in this work of fiction, pseudo-Behn uses a male narrator like Lysander, Dangerfield. See "'Prentices of State': Aphra Behn and the Female Plot," in *Rereading Aphra Behn*, ed. Hutner, 197.

14. Todd describes Behn as "a patriarchalist in state politics, a Cartesian in psychology, and a contract theorist in family matters" (*Secret Life*, 5). Snider analyzes her Cartesian leanings in great detail in "Cartesian Bodies."

15. Doody applies this observation to her reading of the psychology of Rochester's speakers. See *The Daring Muse*, 73.

16. Doody discusses these matters, again concerning Rochester, in her study (68, 130–31).

17. See *The Complete Works of William Wycherley*, ed. Summers, 3:155. In similar language but without the coarse good humor, Robert Gould says of women writers: "Their Verses are as vitious as their Tails: / Both are expos'd alike to publick View, / And both of 'em have their Admirers too" ("To a Gentlewoman who had written many fine Things, and not seen Mrs. *Phillips's* Poems"). See *Works*, 1:101.

18. "Androcentric literature is all the more efficient as an instrument of sexual politics because it does not allow the woman reader to seek refuge in her difference. Instead, it draws her into a process that uses her against herself. It solicits her complicity in the elevation of male difference into universality and, accordingly, the denigration of female difference into otherness without reciprocity. . . . Androcentricity is a sufficient condition for the process of immasculation." See "Reading Ourselves: Toward a Feminist Theory of Reading," in *Gender and Reading: Essays on Readers, Texts, and Contexts*, ed. Elizabeth Flynn and Patrocinio P. Schweickart (Baltimore: Johns Hopkins University Press, 1986), 41.

19. Todd analyzes the "cavalier" attitude to rape as follows: "First, Puritans and Dissenters tended to condemn rape and wife-beating, so that male violence had a whiff of the cavalier about it. Secondly, in heroic plays of the 1660's and early 1670's, rape had become the ultimate property crime; Behn's tendency to trivialise it was an escape from this degrading circumstance. And thirdly, when the tragic presentation of rape by male playwrights in the theatre was always voyeuristic, Behn's resolute refusal to allow rape dramatic seriousness can appear decently reactionary." See *Secret Life*, 216.

20. Compare Barash, who argues that in *A Voyage*, "Behn does not explicitly challenge the male-male frame of erotic reading, but she exposes it to be repetitive, self-indulgent, and, in the end, rather silly." See *English Women's Poetry*, 114.

21. For Cixous, see "The Laugh of the Medusa," trans. Keith Cohen and Paula Cohen, in *The Critical Tradition: Classic Texts and Contemporary Trends*, 2d ed., ed. David H. Richter (Boston: Bedford, 2000), 1454. It is hard to imagine Behn feeling Cixous's "torment of getting up to speak," with "heart racing, at times entirely lost for words" (1457). Yet this sentence seems particularly applicable to Behn in her milieu: "even if she transgresses, her words fall almost always upon the deaf male ear, which hears in language only that which speaks in the masculine" (1457). Todd has noted the unhappy inapplicability of much contemporary feminist literary theory to Behn, suggesting instead that she "made a public space

for women" (*Secret Life*, 4). David Roberts comments on women as a large and vital part of the Restoration theater audience: "There is . . . no indication that the unexceptional, inconspicuous majority needed to attend with a male escort any more than they had to worry about the damaging effects of a new play upon their reputations. It was for those who felt entitled to be conspicuous to retreat from view, behind a mask or away from the playhouse altogether, when embarrassment and self-betrayal threatened." See *The Ladies: Female Patronage of Restoration Drama 1660–1700* (Oxford: Clarendon Press, 1989), 94.

22. Barash, *English Women's Poetry*, 102–3.

23. Todd notes this in W 1:404.

24. *English Women's Poetry*, 114.

25. Gould, *Works*, 1:101.

26. See Todd for information about Carola Harsnett, and Lady Morland (1652–74), as well as speculation about Behn's relationship with her (*Secret Life*, 125–26; W 1:392).

27. "Lady *Morland*" is one of three pentameter verse epistles in *Poems upon Several Occasions*: the others are "*Oenone* to *Paris*" and "To a Brother of the Pen in *Tribulation*." Although Doody makes no mention of Behn in her study, her description of the "heroic epistle" is applicable here: "an expression of emotion which may or may not affect the addressee. Such an epistle is particularly suited, on the overt level of narrative, to feminine discourse, and, being female, it can thus forsake altogether the bounds of rhetorical styles or decorums, is not even required to be aware of generic distinctions" (87).

AFTERWORD

The epigraph is from Gould, *Works*, 2:22.

1. Respectively: "Women Becoming Poets," 335–55; *English Women's Poetry*.

2. Respectively: "Aphra Behn and the Ideological Construction of Restoration Literary Theory"; "'Prentices of State': Aphra Behn and the Female Plot," in *Rereading Aphra Behn*, ed. Hutner, 17–43, 187–211.

3. *The Works of Aphra Behn*, 6 vols. (London: 1915).

4. Doody, *The Daring Muse*, 130.

Bibliography

Agorni, Mirella. "The Voice of the 'Translatress': From Aphra Behn to Elizabeth Carter." *Yearbook of English Studies* 28 (1998): 181–95.

Alpers, Paul. *What Is Pastoral?* Chicago: University of Chicago Press, 1996.

Astbury, Raymond. "The Renewal of the Licensing Act in 1693 and Its Lapse in 1695." *The Library*, 5th ser., 33 (1978): 296–322.

Atwood, William. *The Idea of Christian Love, Being a Translation at the Instance of Mr. Waller of a Latin Sermon upon John XIII. 34, 35.* London: Jonathan Robinson, 1688.

Ballaster, Ros. *Seductive Forms: Women's Amatory Fiction from 1684 to 1740.* Oxford: Clarendon Press, 1992.

———. "'Prentices of State': Aphra Behn and the Female Plot." In *Rereading Aphra Behn: History, Theory, and Criticism,* ed. Heidi Hutner, 187–211. Charlottesville: University Press of Virginia, 1993.

Barash, Carol. *English Women's Poetry, 1649–1714: Politics, Community, and Linguistic Authority.* Oxford: Clarendon Press, 1996.

Barnard, John. "Dryden, Tonson, and the Subscriptions for the 1697 *Virgil.*" *Papers of the Bibliographical Society of America* 57 (1963): 129–51.

Behn, Aphra. *The Works of Aphra Behn.* 6 vols. Ed. Montague Summers. London, 1915. Reprint, New York: Benjamin Blom, 1967.

———. *The Works of Aphra Behn.* 7 vols. Ed. Janet Todd. Columbus: Ohio State University Press, 1993.

———. *Love-Letters between a Nobleman and His Sister.* Ed. Janet Todd. New York: Penguin, 1996.

Belin, Elaine V. *Redeeming Eve: Women Writers of the English Renaissance.* Princeton: Princeton University Press, 1987.

Benedict, Barbara M. *Making the Modern Reader: Cultural Mediation in Early Modern Literary Anthologies.* Princeton: Princeton University Press, 1996.

Bluche, François. *Louis XIV.* Trans. Mark Greengrass. New York: Watt, 1990.

Boebel, Dagny. "In the Carnival World of Adam's Garden: Roving and Rape in Behn's *Rover.*" In *Broken Boundaries: Women and Feminism in Restoration Drama,* ed. Katherine Quinsey, 54–70. Lexington: University Press of Kentucky, 1996.

Boehrer, Bruce Thomas. "Behn's 'Disappointment' and Nashe's 'Choise of Valentines': Pornographic Poetry and the Influence of Anxiety." *Essays in Literature* 16 (1989): 172–87.

Bordieu, Pierre. *Outline of a Theory of Practice*. Trans. Richard Nice. Cambridge: Cambridge University Press, 1977.

Brinks, Ellen. "Meeting Over the Map: Madeleine de Scudéry's *Carte du Pays de Tendre* and Aphra Behn's *Voyage to the Isle of Love*." *Restoration: Studies in English Literary Culture 1660–1700* 17 (1993): 39–52.

Burns, Edward, ed. *Reading Rochester*. New York: St. Martin's, 1995.

Canfield, J. Douglas, and Deborah C. Payne, ed.s *Cultural Readings of Restoration and Eighteenth-Century Theater*. Athens: University of Georgia Press, 1995.

Cixous, Hélène. "The Laugh of the Medusa." Trans. Keith Cohen and Paula Cohen. In *The Critical Tradition: Classic Texts and Contemporary Trends*, 2d ed., ed. David H. Richter, 1454–66. Boston: Bedford, 2000.

Clapp, Sarah Lewis Carol, ed. *Jacob Tonson, In Ten Letters by and about Him*. Austin: University of Texas Press, 1948.

Clifford, Martin. *Notes upon Mr. Dryden's Poems in Four Letters*. London: n.p., 1687.

Corns, Thomas. *Uncloister'd Virtue: English Political Literature, 1640–1660*. Oxford: Clarendon Press, 1992.

Cotgrave, Randle. *A Dictionarie of the French and English Tongues*. London: A. Islip, 1611.

Cowley, Abraham. *Poems*. London: Printed by [Thomas Newcombe] for Humphrey Moseley, 1656.

———. *The Complete Works in Verse and Prose of Abraham Cowley*. 2 vols. Ed. Alexander Grosart. Edinburgh: Constable, 1881. Reprint, New York: AMS Press, 1967.

———. *The Collected Works of Abraham Cowley*. 6 vols. Ed. Thomas O. Calhoun, Laurence Heyworth, Robert B. Hinman, William B. Hunter, and Allan Pritchard. Newark: University of Delaware Press, 1989-.

Creech, Thomas, trans. *T. Lucretius Carus, the Epicurean Philosopher, His Six Books De Natura Rerum, Done into English Verse, with Notes*. 2d ed. Oxford: L. Lichfield for Anthony Stevens, 1683.

———. *The Idylliums of Theocritus, with Rapin's Discourse of Pastorals Done into English*. Oxford: L. Lichfield for Anthony Stephens, 1684.

———. *The Odes, Satyrs, and Epistles of Horace, Done into English*. London: Printed for Jacob Tonson and Anthony Stephens, 1684.

———, ed. *Titi Lucretii Cari De rerum natura libri sex*. Oxford: A. Swall. & Tim. Child., 1695.

———, trans. *The Five Books of M[arcus]. Manilius containing a system of the ancient astronomy and astrology: together with the philosophy of the Stoicks*. London: J. Tonson, 1697.

Cudworth, Ralph. *The True Intellectual System of the Universe*. London: Printed for Richard Royston, 1678.

Denham, John. *The Poetical Works of Sir John Denham*. Ed. Theodore Howard Banks. New Haven: Yale University Press, 1928.

DeRitter, Jones. "The Gypsy, *The Rover*, and the Wanderer: Aphra Behn's Revision of Thomas Killigrew." *Restoration: Studies in English Literary Culture, 1660–1700* 10 (1986): 82–92.

Dhuicq, Bernard. "Aphra Behn: Théorie et pratique de la traduction au xviième siècle." *Franco-British Studies* 10 (1990): 75–98.

Doody, Margaret Anne. *The Daring Muse: Augustan Poetry Reconsidered*. Cambridge: Cambridge University Press, 1985.

Drougge, Helga. "Love, Death, and Mrs. Barry in Thomas Southerne's Plays." *Comparative Drama* 27 (1993–94): 408–25.

Dryden, John. *Essays of John Dryden*. 2 vols. Ed. Walter P. Ker. Oxford: Clarendon Press, 1900.

———. *The Letters of John Dryden, with Letters Addressed to Him*. Ed. Charles Eugene Ward. Durham, N.C.: Duke University Press, 1942.

———. *The Works of John Dryden*. 18 vols. Ed. Alan Roper et al. Berkeley and Los Angeles: University of California Press, 1956-.

Duffy, Maureen. *The Passionate Shepherdess: Aphra Behn 1640–89*. London: Methuen, 1989.

Duyfhuizen, Bernard. " 'That which I dare not name': Aphra Behn's 'The Willing Mistress.' " *English Literary History* 58 (1991): 63–82.

Edmonds, J. M., trans. *The Greek Bucolic Poets*. Cambridge: Harvard University Press, 1977.

Engell, James. *Forming the Critical Mind: Dryden to Coleridge*. Cambridge: Harvard University Press, 1989.

Etherege, George. *The Poems of Sir George Etherege*. Ed. James Thorpe. Princeton: Princeton University Press, 1962.

———. *The Plays of Sir George Etherege*. Ed. Michael Cordner. Cambridge: Cambridge University Press, 1982.

Evelyn, John. *The Diary of John Evelyn*. 6 vols. Ed. E. S. De Beer. Oxford: Clarendon Press, 1955.

Female Poems on Several Occasions. Written by Ephelia. London: William Downing, 1679.

Fink, Beatrice C. "Sade's Libertine: A Pluralistic Approach." *Eighteenth-Century Life* 2 (1975): 34–37.

Finke, Laurie. "Aphra Behn and the Ideological Construction of Restoration Literary Theory." In *Rereading Aphra Behn: History, Theory, and Criticism*, ed. Heidi Hutner, 17–43. Charlottesville: University Press of Virginia, 1993.

Fish, Stanley. *Is There a Text in This Class? The Authority of Interpretive Communities*. Cambridge: Harvard University Press, 1980.

Fisher, Nicholas, ed. *That Second Bottle: Essays on John Wilmot, Earl of Rochester*. Manchester: Manchester University Press, 2000.

Foxon, D. M. *Libertine Literature in England 1660–1745*. New Hyde Park, N.Y.: University Books, 1965.

Free, Lloyd R. "Crebillon fils, Laclos, and the Code of the Libertine." *Eighteenth-Century Life* 1 (1974): 36–40.

Gallagher, Catherine. "Who Was That Masked Woman? The Prostitute and the Playwright in the Comedies of Aphra Behn." *Women's Studies* 15 (1988): 23–42.

———. *Nobody's Story: The Vanishing Act of Women Writers in the Market-place*. Berkeley and Los Angeles: University of California Press, 1994.

Gardiner, Judith Kegan. "Liberty, Equality, Fraternity: Utopian Long-ings in Behn's Lyric Poetry." In *Rereading Aphra Behn: History, Theory, and Criticism*, ed. Heidi Hutner, 273–300. Charlottesville: University Press of Virginia, 1993.

Gardner, Helen, ed. *The Metaphysical Poets*. London: Penguin, 1957. Revised ed. 1966.

Gelber, Michael Werth. *The Just and the Lively: The Literary Criticism of John Dryden*. Manchester: Manchester University Press, 1999.

Goldberg, Jonathan. *Desiring Women Writing: English Renaissance Examples*. Stanford, Calif.: Stanford University Press, 1997.

Goreau, Angeline. *Reconstructing Aphra: A Social Biography of Aphra Behn*. Oxford: Oxford University Press, 1980.

———. "'Last Night's Rambles': Restoration Literature and the War between the Sexes." In *The Sexual Dimension in Literature*, ed. Alan Bold, 49–69. Totowa, N.J.: Barnes and Noble, 1982.

Gould, Robert. *The Works of Mr. Robert Gould*. 2 vols. London: Printed for R. Lewis, 1709.

Gray, Francine du Plessix. *At Home with the Marquis de Sade: A Life*. New York: Penguin, 1999.

Greenblatt, Stephen. *Shakespearean Negotiations: The Circulation of Social Energy in Renaissance England*. Berkeley and Los Angeles: University of California Press, 1988.

Greene, Thomas M. *The Light in Troy: Imitation and Discovery in Renaissance Poetry*. New Haven: Yale University Press, 1982.

Greer, Germaine. "'Alme in Liberate Avvezze': Aphra Behn's Version of Tasso's Golden Age." In Aphra *Behn: Identity, Alterity, Ambiguity*, ed. Mary Ann O'Donnell, Bernard Dhuic, and Guyonne Leduc, 225–33. Paris: L'Harmattan, 2000.

Greer, Germaine, Jeslyn Medoff, Melinda Sansone, and Susan Hastings, eds. *Kissing the Rod: An Anthology of Seventeenth-Century Women's Verse*. New York: Farrar Straus Giroux, 1989.

Hampton, Simon. "Rochester, *The Man of Mode*, and Mrs. Barry." In *That Second Bottle: Essays on John Wilmot, Earl of Rochester*, ed. Nicholas Fisher, 165–78. Manchester: Manchester University Press, 2000.

Helgerson, Richard. *Self-Crowned Laureates: Spenser, Jonson, Milton, and the Literary System*. Berkeley and Los Angeles: University of California Press, 1983.

Hill, Christopher. *The World Turned Upside Down: Radical Ideas During the English Revolution.* New York: Penguin, 1991.

———. *A Nation of Change and Novelty: Radical Politics, Religion and Literature in Seventeenth-Century England.* London: Routledge, 1991.

Hobbes, Thomas. *Leviathan.* Ed. C. B. MacPherson. New York: Pelican, 1968.

Holme, Randle. *The Academy of Armoury: Or, a Storehouse of Armoury and Blazon.* Chester: Printed for the Author, 1688.

Horace. *Q. Horati Flacci Opera.* 2d ed. Ed. E. C. Wickham and H. W. Garrod. Oxford: Clarendon Press, 1912.

Hornblower, Simon, and Anthony Spawnforth. *The Oxford Classical Dictionary.* 3d ed. Oxford: Oxford University Press, 1996.

Howe, Elizabeth. *The First English Actresses: Women and Drama, 1660–1700.* Cambridge: Cambridge University Press, 1992.

Hughes, Derek. *The Theatre of Aphra Behn.* London: Palgrave, 2001.

Hull, Suzanne. *Women According to Men: The World of Tudor-Stuart Women.* Walnut Creek, Calif.: Alta Mira Press, 1996.

Hume, Robert D. *The Development of English Drama in the Late Seventeenth Century.* Oxford: Clarendon Press, 1976.

———. "Elizabeth Barry's First Roles and the Cast of *The Man of Mode,*" *Theatre History Studies* 5 (1985); 16–19

Hutner, Heidi, ed. *Rereading Aphra Behn: History, Theory, and Criticism.* Charlottesville: University Press of Virginia, 1993.

Hutton, Ronald. *Charles II: King of England, Scotland, and Ireland.* Oxford: Clarendon Press, 1989.

Ivker, Barry. "Towards a Definition of Libertinism in 18th-Century French Fiction." *Studies on Voltaire and the Eighteenth Century* 73 (1970): 221–39.

Johnson, Samuel. *Lives of the English Poets.* 3 vols. Ed. George Birkbeck Hill. Oxford: Clarendon Press, 1905.

Jones, Jane. "New Light on the Background and Early Life of Aphra Behn." In *Aphra Behn Studies,* ed. Janet Todd, 310–20. Cambridge: Cambridge University Press, 1996.

Keeble, N. H. "Obedient Subjects? The Loyal Self in Some Later Seventeenth-Century Royalist Women's Memoirs." In *Culture and Society in the Stuart Restoration,* ed. Gerald MacLean, 201–18. Cambridge: Cambridge University Press, 1995.

King, Robert. *Henry Purcell.* London: Thames and Hudson, 1994.

Labio, Catherine. " 'What's in Fashion Vent': Behn, LaFayette, and the Market for Novels and Novelty." *Journal of Medieval and Early Modern Studies* 28 (1998): 119–38.

Langbaine, Gerard. *An Account of the English Dramatick Poets.* Oxford: Printed by L. L. for George West and Henry Clements, 1691.

La Rochefoucauld, Duc François de. *Maximes et Réflections Diverses.* Ed. Jean-Pol Caput. Paris: Larousse, 1975.

Lipking, Joanna. "At London and Paris: Pursuing Behn's French Connections." In *Aphra Behn: Identity, Alterity, Ambiguity*, ed. Mary Ann O'Donnell, Bernard Dhuic, and Guyonne Leduc, 259–76. Paris: L'Harmattan, 2000.

Love, Harold. "The Art of Adaptation: Some Restoration Treatments of Ovid." In *Poetry and Drama 1570–1700: Essays in Honour of Harold F. Brooks*, ed. Antony Coleman and Antony Hammond, 136–55. New York: Methuen, 1981.

Lowenthal, Cynthia. "Sticks, Rags, Bodies and Brocade: Essentializing Discourses and the Late Restoration Playhouse." In *Broken Boundaries: Women and Feminism in Restoration Drama*, ed. Katherine Quinsey, 219–33. Lexington: University Press of Kentucky, 1996.

Lynch, Kathleen. *Jacob Tonson: Kit-Cat Publisher*. Knoxville: University of Tennessee Press, 1971.

MacLean, Gerald. "Literature, Culture, and Society in Restoration England." In *Culture and Society in the Stuart Restoration*, ed. Gerald MacLean, 3–27. Cambridge: Cambridge University Press, 1995.

Markley, Robert. "'Be Impudent, Be Saucy, Forward, Bold, Touzing, and Leud': The Politics of Masculine Sexuality and Feminine Desire in Behn's Tory Comedies." In *Cultural Readings of Restoration and Eighteenth-Century Theater*, ed. J. Douglas Canfield and Deborah C. Payne, 114–40. Athens: University of Georgia Press, 1995.

Markley, Robert, and Molly Rothenberg. "Contestations of Nature: Aphra Behn's 'The Golden Age' and Sexualizing of Politics." In *Rereading Aphra Behn: History, Theory, and Criticism*, ed. Heidi Hutner, 301–21. Charlottesville: University Press of Virginia, 1993.

Maus, Katherine Eisaman. "'Playhouse Flesh and Blood': Sexual Ideology and the Restoration Actress." *English Literary History* 46 (1979): 595–617.

McGhee, Jim. "Obscene Libel and the Language of 'The Imperfect Enjoyment.'" In *Reading Rochester*, ed. Edward Burns, 42–65. New York: St. Martin's, 1995.

Mendelson, Sarah Heller. *The Mental World of Stuart Women: Three Studies*. Amherst: University of Massachusetts Press, 1987.

Mermin, Dorothy. "Women Becoming Poets: Katherine Philips, Aphra Behn, Anne Finch." *English Literary History* 57 (1990): 335–55.

Milton, John. *Complete Prose Works of John Milton*. 8 vols. Don M. Wolfe, general ed. New Haven: Yale University Press, 1953–82.

Munns, Jessica. "'I by a Double Right Thy Bounties Claim': Aphra Behn and Sexual Space." In *Curtain Calls: British and American Women and the Theater, 1660–1820*, ed. Mary Anne Schofield and Cecelia Macheski, 193–210. Athens: Ohio University Press, 1991.

———. "'Good, Sweet, Honey, Sugar-Candied Reader': Aphra Behn's Foreplay in Forewords," *Rereading Aphra Behn: History, Theory, and Criticism*, ed. Heidi Hutner, 44–62. Charlottesville: University Press of Virginia, 1993.

———. "'But to the Touch Were Soft': Pleasure, Power, and Impotence in 'The Disappointment' and 'The Golden Age.'" In *Aphra Behn Studies*, ed. Janet Todd, 178–98. Cambridge: Cambridge University Press, 1996.

Nussbaum, Felicity. *The Brink of All We Hate: English Satires on Women, 1660–1750*. Lexington: University Press of Kentucky, 1984.

O'Donnell, Mary Ann, Bernard Dhuic, and Guyonne Leduc, eds. *Aphra Behn: Identity, Alterity, Ambiguity*. Paris: L'Harmattan, 2000.

Parry, Graham. *The Seventeenth Century: The Intellectual and Cultural Context of English Literature, 1603–1700*. New York: Longman, 1989.

Patterson, Annabel. *Pastoral and Ideology: Virgil to Valéry*. Berkeley and Los Angeles: University of California Press, 1987.

Payne, Deborah C. "The Restoration Dramatic Dedication as Symbolic Capital." *Studies in Eighteenth-Century Culture* 20 (1990): 27–42.

Pearson, Jacqueline. *The Prostituted Muse: Images of Women and Women Dramatists, 1642–1737*. New York: Harvester, 1988.

Pechter, Edward. *Dryden's Classical Theory of Literature*. Cambridge: Cambridge University Press, 1975.

Perkins, Jean A. "Irony and Candour in Certain Libertine Novels." *Studies on Voltaire and the Eighteenth Century* 60 (1968): 248–59.

Pettit, Alexander. "Aphra's Bane." *Seventeenth-Century News* 56 (1998): 1–5.

Philips, Katherine. *Poems by the Most Deservedly Admired Mrs. Katherine Philips, The Matchless Orinda: To Which Is Added Monsieur Corneille's Pompey & Horace, Tragedies, with Several Other Translations Out of French*. London: Printed by T. N. for Henry Herringman, 1678.

Price, Bronwen. "Playing the 'Masculine Part': Finding a Difference within Behn's Poetry." In *Voicing Women: Gender and Sexuality in Early Modern Writing*, ed. Kate Chedgzoy, Melanie Hansen, and Suzanne Trill, 129–51. Pittsburgh: Duquesne University Press, 1997.

Quinsee, Susannah. "Aphra Behn and the Male Muse." In *Aphra Behn: Identity, Alterity, Ambiguity*, ed. Mary Ann O'Donnell, Bernard Dhuic, and Guyonne Leduc, 203–13. Paris: L'Harmattan, 2000.

Quinsey, Katherine, ed. *Broken Boundaries: Women and Feminism in Restoration Drama*. Lexington: University Press of Kentucky, 1996.

Revard, Stella P. "Katherine Philips, Aphra Behn, and the Female Pindaric." In *Representing Women in Renaissance England*, ed. Claude J. Summers and Ted-Larry Pebworth, 227–41. Columbia: University of Missouri Press, 1997.

Roberts, David. *The Ladies: Female Patronage of Restoration Drama 1660–1700*. Oxford: Clarendon Press, 1989.

Rochester, John Wilmot, Second Earl of. *Poems on Several Occasions by the Right Honourable, the E. of R—*. Antwerp: n.p., 1680.

———. *The Letters of John Wilmot, Earl of Rochester*. Ed. Jeremy Treglown. Chicago: University of Chicago Press, 1980.

———. *The Poems of John Wilmot, Earl of Rochester*. Ed. Keith Walker. Oxford: Blackwell, 1984.

———. *The Works of John Wilmot, Earl of Rochester*. Ed. Harold Love. Oxford: Clarendon Press, 1999.

Romanowski, Sylvie. "Montesquieu's *Lettres persanes* and the Libertine Traditions." In *Libertinage and the Art of Writing*, ed. David Rubin, 59–86. New York: AMS Press, 1992.

Roscommon, Wentworth Dillon, Earl of. *Horace's Art of Poetry made English by the Right Honourable Earl of Roscommon*. London: Printed for Henry Herringman, 1680.

Rosenmeyer, Thomas G. *The Green Cabinet: Theocritus and the European Pastoral Lyric*. Berkeley and Los Angeles: University of California Press, 1969.

Rostenberg, Leona. "Robert Stephens, Messenger of the Press: An Episode in 17th-Century Censorship." *Publications of the Bibliographical Society of America* 49 (1955): 131–52.

Rothstein, Eric. *Restoration and Eighteenth-Century Poetry 1660–1780*. London: Routledge & Kegan Paul, 1981.

Russell, Anne. "Aphra Behn's Miscellanies: The Politics and Poetics of Editing." *Philological Quarterly* 77 (1998): 307–28.

Rymer, Thomas. *Monsieur Rapin's Reflections on Aristotle's Treatise of Poesie: Containing the Necessary, Rational and Universal Rules for Epick, Dramatick, and the Other Sorts of Poetry*. London: Printed by T. Warren for H. Herringman, 1694.

Saintsbury, George, ed. *Minor Poets of the Caroline Period*. 3 vols. Oxford: Clarendon Press, 1905–21.

Salzman, Paul. "Aphra Behn: Poetry and Masquerade." In *Aphra Behn Studies*, ed. Janet Todd, 109–29. Cambridge: Cambridge University Press, 1996.

Saunders, David. "Copyright, Obscenity, and Literary History." *English Literary History* 57 (1990): 431–44.

Schweickart, Patrocinio P. "Reading Ourselves: Toward a Feminist Theory of Reading." In *Gender and Reading: Essays on Readers, Texts, and Contexts*, ed. Elizabeth Flynn and Patrocinio P. Schweickart, 39–48. Baltimore: Johns Hopkins University Press, 1986.

Snider, Alvin. "Professing a Libertine in *The Way of the World*." *Papers on Language and Literature* 25 (1989): 376–97.

———. "Cartesian Bodies." *Modern Philology* 98 (2000): 299–319.

Spearing, Elizabeth. "Aphra Behn: The Politics of Translation." In *Aphra Behn Studies*, ed. Janet Todd, 154–177. Cambridge: Cambridge University Press, 1996.

Spencer, Jane. *Aphra Behn's Afterlife*. Oxford: Oxford University Press, 2000.

Spingarn, J. E., ed. *Critical Essays of the Seventeenth Century*. 3 vols. Oxford: Clarendon Press, 1907. Reprint, Bloomington: Indiana University Press, 1963.

Steele, Valerie. *The Corset: A Cultural History.* New Haven: Yale University Press, 2001.

Steibel, Arlene. "Not Since Sappho: The Erotic in Poems of Katherine Philips and Aphra Behn." In *Homosexuality in Renaissance and Enlightenment England: Literary Representations in Historical Context,* ed. Claude J. Summers and Ted-Larry Pebworth, 153–71. New York: Harrington Park, 1992.

———. "Subversive Sexuality: Masking the Erotic in Poems by Katherine Philips and Aphra Behn." In *Renaissance Discourses of Desire,* ed. Claude J. Summers and Ted-Larry Pebworth, 223–36. Columbia: University of Missouri Press, 1993.

Summers, Claude J., and Ted-Larry Pebworth, eds. *Renaissance Discourses of Desire.* Columbia: University of Missouri Press, 1993.

———. *Representing Women in Renaissance England.* Columbia: University of Missouri Press, 1997.

Sutherland, James R. *English Literature of the Late Seventeenth Century.* Oxford: Clarendon Press, 1969.

Swift, Jonathan. *The Writings of Jonathan Swift.* Ed. Robert A. Greenberg and William B. Piper. New York: Norton, 1973.

Thompson, Peggy. "Closure and Subversion in Behn's Comedies." In *Broken Boundaries: Women and Feminism in Restoration Drama,* ed. Katherine Quinsey, 71–88. Lexington: University Press of Kentucky, 1996.

Thompson, Roger. *Unfit for Modest Ears: A Study of Pornographic, Obscene, and Bawdy Works Written or Published in England in the Second Half of the Seventeenth Century.* London: Macmillan, 1979.

Todd, Janet. "Aphra Behn: A Female Poet." *Studies on Voltaire and the Eighteenth Century* 304 (1992): 834–37.

———. "Who Is Silvia? What Is She? Feminine Identity in Aphra Behn's *Love Letters between a Nobleman and His Sister.*" In *Aphra Behn Studies,* ed. Janet Todd, 199–218. Cambridge: Cambridge University Press, 1996.

———. *The Secret Life of Aphra Behn.* New Brunswick, N.J.: Rutgers University Press, 1997.

———, ed. *Aphra Behn Studies.* Cambridge: Cambridge University Press, 1996.

Turner, Cheryl. *Living by the Pen: Women Writers in the Eighteenth Century.* London: Routledge, 1992.

Turner, James Grantham. "The Properties of Libertinism." *Eighteenth-Century Life* 9 (1985): 75–87.

———. *One Flesh: Paradisal Marriage and Sexual Relations in the Age of Milton.* Oxford: Clarendon Press, 1987.

———. "The Libertine Sublime: Love and Death in Restoration England." *Studies in Eighteenth-Century Culture* 19 (1989): 99–115.

———. "Pepys and the Private Parts of Monarchy." In *Culture and Society in the Stuart Restoration,* ed. Gerald MacLean, 95–110. Cambridge: Cambridge University Press, 1995.

———. *Libertines and Radicals in Early Modern London: Sexuality, Politics and Literary Culture, 1630–1685.* Cambridge: Cambridge University Press, 2002.

———. *Schooling Sex: Libertine Literature and Erotic Education in Italy, France, and England, 1534–1685.* Oxford: Oxford University Press, 2003.

Vieth, David. *Attribution in Restoration Poetry: A Study of Rochester's "Poems" of 1680.* New Haven: Yale University Press, 1963.

Wagenknecht, Edward. "In Praise of Mrs. Behn." *Colophon* 18 (1934): 17–32.

Waller, Edmund. *The Works of Edmond Waller Esquire, Lately a Member of the Honourable House of Commons, In this present Parliament.* London: Printed for Thomas Walkley, 1645.

———. *The Poems of Edmund Waller.* Ed. G. Thorn Drury. London: Lawrence & Bullen, 1893.

Ward, Adolphus William. *A History of English Dramatic Literature.* 2d ed. 3 vols. Cambridge: Cambridge University Press, 1899. Reprint, New York: Frederick Ungar, 1970.

Weil, Rachel. "Sometimes a Scepter Is Only a Scepter: Pornography and Politics in Restoration England." In *The Invention of Pornography: Obscenity and the Origins of Modernity, 1500–1800,* ed. Lynn Hunt, 124–53. New York: Zone Books, 1993.

Weinbrot, Howard D. *The Formal Strain: Studies in Augustan Imitation and Satire.* Chicago: University of Chicago Press, 1969.

———. "'An Ambition to Excell': The Aesthetics of Emulation in the Seventeenth and Eighteenth Centuries." *Huntington Library Quarterly* 48 (1985): 121–39.

Williams, Andrew. "Soft Women and Softer Men: The Libertine Maintenance of the Masculine." In *The Image of Manhood in Early Modern Literature,* ed. Andrew Williams, 95–118. Westport, Conn.: Greenwood Press, 1999.

Winchilsea, Anne Finch, Countess of. *Selected Poems of Anne Finch, Countess of Winchilsea.* Ed. Katharine M. Rogers. New York: Ungar, 1979.

Winn, James Anderson. *John Dryden and His World.* New Haven: Yale University Press, 1987.

———. "Dryden's Epistle before Creech's Lucretius: A Study in Restoration Ghostwriting." *Philological Quarterly* 71 (1992): 47–68.

Woolf, Virginia. *A Room of One's Own and Three Guineas.* London: Chatto & Windus, 1984.

Wycherley, William. *The Complete Works of William Wycherley.* 4 vols. Ed. Montague Summers. London, 1924. Reprint, New York: Russell and Russell, 1964.

———. *The Complete Plays of William Wycherley.* Ed. Gerald Weales. New York: Anchor, 1966.

Young, Elizabeth V. "Aphra Behn, Gender, and Pastoral." *Studies in English Literature* 33 (1993): 523–43.

———. "Aphra Behn's Horace." *Restoration: Studies in English Literary Culture 1660–1700* 23 (1999): 76–90.

Zeitz, Lisa, and Peter Thoms. "Power, Gender, and Identity in Aphra Behn's 'The Disappointment.'" *Studies in English Literature* 37 (1997): 501–16.

Index

Adams, John, 20
Addison, Joseph, 36
Agorni, Mirella, 146
Alighieri, Dante, 47, 77, 128, 165, 208 n. 8
allegory, 72, 155; in *A Voyage to the Isle of Love*, 165, 167, 169–73, 177
Alpers, Paul, 211 n. 6
androgyny: and Behn, 21, 22, 23, 34, 150, 178, 213 n. 15; and Cowley, 73–74, 78; in "To the Fair *Clarinda*," 24, 25, 63, 74, 141, 150; in *A Voyage to the Isle of Love*, 164–97
Aristotle, 88–89, 111, 211 n. 7
Ascham, Roger, 77–78
Astbury, Raymond, 209 n. 13
Atwood, William, 45
Augustine, 87

Ballaster, Ros, 18, 25, 84, 199, 203 n. 7, 225 n. 13
Banister, John, 212 n. 12
Barash, Carol, 25, 78, 190, 199, 201 n. 1 and 216 n. 10, 217 n. 21 and 226 n. 20
Barber, Mary, 47
Barker, Jane, 200
Barnard, John, 208 n. 11
Barry, Elizabeth, 121–22, 142, 215 n. 5, 225 n. 8
Behn, Aphra: and Cowley, 24, 28, 40, 48, 60, 64, 65–85, 146–47, 155, 174; and Dryden, 19, 23, 44, 58, 118, 204 n. 11; effect on her successors, 25, 151–52, 154–55, 199–202, 205 n. 21, 205 n. 31; and John Hoyle, 49–50, 55–56, 58, 60, 92, 96, 98, 101, 103, 108, 116, 127;

knowledge of French, Latin, 23, 55, 57–58, 78, 85, 86–118, 146–47, 164–97, 199–201, 211 n. 1 and 212 n. 8, 212 n. 14, 213 n. 15, 213 n. 16, 221 n. 7, 222 n. 11, 224 n. 2, 224 n. 4; and libertinism, 118, 119–42, 147, 216 n. 10 and 218 n. 30 and 219 n. 31; and music, 50–51, 53–55, 72, 93, 212 n. 12; and Philips, 149–55, 160; political conservatism of, 18, 38, 204 n. 8 and 205 n. 26 and 226 n. 14; portrayal of female sexuality, 53, 91–92, 96, 99, 119, 140, 143–63, 219 n. 34; portrayal of male sexuality, 53, 76, 95, 99, 119, 133–36, 140, 143–63; 164–97, 205 n. 26, 224 n. 5; reception of her poetry, 17–29, 34–35, 43–45, 66, 103, 150–52, 154–55, 198–202, 203 n. 4, 205 n. 21, 210 n. 19; and Rochester, 28, 46; 118, 119–42; self-display, subjectivity, 17–18; 19–23, 25, 26, 34, 39, 73, 94, 114, 120, 143, 151, 164–97, 200–202, 203 n. 2, 204 n. 13, 204 n. 16, 205 n. 31, 216 n. 10, 221 n. 2, 224 n. 4; and translation theory, 78, 86–118, 146–47, 210 n. 16, 221 n. 7, 224 n. 2, 224 n. 4; dramatic works: *The Amorous Prince*, 168, 185; *The City Heiress*, 129–31, 137, 189; *The Debauchee*, 126; *The Dutch Lover*, 129–31, 168; *The False Count*, 214 n. 18; *The Feign'd Curtizans*, 129–31; *The Forc'd Marriage*, 185; *The Luckey Chance*, 145; *The Roundheads*, 125, 137, 145; *1 Rover*, 24, 121–22, 132–36, 176,

178, 185, 216 n. 8, 225 n. 8; *2 Rover*, 122, 135, 216 n. 9; *Sir Patient Fancy*, 45, 131, 139, 141, 185, 211 n. 3; *The Town-Fopp*, 129–31; *Poems upon Several Occasions*: "The Answer," 52; "A Ballad on Mr. *J. H.* to *Amoret*," 49–50, 60, 96, 108, 116, 176, 182; "The Cabal at *Nickey Nackeys*," 57; "The Complaint," 50–51, 174; "The Counsel," 54, 136; "A Dialogue for an Entertainment at Court," 55–56, 93; "The Disappointment," 24, 25, 52–53, 61, 63, 82, 91, 98, 100, 116, 136, 138, 140, 153, 162–63, 167–68, 176, 180, 183–84, 186, 190, 200, 202; "The Dream," 53, 61, 97; "A Farewel to *Celladon*," 19, 49–50, 60, 63–64, 68, 103, 116, 141, 169; "The Golden Age," 42, 49–50, 53, 60, 62–64, 76, 81, 83, 93, 103, 105, 115, 117, 126, 137, 142, 145, 157, 173, 180, 186, 188, 190, 202; "In Imitation of *Horace*," 55, 62, 105, 173; "The Invitation [Damon, I cannot blame your will]," 50–51, 55, 60–61, 103; "The Invitation: A Song," 61, 97; "A letter to a Brother of the Pen," 53, 61, 129, 201, 225 n. 8, 227 n. 27; "Love Arm'd," 50–51, 60, 97, 117, 176; "Love Reveng'd," 57; "An *Ode* to *Love*," 57; "On a Copy of Verses made in a Dream," 51–52, 60, 97, 117, 174–75, 193; "On the Death of the Late Earl of *Rochester*," 119–20; "On the Death of Mr. *Grinhil*," 49–50, 59, 68, 116–17, 142, 201, 222 n. 14; "On her Loving Two Equally," 54, 107, 118, 141, 165, 183; "On a *Juniper-Tree*," 24, 28, 49, 53, 58, 60–61, 63–64, 74, 91, 95, 96, 98, 99, 103, 116, 141–42, 143–63, 167–68, 180, 186, 202; "On a Locket of Hair," 53, 62; "On Mr. *J. H.* in a fit of sickness," 55–56, 60, 68, 96, 138, 175; "Our Cabal,"

26, 49–50, 60, 74, 93, 107–8, 127, 175, 179; "A Paraphrase on the Eleventh Ode . . . of . . . *Horace*," 42, 136; "A Paraphrase on *Oenone* to *Paris*," 23, 57–58, 62, 76, 84, 91, 97, 98, 127, 141, 175, 182, 201, 227 n. 27; "The Reflection," 54, 61, 97, 105, 130, 140, 193; "The Return," 51–52, 61, 93, 97, 140; "The Sence of a Letter sent me," 51–52, 61, 93; "Silvio's Complaint," 55, 174; "Song to *Ceres*," 51–52, 186; "A Song in the same Play," 51–52, 118; "Song: To *Pesibles* Tune," 54, 174; "Song [When *Jemmy* first began to love]," 50–51, 61, 97; "The Surprize," 55; "To *Henry Higden*," 33, 69, 219 n. 31; "To the Honourable *Edward Howard*," 59, 68; "To *Lysander*, . . . Loves Fire," 55–56, 62, 64, 78–84, 96, 137, 168, 188; "To *Lysander* at the *Musick-Meeting*," 56–57, 62, 72, 76, 107, 118, 168, 184; "To *Lysander* on some Verses he writ," 55–56, 62, 97, 105, 140, 168, 173; "To Mr. *Creech*," 19, 51–52, 60, 86, 99, 108, 116, 118, 147–48, 211 n. 1, 211 n. 4, 214 n. 20; "To Mrs. *W*.," 51–52, 59, 135, 186, 204 n. 12; "To My Lady *Morland*," 51–52, 61, 191–97; 201, 227 n. 27; "A Translation," 57, 136; *A Voyage to the Isle of Love*, 21, 26, 27, 28, 46, 48, 57–58, 63–65, 72, 75, 76, 83, 87, 99, 102, 107, 142, 145, 164–97, 201; "The Willing Mistriss," 50–51, 61, 91, 157; "The Wish," 71; poetical works (miscellaneous): *La Montre: Or, The Lover's Watch*, 24, 128–31, 136, 168, 217 n. 25; (dedication); "A Letter to Mr. *Creech* at Oxford," 41; *Lycidus*, 48, 152; "On the Author of . . . *The way to Health*" (i.e., Thomas Tryon), 220 n. 38; "On the Death of *E. Waller*, Esq.," 42, 45, 46, 206 n. 43;

"On Desire," 75; "A Pindaric Poem to the Reverend Doctor *Burnet*," 70, 218 n. 29; "A Satyr on Doctor Dryden," 204 n. 11; *Sylva*, 146–47, 222 n. 11; "To *Alexis* in Answer to His Poem against Fruition," 130, 141, 151, 186, 189; "To the Fair *Clarinda*," 24, 25, 63, 74, 141, 150, 214 n. 18; prose works: *A Discovery of New Worlds*, 210 n. 16, 221 n. 7, 224 n. 4; *The Fair Jilt*, 137, 139–40, 178, 218 n. 26, 219 n. 34; "The History of the Nun," 62, 127; *Love-Letters between a Nobleman and His Sister*, 123, 132, 137–39, 216 n. 9, 219 n. 33; *Oroonoko*, 19, 24, 178, 200; Preface to *The Dutch Lover*, 29, 120–21, 125–26; Preface to *The Fair Jilt*, 29; Preface to *The Luckey Chance*, 62, 203 n. 2; Preface to *2 Rover*, 218 n. 27; Preface to *Sir Patient Fancy*, 136, 219 n. 31; *Seneca Unmasqued*, 126, 131

Benedict, Barbara M., 204 n. 13
Blackmore, Richard, 43–45
Bluche, François, 207 n. 45
Boebel, Dagny, 218 n. 28
Boehrer, Bruce Thomas, 223 n. 34
Boethius, 128, 165
Bonnecorse, Balthazar de, 24, 128, 164, 168
Bordieu, Pierre, 207 n. 5
Bosch, Hieronymus, 177
Brinks, Ellen, 225 n. 5
Broome, William, 47
Buckingham, George Villiers, Second duke of, 47
Bunyan, John, 36
Burnet, Gilbert, 36, 70, 135, 199, 218 n. 29
Burnet, Thomas, 36
Burns, Edward, 220 n. 37

Cantenac, de, 224 n. 35
Carew, Thomas, 157
Carter, Elizabeth, 47
Cassini, Giovanni, 36

Catharine of Braganza, 37
Catullus, 57
cavalier poetry, 71, 161, 179, 226 n. 19
Cavendish, Margaret, duchess of Newcastle, 204 n. 8
Charles II, 34, 36–39, 75, 124–25, 146, 151, 213 n. 17
Chaucer, Geoffrey, 65, 202
Chudleigh, lady Mary, 47
Cicero, 77
Cixous, Hélène, 185, 226 n. 21
Clapp, Sarah Lewis Carol, 205 n. 30
Clef d'Amors, La, 177
Cleveland, Barbara Palmer (or Villiers), duchess of, 34, 37, 39, 125, 155
Cleveland, John, 33
Clifford, Martin, 205 n. 33
Congreve, William: and *The Way of the World*, 35, 47, 121, 141
Cooper, John, 20, 22, 23
Corneille, Pierre, 36, 166
Corns, Thomas, 207 n. 50
Cotgrave, Randle, 160
Cotton, Charles, 47
couplet, heroic, 50, 53, 59–60, 61, 69, 169, 221 n. 5
Cowley, Abraham, 21, 22, 34, 55, 58, 86, 103, 202, 204 n. 17; and androgyny, 73–74, 165; and eroticism, 72–76; influence on Behn, 24, 28, 40, 48, 60, 64, 65–85, 146–47, 155, 165–66, 174; poetic form and meter, 65–71; reputation, 32, 65–70, 209 n. 5; influence on Rochester, 65–66
Crashaw, Richard, 33
Crawford, Joan, 127
Creech, Thomas, 20, 21, 22, 23, 27, 35, 46, 51, 86–118, 209 n. 5; editor of Lucretius, 211 n. 2; homosexuality, 91–95, 105–8; knowledge of classical prosody, 102; relationship with Behn, 85, 86–87, 91–101, 166; translations: of Horace, 101–08, 147–49, 154, 159, 212 n.

13, 213 n. 14, 213 n. 17; of Lucretius, 108–18, 122, 124, 135, 165,
211 n. 4, 214 n. 23; of Marcus Manilius and Plutarch, 211 n. 2; of
Rapin, 87–91; of Theocritus, 91–
101, 105, 146, 147
Crisp, Tobias, 123
Crowne, John, 35

Davenant, William, 31, 32, 77,
210 n. 21
Davys, Mary, 126
Defoe, Daniel, 35
Democritus, 111
Denham, John, 32, 47, 78
DeRitter, Jones, 216 n. 8
Descartes, René, 175, 221 n. 7,
226 n. 14
Dickinson, Emily, 61, 198
Dietrich, Marlene, 163
Donne, John, 24, 32, 33, 60, 68, 72,
73, 157–58
Doody, Margaret Anne, 201, 206 n.
37, 206 n. 38, 206 n. 40, 208 n. 17,
208 n. 18, 212 n. 13, , 226 n. 15,
227 n. 27, 227 n. 4
Drougge, Helga, 215 n. 5, 225 n. 8
Dryden, John, 29, 35, 36, 39, 47, 56,
109, 194, 204 n. 19, 206 n. 43, 208 n.
11; and Behn, 19, 23, 44, 58, 118,
155, 204 n. 11, 215 n. 25; and
Creech's translation of Lucretius, 111, 114, 125, 214 n. 23;
definition of wit, 26–27, 33, 210 n.
21; dramatic and poetic theory,
30–32, 45, 48, 61–62, 115, 143,
206 n. 39, 220 n. 2; imitation theory, 77–78, 85, 110; translation
theory, 77, 209 n. 15
Duffy, Maureen, 215 n. 25
D'Urfey, Thomas, 133
Duyfhuizen, Bernard, 214 n. 18

Egerton, Sarah Fyge, 47
Eliot, T. S., 34, 59, 65, 67, 74
Elys, Edmund, 70, 75
Engell, James, 30
"Ephelia," 17, 47

Epicurus, epicureanism, 108–18,
124, 131, 216 n. 14
Etherege, George (and *The Man of
Mode*), 35, 47, 120, 129, 133, 152,
158, 223 n. 24
Evelyn, John, 35, 40–42, 109, 207 n.
52

femininity, construction of: in
Behn as poet, 20–22, 23, 26, 27,
69, 74, 120; and Philips, 152–53;
in "On a *Juniper-Tree*," 154–59,
161; in *A Voyage to the Isle of
Love*, 181–86; and women writers, 198–202
feminism, 18, 25, 120–22, 154, 161,
167, 185, 198–202, 203 n. 2, 213 n.
15, 226 n. 21
Finch, Anne Kingsmill, countess
of Winchilsea, 44, 47, 199
Fink, Beatrice C., 217 n. 16
Finke, Laurie, 18, 20, 29, 30, 199,
204 n. 15, 209 n. 4, 217 n. 17, 218 n.
30
Fish, Stanley, 79
Flatman, Thomas, 28, 35, 204 n. 17
Flecknoe, Richard, 32
Fletcher, Thomas, 47
Fontenelle, Bernard le Bovier de,
78, 164, 199, 221 n. 7, 224 n. 4
form, poetic, 22–24, 208 n. 15, 208 n.
17, 209 n. 2, 221 n. 5; Behn's ex-
periments with, 50, 53, 58–62,
78–84, 169, 212 n. 14; influence of
Cowley, 66–70
Foxon, D. M., 216 n. 13
Frazer, Cary, 155
Free, Lloyd R., 217 n. 16

Gallagher, Catherine, 203 n. 4,
204 n. 16
Gardiner, Judith Kegan, 26, 84,
221 n. 7, 222 n. 17, 222 n. 19, 223 n.
29
Gardner, Helen, 66, 145, 208 n. 2
Gelber, Michael Werth, 30–31,
206 n. 39, 206 n. 44, 208 n. 1
gender roles: and Behn's plays,
133–36, 225 n. 8; and Behn's

poetry, 20–22, 120, 140, 152–53, 166, 215 n. 2; and libertinism, 218 n. 30; and women writers, 17–18; 23, 25, 152–53, 198–202, 203 n. 2; and *A Voyage to the Isle of Love*, 165–97, 225 n. 5, 225 n. 9
Gildon, Charles, 47
Godolphin, Sidney, 38
Goldberg, Jonathan, 205 n. 31
Goreau, Angeline, 18, 203 n. 4, 203 n. 7, 204 n. 16, 204 n. 19
Gould, Robert, 17, 26, 44–45, 72, 120, 155, 191, 198, 202, 226 n. 17
Gray, Francine du Plessix, 217 n. 16
Greenblatt, Stephen, 46
Greene, Thomas M., 209 n. 14, 210 n. 16
Greer, Germaine, 221 n. 4, 222 n. 10, 223 n. 22, 223 n. 30
Gwyn, Nell, 37, 125, 211 n. 3

Halifax, George Savile, marquis of, 36
Hampton, Simon, 215 n. 5
Harvey, William, 46
Helgerson, Richard, 19
Herbert, George, 33, 60
Herrick, Robert, 33, 91
Hill, Christopher, 207 n. 50, 216 n. 12
Hobbes, Thomas: and libertinism, 111, 123, 124–25, 131, 216 n. 15; poetic theory, 31, 59, 115; politics, 128
Hogarth, William, 177
Holme, Randle, 160
Homer, 208 n. 8
homosexuality: in Behn's poetry, 214 n. 18; in Creech's Horace, 105–08; in Creech's Theocritus, 91–95; and libertinism, 124
Hondius, Abraham, 40, 207 n. 51
Honour, 64, 72, 83, 137, 145, 152, 159, 219 n. 32; in *A Voyage to the Isle of Love*, 167, 171, 176, 181, 182, 188–89
Horace, 28, 35, 55, 57, 63, 85, 201,

208 n. 8; Creech's translation, 94, 95, 101–08, 147–49, 154, 159; Roscommon's translation of *Ars poetica*, 212 n. 13
Howard, Edward, 56, 208 n. 14
Howard, Robert, 26, 31, 47, 56, 210 n. 21
Hoyle, John (also Mr. J. H.), 49–50, 55–56, 58, 60, 92, 96, 98, 101, 103, 108, 116, 127, 175, 182, 202
Hughes, Derek, 203 n. 1, 208 n. 10, 220–21 n. 2
Hume, Robert D., 206 n. 39, 215 n. 5
Hutton, Ronald, 207 n. 45
Hyde, Laurence, Earl of Rochester, 36, 39

imitation/emulation, 28, 29, 55, 66–85, 148, 166, 206 n. 41, 209 n. 4, 209 n. 14, 210 n. 16, 210 n. 19, 211 n. 1
Innocent XI, 39
Ivker, Barry, 217 n. 16

Jakobson, Roman, 206 n. 41
James, duke of York (afterward James II), 23, 37, 38, 39, 41, 132, 135, 204 n. 11, 208 n. 20
James, earl of Salisbury, 45
Jenkins, George, 24
Jermyn, Henry, earl of St. Albans, 36
Johnson, Samuel, 59, 65, 67, 69, 74, 75, 206 n. 39
Jones, Jane, 224 n. 4
Jonson, Ben, 56, 61, 120–21, 208 n. 14
Juvenal, 33, 86, 211 n. 2

Keats, John, 61, 160
Keeble, N. H., 25, 204 n. 8, 204 n. 20
Kendrick, Dr. Daniel, 34, 152
Killigrew, Anne, 18
Killigrew, Thomas, 122, 216 n. 8
King, Robert, 207 n. 48

Labio, Catherine, 204 n. 10, 204 n. 16

Langbaine, Gerard, 78, 165, 210 n. 19, 224 n. 2

La Rochefoucauld, François, duc de, 124, 175–76; Behn's translation of (*Seneca Unmasqued*), 126, 131, 164

Lee, Nathaniel, 35

Leibniz, Baron Gottfried Wilhelm von, 36

Lely, Peter, 202

libertinism, 64, 86, 111, 118, 119–42, 217 n. 16; and Behn, 73, 119–42, 144, 147, 186, 216 n. 10, 217 n. 25, 221 n. 7; and Charles II, 75, 124–25; defined, 123–25; and Dryden, 19, 110; and Milton, 123; and Rochester, 28, 118, 119–42, 218 n. 29; and Sade, 124; Turner's work on, 216 n. 13, 216 n. 14

Lipking, Joanna, 224 n. 4

Locke, John, 36, 37, 176

Louis XIV, 37, 39, 41, 214 n. 17

Love, Harold, 77; and seven Restoration modes of translation, 209 n. 16

Lovelace, Richard, 63, 91, 208 n. 19

Lowenthal, Cynthia, 215 n. 5

Lucan, 208 n. 8

"lucky minute." *See also* "blessed", "happy", 58, 63, 76, 111; and "On a *Juniper-Tree*," 144, 149, 157–59

Lucretius, 28, 124, 136, 201; Creech's translation, 85, 86, 94, 108–18, 122, 125, 165; Dryden's translation, 111, 114, 125; materialism of, 110–12

Lynch, Kathleen, 208 n. 9

MacLean, Gerald, 18, 59, 207 n. 50

Malone, Edmund, 34

Mapplethorpe, Robert, 155

Marcus Manilius, 86, 211 n. 2

Markley, Robert, 25, 222 n. 10

Marvell, Andrew, 35, 57, 60, 213 n. 17

Mary II, 37

materialism, philosophical: and Behn, 126, 186; and Hobbes, 126, 144; and Lucretius, 110–12, 124, 144

Maus, Katherine Eisamann, 203 n. 4

Mazarin, Hortense Mancini, duchess of, 37, 125

McGhee, Jim, 223 n. 34

McWhir, Anne, 204 n. 11

Mermin, Dorothy, 25, 145, 199, 205 n. 21, 212 n. 9

meter, poetic, 24, 50, 208 n. 18, 221 n. 5; Behn's facility with, 58–62, 72, 103, 107, 212 n. 14; influence of Cowley, 66–70, 72; influence of Creech, 93

Milton, John: and *Paradise Lost*, 35, 43, 61, 63, 76, 94, 123, 151, 156, 158, 167, 172

misogyny, 72–73, 154–56; and Behn's theatrical milieu, 119–21; and Blackmore, 43–45; and Gould, 17–18, 191, 202, 226 n. 17; and Rochester, 119–20, 167

Monmouth, James Scott, duke of. *See also* "Jemmy", 23, 36–37, 39, 41, 46, 50–51, 55, 109, 174, 190, 213 n. 17, 219 n. 33

Morgan, Henry, 35

Morley, George, 36

Mulgrave, John Sheffield, earl of, 33, 115, 210 n. 21

Munns, Jessica, 203 n. 4, 215 n. 4, 219 n. 36, 222 n. 10

Newton, Isaac, 36

Oldham, John, 194–95

Osborne, Thomas, earl of Danby, 38

Otway, Thomas, 35, 109, 114

Ovid, 23, 46, 57–58, 62, 83, 101, 103, 132, 139, 141, 147, 158, 201, 208 n. 8, 220 n. 37, 222 n. 14

Parry, Graham, 71

pastoral, 28, 36, 49, 50, 63, 71, 141, 182, 211 n. 5, 211 n. 6, 212 n. 8, 225 n. 9; and "On a *Juniper-Tree*,"

143–63; and Philips, 149–54; and Rapin, 87–91; and Theocritus, 91–101; and Virgil, 87–91, 93, 94, 146, 194, 222 n. 12

Patterson, Annabel, 211 n. 6

Payne, Deborah C., 207 n. 5

Pepys, Samuel, 35

Perkins, Jean A., 217 n. 16

Petrarch, Francis (i.e., Francesco Petrarca), 77–78, 87

Philips, Katherine (also Orinda), 17, 186, 197–98, 222 n. 18, 222 n. 21; Behn's response to, 145; 149–55, 160, 162, 180; influence on Behn, 20, 24, 40, 48, 147, 166

Phillips, Ambrose, 156

Phillips, Edward, 26, 43–45

Pindar, 59, 66, 68, 102, 209 n. 5

Pindaric ode/pindarics, 208 n. 15, 208 n. 17, 209 n. 2; Behn's use of, 22, 28, 46, 50–52, 54, 56, 59–60, 63, 87, 94, 170–71, 180; influence of Cowley, 65–85

Plath, Sylvia, 200

Plutarch, 86, 211 n. 2

Pope, Alexander, 33, 59, 87, 93

Pordage, Samuel, 47

Portsmouth, Louise de Kéroualle, duchess of, 37, 125, 214 n. 17

Price, Bronwen, 215 n. 2

Prior, Matthew, 47

Purcell, Henry, 35, 38, 93

Puritans, 61

Quinsee, Susannah, 225 n. 9

Rainger, Ralph, 224 n. 36

rakes/rakishness, 122, 124, 126–31, 168, 217 n. 17, 217 n. 26

Randolph, Thomas, 52

rape, 90, 134, 179, 218 n. 28, 226 n. 19

Rapin, René, 36, 87–91, 93, 111, 118, 211 n. 6, 211 n. 7

Ravenscroft, Edward, 28, 35, 121

Revard, Stella, 209 n. 4

Rich, Adrienne, 198

Richardson, Samuel, 189

Roberts, David, 227 n. 21

Rochester, John Wilmot, Second earl of, 22, 24, 35, 39, 70, 72, 111, 116, 121, 143, 154, 156, 177, 186, 214 n. 22, 215 n. 7, 226 n. 15; and Cowley, 65; influence on Behn, 28, 46, 160, 165, 204 n. 12; and libertinism, 118, 119–42, 218 n. 29; misattribution of Behn's poetry to, 143, 220 n. 1

Roman de la Rose, La, 165, 177

Romanowski, Sylvie, 217 n. 16

Roscommon, Wentworth Dillon, earl of, 33, 35, 48, 49, 78, 204 n. 17, 212 n. 13

Rosenmeyer, Thomas G., 211 n. 6

Rostenberg, Leona, 217 n. 15

Rothernberg, Molly, 222 n. 10

Rothstein, Eric, 31, 206 n. 37, 206 n. 38, 206 n. 40, 206 n. 41, 208 n. 15, 209 n. 3, 221 n. 5, 223 n. 21

Rowe, Nicholas, 34

Royal Society, 36, 65, 206 n. 44

Ruskin, John, 156

Rymer, Thomas, 32, 67, 69, 88, 211 n. 7

Sade, Donatien-Alphonse-François, marquis de, 124–25, 216 n. 15

Salzman, Paul, 20, 25, 204 n. 15, 205 n. 24

Sandys, George, 147

Sappho, 147, 214 n. 18

satire, 53, 61, 177–78, 215 n. 1

Saunders, David, 217 n. 15

Scaliger, Julius Caesar, 89

Schweickart, Patrocinio P., 178, 226 n. 18

Scot, William, 208 n. 12

Scudéry, Madeline de, 225 n. 5

Settle, Elkanah, 215 n. 1

Shadwell, Thomas, 32, 35, 126, 199, 206 n. 43

Shaftesbury, Antony Ashley Cooper, earl of, 57

Shakespeare, William, 34, 54, 61, 74, 120–21, 134, 151

Sidney, Philip, 75

Snider, Alvin, 216 n. 14, 221 n. 7, 226 n. 14

Southerne, Thomas, 133, 167, 225 n. 8

Spearing, Elizabeth, 20, 26, 68–69, 166, 204 n. 15, 210 n. 16, 224 n. 5, 225 n. 8

Spencer, Jane, 205 n. 21, 205 n. 31

Spenser, Edmund (and *The Faerie Queene*), 19, 61, 65, 151, 158, 167, 172, 202, 204 n. 14

Sprat, Thomas, 21, 58, 65–66, 69, 71, 75, 210 n. 21

Steele, Richard, 36

Steele, Valerie, 223 n. 33

Steibel, Arlene, 214 n. 18

Stevens, Anthony, 214 n. 20, 215 n. 24

Summers, Montague, 147, 199, 221 n. 4

Sutherland, James, 202, 203 n. 3, 206 n. 37, 209 n. 2, 223 n. 21

Swift, Jonathan, 35, 60, 66, 209 n. 5

Tallemant, Paul, 46, 72, 87, 164–97

Tate, Nahum, 109, 114, 136

Temple, William, 34

Theocritus, 28, 35, 87, 118, 156, 201; Creech's translation, 85, 91–101, 146

theory, seventeenth-century dramatic, 30, 48–49, 205 n. 33, 206 n. 39, 219 n. 31

theory, seventeenth-century poetic, 22, 28, 29, 30–34, 46, 48, 50, 102, 204 n. 15, 206 n. 37, 221 n. 5

Thomas, Elizabeth, 19, 204 n. 11

Thompson, Peggy, 217 n. 21

Thompson, Roger, 216 n. 13

Thoms, Peter, 220 n. 36, 223 n. 34

Todd, Janet, 18, 73, 208 n. 12, 208 n. 19, 212 n. 12, 215 n. 1, 218 n. 30, 219 n. 33, 221 n. 4, 226 n. 14, 226 n. 19

Tonson, Jacob, 20, 27, 36, 40, 45, 102, 106, 118, 144, 147, 204 n. 16, 208 n. 11; Behn's letter to, 47–48, 164, 166

Tories, royalism, 18, 38, 204 n. 8, 205 n. 26, 226 n. 14

Traherne, Thomas, 60

translation, 23, 28, 35, 49, 50, 57–58, 69, 77–78, 204 n. 15; and Creech's Horace, Lucretius, Rapin, Theocritus, 86–118, 146–47; Dryden's tripartite distinctions, 209 n. 15; Love's seven Restoration modes of, 209 n. 16; and *A Voyage to the Isle of Love*, 164–97, 224 n. 2, 224 n. 5

Tryon, Thomas, 142, 220 n. 38

Turner, James Grantham, 123–25, 216 n. 13

Vaughan, Henry, 33, 35

Velleius Paterculus, 29

verse epistle, 23, 52, 57–58, 62, 220 n. 37; and "To My Lady Morland," 191–97, 227 n. 27; and *A Voyage to the Isle of Love*, 164–97

Vieth, David M., 220 n. 1

Virgil, 33, 103, 208 n. 8; and pastoral, 87–91, 93, 94, 146, 194, 222 n. 12

Voltaire, 216 n. 15

Wagenknecht, Edward, 17, 30, 202

Waller, Edmund, 32, 35, 39, 42, 44, 47, 68, 91, 109, 161

Walters, Lucy, 190

Ward, Adolphus William, 154–55

Ward, Edward, 126

Watson, Henry, 20

Watteau, Jean Antoine, 36

Weinbrot, Howard D., 77, 210 n. 16

West, Mae, 224 n. 36

Wharton, Anne, 51, 135, 186, 218 n. 29

Whigs, 23, 38

Wilde, Oscar, 193

Wilhelm of Orange (William III of England), 37, 38, 41, 70

Willis, Sue, 155

Winn, James Anderson, 207 n. 47, 208 n. 11, 208 n. 14, 214 n. 23

wit: definitions: Behn 33, 80–81; Cowley, 78–79 ("Ode: Of Wit");

Davenant, 210n. 21; Dryden, 27, 29, 33, 210n. 21; Robert Howard, 210n. 21; Mulgrave, 33, 210n. 21; Roscommon, 33; Sprat, 210n. 21
wit: and poetic language, 31–32, 80–81, 103, 206n. 44
Wolseley, Robert, 154
Wood, Anthony à, 35
Woolf, Virginia, 26, 205n. 29

Wycherley, William (and *The Country-Wife*), 34, 72, 120, 137, 178, 199, 219n. 32, 226n. 17

Young, Elizabeth V., 145, 212n. 8, 212n. 14, 213n. 15, 213n. 16, 221n. 7, 223n. 28

Zeitz, Lisa, 220n. 36, 223n. 34